SOLWAY WINDS

Lord Senhouse founder of Maryport, 1706-1770.

SOLWAY WINDS

Compiled by

John D. Wells

ISBN 0 9549240 0 2

Printed by
Titus Wilson & Son, Kendal
2004

TO THE MEMORY
OF
JOHN S. M. BIRKETT
1872-1950
AND TO
THE SEAFARING MEN
OF WEST CUMBRIA

SEA BREEZES

THE WORLDWIDE MAGAZINE OF SHIPS AND THE SEA

Contents

Acknowledgements

FOR help with the preparation of this book, I am most deeply grateful to the following people for giving me their valued time.

Firstly to the Editor of *Sea Breezes* for his kind permission to reproduce a number of photographs and written material, from past editions of the well-known and long standing magazine of *Ships and the Sea*.

To Mr. Les Donnan of the Beacon, Whitehaven.

Mr. Steve White, Carlisle Library, 11 Globe Lane.

Mr. Robin Burgess, The CN Group Limited, Newspaper House, Dalston Road, Carlisle.

The Glasgow University (Archive Service, *DC101/0035*).

The Newcastle City Library and Local Studies.

The County Archives, Carlisle.

Mr. Graham Hindle, 39 Moorland Road, Langho, Blackburn.

The Merseyside Maritime Museum, Liverpool.

Mr. Roger Bentley, 11 Dorset Close, Harrogate, Yorks.

Dr. John Naylon, Smithy House, Highway Lane, Keele, Staffs.

Mr. Phil Cram, Editor, *West Cumberland Times and Star*.

The Huddersfield Examiner, Queen Street South, Huddersfield.

Mr. John Whitwell, 37 St Andrews Road, Stainburn, Workington.

The Maryport Town Library.

The Maritime Museum, Shipping Brow, Maryport.

The Maritime National Museum, Greenwich.

The Dumfries and Galloway Archive Service.

Mr. Barry Burns, ex-merchant seaman of Workington.

Mr. Michael Rhodes, 5 Pennine View, Linthwaite, Huddersfield.

To my dear friends, George and Hannah Miller, of 50 High Street Maryport, with whom a long association has been held. I wish to thank them for their help and kind hospitality.

To Mrs. Jean Law, Lindenside, Papcastle, Cockermouth.

To Mr. and Mrs. J. P. Fitzsimons, 5 The Promenade, Maryport, for photographs supplied. Again friends of long standing.

To Mr. Jim Thorburn, 17 Brookside, Maryport, for his help and loan of photographs.

To Shaun Drummond, Bryan Harper, Phil Hayhurst and David Pointon and all at Titus Wilson & Son, Printers, Kendal.

Last but by no means least, to my wife Sheila, to whom I am most grateful, for her time, help and most of all her patience in the compiling of this manuscript.

Introduction

THIS book is mainly focused on the small seafaring town of Maryport which is situated on the West Cumbrian coast of the Solway Firth. Maryport was a planned town and came into prominence toward the mid-eighteenth century, a once thriving seaport which in its heyday could match many towns of much larger size and population with its commerce and thriving industries, these involved the export of coal to Ireland; steel rails, cast iron, this was mainly due to the opening of its two docks, the Elizabeth Dock in 1857, and the Senhouse Dock in 1884, the Maryport and Carlisle railway in 1845 which transported coal from the local collieries and neighbouring districts.

There was a smelting furnace at Furnace Mill, foundries and engineering yards, the town had its own brewery, a paper mill and glass works, there were shipbuilding yards and a wealthy fishing industry, also two tanneries and many more smaller industries that can be of mention.

Maryport had the two largest docks on the West Cumbrian coastline, until Workington its neighbouring town opened the Prince of Wales dock in 1927, this brought on a steady decline to the harbour industries. Maryport had its own small but highly respected shipping line, The Holme Line, which was known throughout the seafaring world. It could boast some very fine Clipper Barques, notably the *Briar Holme*, the *Hazel Holme*, the *Myrtle Holme*, the *Eden Holme*, the *Castle Holme*, these vessels could hold their own against any other companies sailing in that period, they brought home wool from the Australian ports of Adelaide, and Brisbane, and also from the two Tasmanian ports, they were rarely much over 80 days outward bound, and usually under 90 days on the return voyage home, this also spoke highly of the ships masters and their crews. Maryport produced some very fine seafaring men, from ships Masters to able seamen, many of these fine men met there fate in deep waters. In the churchyard of St. Mary's, also in the Maryport cemetery, are many headstones erected to the memory of these fine men who braved storm and tempest in the life they chose, but to most of them a life they would never have changed.

My own family on the maternal side played their part in Maryport's growth, they were involved with seafaring, the shipyards, docks, and the fishing industry, but sadly all this was eventually to go into a decline from which to this day the town has never fully recovered.

Maryport was in its glory in the 1800s, this was to last only into the mid-1920s, it was then the seed was sown for the big depression which was to come and make its mark in the 1930s.

I was born and raised in Maryport, and even though I do not reside in the town today, I hold a deep affection and loyalty to the place of my roots which will always stay close to my heart, for I have many happy memories of my childhood and teenage years, but I like many other of Maryport's sons had to leave and set out for greener pastures, this was not of choice, but necessity, the lack of employment and circumstance, but I have always had the town in heart and mind, and kept in communication with friends who keep me informed with news of the town be it good or bad.

I now reside in Kendal where my family moved to in the early 1970s, where since that time my parents sadly passed away, I married and decided to stay here, for the town has been kind employment wise, also where I have made many good friends, it is also an ideally well situated town, especially when I decide to visit Maryport, which is just over an hours drive away, with some of the most beautiful scenery to view on route.

I always look forward to my visits to the old home town, to view the progress which is at present taking place after many years in the doldrums, also to enjoy the company of old friends and people of the town, who always give a warm and friendly welcome to any visitor who may be just passing through or with a view to spending some time in the town or surrounding areas.

My inspiration to write or to compile a book on the town and its people came into my mind a good number of years ago, it was while I was making a visit that I witnessed the dereliction of the docks and harbour area, also many dilapidated buildings within the town itself, the unemployment situation was also in a bad way. It was my first visit to the town for almost ten years, I had left in the very early 1960s and I was deeply saddened by what I saw.

As a young boy I can clearly recall visits to Netherhall, the stately home of the Senhouse family, the founders of the town, I accompanied my grandparents on occasion to garden parties which were held there, my grandmother was quite friendly with Colonel Senhouse, and often on these occasions was asked to give a song, having been gifted with a beautiful singing voice. One day in particular I was shown around the grounds, the large cobbled courtyard where the horses were stabled, the dog pens were also housed in the same area, Colonel Senhouse was very fond of his dogs which were Beagles, a breed of which he always favoured, whenever one of his dogs passed away it was always buried to the rear of the mansion near the weir, where a small headstone would be erected in its memory.

What I now gazed upon on my visit to Netherhall was a scene of devastation, this once stately home had been vandalised beyond belief, how and why this had been allowed to happen was beyond ones imagination, many areas of roofing and lead were missing, what remained of the guttering was overgrown with grass and weeds, windows all smashed and frames missing, the beautiful solid oak doors to the building were all missing. I walked into the portico which once housed most of the Senhouse collection of Roman alters and artifacts, then through the main entrance and then into the main hallway, the once costly tapestries which were hanging from the walls were in shreds, the oak staircase leading to the first floor had been torn out, most of it gone, all around lay

Netherhall, Maryport. Home of the Senhouse Family.
Lords of the Manor and Founders of the Town (Photo – 1902).

smashed porcelain and plaster. I had witnessed enough of this heartbreaking scene, how anyone could have taken part in this devastation to the home of the founders of the town was beyond me, they must carry a very guilty conscience, if they at all posessed one. Having my camera on hand, but with only four exposures left on reel, I took what I would think would be the last photographs of that once stately home, on my next visit to the Netherhall Mansion all that remained was the 14th century peel tower, a cleared area of surrounding ground that once housed many historical memories and stories. Apparently at one time it was hoped that the grounds would be turned into a garden centre, with restaurant and a motel, with some of the ground reserved for private housing, but at the present time this idea seems to have fallen by the wayside.

This book has been compiled with the kind permission from various sources of information, namely that long established magazine published each month the *Sea Breezes*, without the information from this particular magazine this book would not have been available, its source of historical information has been most valuable in the completion of this manuscript, also permission from local newspapers and archives, libraries, and individual people who have contributed with information, to these sources I am most grateful.

Numerous books over many years have been written relating to the towns of the West Cumbrian coast, I make reference to two people in particular, the late Herbert Jackson and his wife Mary, who had many books published over the years on the West Coast history, but mainly on their own town of Maryport, of which its welfare they always had at heart. Another lady I may refer to, maybe not as a writer of books, but a lady who has worked solidly over many years for the welfare of the town, and should be honoured for her labours, I refer to Mrs. Kathleen Wallace, formerly English, who with her sister Bessie operated the family café at the lower end of Senhouse Street for many years, and were good friends with my own family, Kathleen now lives in the lodge of the Netherhall Estate, and has done so for quite a number of years looking after the property and being responsible for it.

I previously make mention to the *Sea Breezes* monthly magazine, in publication for many years, my grandfather was an old Maryport sailor, whose life and times are given mention to in this manuscript. I recall as a boy he would often purchase these magazines, so I became familiar with them at an early age which made me realise his passion for the sea, and the sight of a fully rigged sailing ship.

Naturally a book like *Sea Breezes* relates to the sea and of seafaring men and their ships. If I may use the word landlubber, the latter having no interest whatsoever in the sea and ships, may get a pleasant surprise if at sometime he came across an old *Breezes* magazine, and out of curiosity gave himself time to browse through its pages, he would read stories of exploits and voyages from ships Masters to the man of the deck, also to those whose interests include poetry, there are many beautiful poems sent in by these unknown seafaring men that relate to the sea, of its tranquillity, and its awesome moods and power, poems of their fellow men and life aboard ship, and many with a touch of humour which will raise a smile to the reader. I have collected as many of these rare old magazines as possible, and have used quite a lot of their content in this manuscript as I have already mentioned. The contents relates to these fine men, many of them local men, men who went down to the sea in ships.

I have included also notable people of the town. People who deserve recognition, people of the past. Also my own family the Birketts of Maryport and of their origins in Scotland.

To conclude the book I have finished on a more humerous side, having always been interested in the local dialect, and being a member of the Cumbrian dialect society, I thought this would be a good way to close the pages of the book, the Cumbrian dialect is slowly and sadly on the decline, I feel strongly about this, It is a unique dialect, and is a major part of our heritage and should be kept alive. With the influx of people moving from the South to settle in the County the local dialect is fading, the young are picking up new words and expressions, this also stems from the amount of television programmes viewed by the youth, another source of new words and expressions.

Regarding dialect and returning to Maryport, the town has always been noted for its own brand of dialect, which certainly does differ from most, also a lot of expressions and sayings. Whenever I visit the town I automatically fall back into the local dialect without ever thinking about it. I'm known as a Marra in Kendal, of which I am quite proud. (The word 'Marra' relates to a person or persons of West Cumbria and the meaning is mate or pal).

I have penned some Cumbrian wit and humour, funny stories most of which are true, some in which I have been involved myself, also words and expressions, that to a non Cumbrian reader he or she may require the help of a translator.

To some readers of the book the contents will be rather familiar, as I mentioned previously Maryports history has already been written on before, but a lot of these books are now out of print and unavailable. I have endeavoured to make the book as interesting as possible by adding a little variety to which I think the reader will find interesting. It has taken time and effort and has given me great pleasure in doing so. I have spent many hours on the computer for which I must offer many thanks to my wife for her instruction and patience, especially when the calm waters turned stormy, which they did with some regularity, the storms have now abated, and the computer is at rest.

John D. Wells, 14th May 2004.

Outward Bound for Lands Afar.

Solway Winds

(REFLECTIONS)

Its many years since leaving
We crossed the seas and roamed,
To distant lands, horizons far
So many miles from home.

But home is where the heart is
And our young hearts did truly know,
One day we would return to where
The Solway winds they blow.

In youth we were dreamers
We dreamed of being free,
To leave the township of our birth
And sail the seven seas.

To the north south east and west
And out where the trade winds blow,
To venture into the great unknown
Where only the brave dare go.

As boys we used to wander
Like the tides we'd come and go,
We'd walk the sands and make our plans
Where the Solway winds they blow.

We would watch the evening sun go down
As the ships sailed out to sea,
Then dreams and plans from boy to man
Became reality.

We stowed away on a Clipper ship
She was bound for lands afar,
Africa, China, Australia
And Quebec in Canada.

With windfilled sail she rode the waves
As they heaved and tossed below,
As we left the township of our birth
The harbour lights they were aglow.

Before the mast we served our time
Through gales and storms to foreign climes,
On lonely watch our thoughts would go
Home, where the Solway winds they blow.

Where the seabirds cry o'er the shingle beach
The plover scurries out of reach,
The ryegrass weaving to and fro
Home where the Solway winds they blow.

Yes it's many years since leaving
That we crossed the seas to roam,
To those distant lands, horizons far
So many miles from home.

But home is where the heart is
And our young hearts did truly know,
One day we'd drop our final anchor
Where the Solway winds they blow.

J. D. Wells

'The Stowaways' John Birkett pictured right,
aged 14 years 7 months.

The History of Maryport

THE opening of the Senhouse Dock on Tuesday last, affords a suitable opportunity of tracing the rise and progress of Maryport. The town has no bread-roll of antiquity or tradition of which to boast. It is the outcome altogether of the energy and enterprise of modern times, and the growth of little more than a century. It was originally a fishing village called Ellenfoot, within the manor of Ellenborough, the property of the family of Senhouse, who acquired it by intermarriage in the year 1528 with Elizabeth Eaglesfield, and owes its establishment to Humphrey Senhouse of Alneburgh, otherwise Netherhall, the lord of the soil, who founded it about the year 1749. He assigned it to the name it now bears in honour of his wife Mary, a daughter of Sir George Fleming, Bart, of Rydal, Bishop of Carlisle. For hundreds of years the Senhouses have been a county family of note, and for many generations one branch of the family has been settled at Netherhall. One member of the family became Bishop of Carlisle, and another fought on the side of the King in the Great Rebellion. In reference to this we may introduce the following letter, written by Southey, the Poet Laureate in 1821:

Since I received your letter I made my proposed visit to the sea coast with the two Ediths and Cuthbert. We were at Netherhall. The *solar* of my friend and fellow-traveller, Senhouse, where his ancestors have interruptedly resided since the days of Edward II (when part of the present building is known to have been standing), and how long before that no one knows. Some of his deeds are of Edward I's reign, some of Henry III's, and one is as far back as King John. We slept in the tower, the walls which are nine feet thick. In the time of the Great Rebellion the second of the two sons of this house went to serve the King, the elder brother (whose illness had probably detained him at home) died, and the parents then wished their only surviving child to return, lest their ancient line should be extinct. A man who held an estate under the family was sent to persuade him to this, his unwillingness to leave the service in such disastrous times being anticipated; but the result of this endeavour was that Senhouse, instead of returning, persuaded the messenger to remain and follow the King's fortunes. They were at Marston Moor together, and at Naesby. In the last of those unhappy fields Senhouse was dreadfully wounded, his skull was fractured, and he was left for dead. After the battle his faithfull friend searched for the body, and found him still breathing. His preserver was rewarded by having his estate enfranchised; and both properties continue to this day in their respective descendants. This is an interesting story, and the more so when related as it was to me, on the spot. The sword which did such good service in those wars is still preserved. It was made for a twofold use, the back being cut so as to form a double-toothed saw.

Netherhall stands upon the little river Ellen, about half a mile from the sea, but completely sheltered from the sea by a long high hill, under cover of which some fine old trees have grown up. The Ellen rises on Skiddaw, forming the little and unpicturesque lake or rather pool which is called Overwater, near the foot of that mountain, though a very small stream, makes a port where a town containing 4,000 inhabitants has grown up within the memory of a man, on the Senhouse estate. It was called Maryport, after Senhouse's grandmother, a very beautiful woman, whose portrait is in his dining-room. His father remembered when a single summer-house standing in the garden was the only building upon the whole of the ground, which is now covered with streets. The first sash windows in Cumberland were placed in the tower in which we slept, by the founder of this town; and when his son (who died about six years ago at the age of eighty-four or five) first went to Cambridge, there was no stagecoach north of York. Old as Netherhall is, the stones of which it is built were hewn from the quarry more than a thousand years before it was begun. They were taken from a Roman station on the hill between it and the sea, where a great number of Roman alters and artifacts have been found. Some of them described by Camden who praises the Mr. Senhouse of his time for the hospitality with which he received him, and the care with which he preserved these remains of antiquity. It was a Bishop of this family who preached Charles I's coronation sermon, and the text which he took was afterwards noted as ominous, – "I will give him a crown of glory." The gold signet that he wore is now at Netherhall.

The Senhouse mentioned by Southey as having fought at Marston Moor and Naesby was no doubt John Senhouse, who is described in some of the local histories as having been a captain in King Charles the First's army. He succeeded his father in 1667, and was twice married, having by his second wife (Mary, the wife of Andrew Huddleston, Esq., of Hutton John) five sons, of whom the second Andrew was killed at sea, fighting against the French. Johns fifth son, Humphrey, ultimately possessed of the demise of Netherhall and Ellenborough. Bridget, one of his daughters, married John Christian, Esq., of Ewanrigg Hall, whose daughter, Mary married Edmund Law, Bishop of Carlisle. The students of local history and biography do not need to be told that Bishop Law was the father of Lord Ellenborough, Chief justice of England, whom Lord Campbell (who was not given to needless eulogy) admits to have been a man of gigantic intellect. When he was made a peer he took as his title the barony of Ellenborough the township in which Ewanrigg Hall is situated. The second Lord Ellenborough was famous as an administrator and statesman, and may be said to have added fresh lustre to the name. This, however, is somewhat of a digression. The Humphrey Senhouse, already mentioned, was succeeded by his son, also Humphrey, the great-grandfather of Mrs, Senhouse, of Netherhall, the present esteemed and venerated head of the family.

The first grant of land for building purposes was made to John Sharpe, and bears the date January 31st, 1749. On this land, was subsequently built the Queen's Head Inn at the corner of Senhouse Street and King Street. With the exception of a few fishermen's cottages placed here and there along the estuary of the Ellen, the only building of any importance prior to that time was a farmstead called Valentia House, now the Golden Lion Hotel. Under the fostering care of its founder, and in consequence of the encouragement which he gave to building and to commerce, Maryport progressed rapidly. In the year 1791 there were about 90 ships trading to the port. They averaged about 120 tons each, but merely ran into the creek, and were laden as well as possible with coal taken on the backs of pack horses. There was no lighthouse, and the only guide of the mariner on the sea at night was a lamp placed in the shop window of a man named William Corry, who built a house and a place of business in March, 1749, on the opposite side of the road to the Queen's Head Inn. As time went on a few planks placed on piles driven into the ground formed a pier and quay; and William Corry's lamp was superseded by one placed upon a post.

The control of the business of the harbour was vested solely in the Lord of the Manor; and the harbour master was the collector of dues from the shipping and rates from the town. In the year 1760 the Episcopal proprietary Church of St. Mary's was built, and as the population increased a Roman Catholic Church and several Dissenting Chapels were provided to meet the spiritual wants of people. In what may be termed the infancy of the place, the manufacture of glass was carried out at Glasson, behind the present Customs House. In 1752 a lease was granted for a term of 50 years of land near the Mote Hill, to Messers. Hartley, Postlethwaite, Lewthwaite, and other gentlemen of influence belonging to Whitehaven and the neighbourhood, on which to erect ironworks. These consisted of a blast furnace 36 feet high, standing on a base of about 30 feet square, a foundry for making iron castings, 17 coke ovens, three large coal-houses, and dwelling-houses for workmen. The ore used at these works was brought from the district of Millom up the Ellen in small sloops or lighters. The local coal was made into coke in ovens adjoining the furnace and used for fuel. Owing to a deficiency of water and other causes the lease was broken in 1784, and the works were abandoned. A "pig" of iron made at them, with the initials "H. S.," and the date "1769" is preserved at Netherhall.

The Lord of the Manor to whom Maryport owes its foundation, had no wish to retain, as he might have done, the exclusive right to administer the affairs of the place of his creation, but adopted the better and wiser plan of what may be termed Constitutional government. In the year 1883, an Act of Parliament was obtained by which the affairs of Maryport were placed under the control Trustees. The pack horse system of loading ships was abandoned, and the substitution of the system of loading by means of horses and carts had the effect of increasing the trade so much that the Trustees found it necessary to enlarge the harbour accommodation. This was done by making in 1836 a tidal dock – now the basin of the Elizabeth Dock – with an area of a little over two acres. The registration of ships commenced at Maryport in 1838, when the Customs House and Harbour Office were built; and on the third of February, 1842, the port was entirely separated from Whitehaven, to which place it had been previously subsidiary. In 1846 a lighthouse was erected, the harbour was widened in the following year, and after a storm on the 26th of December, 1852 the pier was extended.

Additional energy was infused into the management of the harbour, and the result was the following remarkable increase during 23 years in the revenue of the port: 1834, £1,654, 17s. 10d; 1851, £3,850. 8s. 5d; 1854, £6, 094. 13s. 8d.; 1857, £6,636 5s. 4d.

In the year 1837, an event occurred which was undoubtedly an important factor in the changes at Maryport. In that year parliamentary sanction for making the railway between Maryport and Carlisle was obtained. The committee for the promotion of this undertaking were – Sir Wilfrid Lawson, Bart., Brayton Hall; Sir Wastel Brisco, Bart., Crofton Hall; Messers. Richard Hodgson, Benwell House, Northuumberland; Humphrey Senhouse, Netherhall; Sir Humphrey Le Fleming Senhouse, Seascale Hall; Messers F. L. B. Dykes, Dovenby Hall; Samson Senhouse, Ponsonby; Joseph Pocklington, Barrow House; Charles Ray, Lesson Hall; Joseph Harris, Greysouthen; Jeremiah Spencer, South Lodge, Cockermouth; John Wilson Fletcher, Greysouthen; George Cowen, Dalston; John Ritson, John Inman, Kelsick Wood, John Wood, William Ostle, George Rae, and Nicholas Ross, Maryport; William Quayle and Joseph Tyson, Whitehaven; Edward Fidler and Robert Lawson, Wigton; Joseph Thomlinson, Liverpool; and Jonathan Harris, jun., Cockermouth. The scheme was warmly supported by Mr. Robert Adair in

Maryport in 1837, taken from The Mount. Where the group of 5 people are standing is now the site of the Golden Lion Hotel.

the newspaper of which he was then the proprieter. The engineer was the celebrated George Stephenson the pioneer of railway enterprise and the selector for promoting the bill in Parliament. Authorising the construction of the line were the late Mr. George Gill Mounsey, of Carlisle; and our veteran and respected townsman, Mr Edward Tyson.

The line was opened from Maryport to Aspatria on the 15th of July, 1840; from Carlisle to Wigton in the month of May, 1844; and the whole line was opened on the 10th of May, 1845. At its commencement the undertaking was not successful, and at some of the meetings of the shareholders there was a considerable amount of what is called in Cumberland "fratching". But gradually the position of the company improved, until under the table management of Mr. Addison it became one of the best properties of its kind in the kingdom. The supremacy which it acquired under Mr Addisons management it still retains, and is likely to do so; for Mr. Carr, the present secretary, has already shown himself thoroughly capable of discharging the duties of his office efficiently.

The increase from the causes we have indicated in the trade of Maryport necessitated a further increase of harbour accommodation, and a wet area of nearly four acres. Work on the dock commenced in 1854. The engineer was Mr. Dees, of Whitehaven; and the contract was let to Mr. Nelson, of Carlisle. The dock was completed and opened amid universal rejoicing on the 20th of October, 1857, by Mr. Joseph Pocklington-Senhouse, and was named the "Elizabeth" Dock, in honour of the present lady of the Manor. This undertaking proved a great acquisition to the port, and the axiom of the late Sir William Cubitt, that "Ships follow docks," was certainly verified in this instance. The export and import trade extended so rapidly and assumed such large proportions that in the year 1866 the Trustees applied to Parliament for power to construct a wet dock on the north side of the harbour. This dock was designed by an engineer named Page. His scheme was thoroughly Utopian, and it was successfully opposed by the coal owners shipping at the port. For some time nothing was done by the Trustees to relieve the pressure upon the resources of the harbour; but at last Mr. Henry Oldknow Huthwaite, at that time a solicitor in Maryport, and a member of the Trust – submitted a motion to the Board to the effect that Sir John Hawkshaw, the eminent engineer, should be engaged to make a survey and report as to the most suitable site for a new dock. The motion was carried; the survey was made; and in a report remarkable for clearness and conciseness, Sir John indicated the south side of the harbour as the best site for the purpose specified. He was instructed to prepare the necessary plans, and in 1868 the Trustees again applied to Parliament for power to make a dock. The application was opposed by the coal owners, who went so far as to submit a bill of their own, which had for its object the severance of the government of the town from that of the harbour. A satisfactory settlement of the dispute, however was effected. The Trustees obtained their bill; that of the coal owners was abandoned; and Parliament, acting on the Constitutional maxim that taxation and representation should go together – for by the bill of the Trustees the coal owners were to assist in paying the cost of constructing the dock

– inserted a clause giving the colliery proprietors shipping at Maryport the power of electing four representatives to watch over interest at the Trustees Board. Shortly after the bill became law, the Trustees made an application to the Public Works Loan Commissioners for a loan of £80,000, the amount estimated as necessary to complete the new undertaking. The loan was refused on the ground that the Commissioners were unable to make an advance of money for any other purpose than building harbours of refuge. For some time nothing was done; but in 1872 a feeble and unsuccessful attempt was made by the Trustees to give effect to the plan of Sir John Hawkshaw. The compulsory purchase clauses in the Act which had been obtained expired at the end of four years from the time that it was passed, and in ten years the Parliamentary powers of the Trustees to make the dock, also lapsed through effluxion of time.

The trade of the port, however, continued to increase, and it became absolutely necessary to make some provision for it. In the year 1879 the Trustees applied to Parliament again for permission to carry out an amended and improved plan for a new dock by Sir John Hawkshaw. The permission was granted, and the bill received the Royal Assent on the 3rd of July in that year. The preparation and promotion of the new bill in Parliament was entrusted to Messrs. Tyson and Hobson, and by then it was cleverly piloted until it became law.

Tenders were towards the end of the year invited for the carrying out of the work, and the contract was let to Mr. William James Doherty, of Dublin, for the sum of £91,000. The borrowing powers of the Trustees were by the Act fixed at £110,000, and a large amount of money was subscribed by the public, a proof of confidence in the success of the undertaking and the financial soundness of the Trust. Mrs. Senhouse, the lady of the Manor, consented to take the price of the land required – 54 acres in extent – for the construction of the dock and railway approaches to it. Mr. Richmond, of Crosscanonby, has largely assisted the under-taking; and as our readers know, the London and North-Western and Maryport and Carlisle Railway Companies each lent £10,000 recently to promote its completion.

The first sod of the new dock was cut on Thursday, the 26th of February, 1880. It was thought desirable by many gentlemen in the town that there should be a demonstration on the occasion, and for the purpose of promoting one a com-mittee was formed consisting of Mr. R. Adair, Mr. M. Wilson, Mr. A. Hine, Mr. J. Adair, Mr. J. Campbell, Mr. P. Dodgson, Mr. E. G. Mitchell, Mr. J. Jones, Mr. J. Nicholson, Mr. J. Gibson, Mr. T. S. M'Graa, Mr. T. Boyd, Mr. J. Carr, Mr. W. Armstrong, Mr. J. Shippen, Mr. W. S. Eckersley, and Mr. J. Robinson – the two last named gentlemen acting as honorary secretaries. The result of their deliberations was that a formal demonstration – commensurate with the importance of the project – should take place, and that luncheon should afterwards be served to wish the Trustees, the contractor, and others interested should be invited. Mr Doherty reciprocated the feeling of the committee, and provided for the occasion by gratuitously arranging everything on the ground for the selected area for the cutting of the sod, inside the railings of the Battery. A portion of the ground was there boarded over, carpeted, and railed in for the accommodation and convenience of those who had to take part in the proceedings. Shortly after noon the enclosure – at the entrance to which a triumphal arch gaily decorated had been erected – was surrounded by a large crowd, which had assembled to witness the inauguration of a great work by the Lady of the Manor. The shipping in the harbour displayed an abundance of flags, which also floated in the breeze from various points in the town. The business commenced by the presentation to Mrs. Senhouse of a handsome silver spade – a gift from the contractor, the handle only being of wood made by Messers. Francis Martin and Company, of Dame Street Dublin; and a neat little barrow that had been made at Dublin by the workmen in the employ of the contractor. On the body of the spade was beautifully engraved the arms of the Senhouse family, with the mottoes, *Deo gratias* ("Thanks to God") and *Voe victio.* ("Woe to the vanquished"), underneath being the inscription; "Presented to Mrs. Elizabeth Senhouse, the Lady of the Manor, on the occasion of cutting the the first sod of the second dock. Maryport, 26th February 1880. Sir John Hawkshaw., Son and Hayter, engineers. H. P. Senhouse, Esq., Chairman of the Harbour Trustees. By William James Doherty, contractor for the works. On a neat silver plate attached to the inside of the barrow was a similar inscription. The spade and wheelbarrow were presented to Mrs. Senhouse by Mrs. Doherty, the wife of the contractor. The lady of the Manor acknowledged the presentation in a few appropriate words, and then lifted the first sod with the spade and deposited it into the wheelbarrow amid general cheering from the spectators. This done, Mrs Senhouse thanked all who were connected with the proceedings for the kindness they had shown to herself and her family, and added, I take it as a privilege to have been able to comply with their request, because I believe that it is the very last ceremony connected with this dock that I can expect to take part in. Life at my age is very uncertain, and I dont expect to live to see the dock opened; but while I do live I shall never cease to take a warm interest in all that concerns Maryport and tends to increase its prosperity, and I believe that this dock will greatly increase it. It is gratifying to be able to record that the Lady of the Manor was mistaken in her anticipation that she would not live to see the opening of the dock. Not only has she lived to see it opened, but she has taken the principal part in the ceremony; and there are thousands of people in Maryport who heartily and sincerely trust that her pure and useful life may be spared for many years to come. That her belief in the dock tending to increase very largely the prosperity of Maryport will be realised to the fullest extent, there cannot be a shadow of a doubt. At the close of the remarks of Mrs. Senhouse, Mr. H. P. Senhouse wheeled the barrow to the end of the platform and tipped the sod out amid general cheering. The ceremony was followed by a luncheon in the Athenaeum.

Maryport and It's Harbour
Carlisle Patriot and Journal
1850-1854

TO-MORROW (Saturday) the messers. Ritson, of Maryport will launch from their building yard a ship of 1,000 tons, the model and workmanship of which we are informed by competent judges, are among the finest specimens of navel construction. The consignment of so large and noble a vessel to the great waters is naturally looked upon as an event in Maryport's history; to-morrow, therefore, will be a gala-day at the mouth of the Ellen.

Even in these times of "progress" the progress of Maryport is as remarkable as it is gratifying to all persons connected with the port by birth or interest. Trade and population are rapidly increasing; and the public spirit of the local authorities and the enterprise of the local inhabitants keep pace with them. This is not only a pleasant sign of the present times; it indicates a prosperous future.

Our readers are aware of the works going on for the enlargement and improvement of the harbour. Considering their extent, and range of means and appliances, we believe that no undertaking was ever more steadily or energetically carried forward. For some time past the state of the money market has not been favourable to enterprise. But difficulties have been met and overcome. The Harbour Trustees, by an effort most honourable to themselves, have just concluded an argument by which they raise, on favourable terms, the important sum of Ten Thousand Pounds. This ensures the completion of the Dock, or thereabout, in due season; and the achievement will not only reflect lasting credit on all parties concerned, but will confer great public benefit, for Maryport is evidently destined to attain commercial eminence. It is undoubtedly the natural outlet for the eastern traffic; and the coal-shippers and merchants on that side of the island are looking forward with lively expectation to the benefits derivable from the Harbour and Railway improvements.

The new dock as we have stated on former occasions, is about four acres in extent, the length being 600 feet. It will contain a hundred vessels at one time, the average burthen of 300 tons. The south-east side will be appropriated to the shipment of coals. The railway company will put up, at the commencement, four coal-drops, of improved construction; and other drops will be provided as the necessity for them arises. The south-west end, or head of the Dock, will be formed into a timber-slip, so as to allow three timber-vessels to discharge at the same time on to an inclined plane. The north-west side is to be appropriated to steamers, and the shipment and discharge of dry goods, and a capacious shed will be erected on the wharf. The tidal basin to this floating dock is about two acres in extent, and will afford room for at least fifty sail of shipping; shipping places for coal are also provided along the sides of the Basin. The Old Harbour is likewise capable of containing one hundred vessels. The total quantity of coals shipped at Maryport in the last year exceeded 300,000 tons.

Construction of the Senhouse Dock, the old breakwater in the Middle of the Senhouse Dock Basin. 1880-1884.

Equally satisfactory are the facts relating to the depth of water, about which, for particular purposes, there has been much misrepresentation. In time of ordinary spring-tides the depth in the Dock and Basin will be 20 feet; at neaps, 14 feet. The Dock Sill is about 2 feet above the level of the Dock and Basin. The sill is laid 2 feet below the datum line, as given in Holden's Tide-Table; by which table, most of our Maritime and commercial readers are aware, all the West Cumberland Ports are governed; so that, at Maryport, they have 2 feet more water than is shown in Holden's useful record – a fact which should be remembered by persons having anything to do with the shipping affairs of Maryport. Besides the depth of water thus given, the water in the channel leading to the old Harbour, as far as the mouth or entrance of the tidal Basin, is still greater by about 4 feet; under almost all ordinary circumstances, therefore, vessels ought to experience no difficulty in either entering or departing from the Port, without being subject to grounding. Within the last few years the old Harbour has been considerably deepened and improved. The uniform consequence has resulted – there is a continuous influx of shipping and a progressive increase. For the last three years the harbour revenue has amounted upwards of £6,000 per annum; and in the half-year ended in March last there was an increase exceeding the revenue of the corresponding half of last year by several hundred pounds; this would have appeared greater still if the recent alterations in the admeasurement of vessels had not taken place, the effect of which was the reduction of tonnage something like ten per cent. Yet, despite of this reduction, such was the elastic spring of trade of the Port that the tonnage dues are in a state of continual increase. The revenue at present derivable from the Harbour is not only sufficient to pay the current expenses of the Port and the interest of all moneys borrowed thereon, inclusive of the sums raised for the construction of the new Dock, and what may be hereafter borrowed for that purpose, but affords a large surplus for contingencies. It is evident therefore, that the revenue arising from the use of the New Dock will be large; and its application will be directed to future improvements and enlargements; so that the harbour fund bids fair to be equal in stability to any other in the three kingdoms. Such an investment is what capitalists are prone to look to, especially those who desire permanency, as the Trustees, we understand, offer 5 per cent, interest on all loans.

This is not all. The completion of the dock may be expected to augment the receipts of the Maryport and Carlisle railway, the harbour being a most valuable water outlet to that undertaking. The effect upon the whole of the western part of the county is likely to be considerable. Even in the present stage of the undertaking there is a manifest advancement. New and extensive iron-works are about to be established at Beerpot, Workington, and Harrington. The iron ore in the West is apparently inexhaustible. It is sent into Wales – in great quantities to Glasgow – and likewise goes in large consignments into Durham and Northumberland, whose affinities should be, and doubtless will be, towards the Western Lines, its natural and best allies.

It is clear, therefore, as we have said, that a bright future awaits Maryport. Those who occupy the honourable post of leaders appear to be duly sensible of the importance of their position. They were perhaps somewhat late in putting forth their strength; but having put their hands to the plough the have not looked back; on the contrary they have gone forward in the spirit of the age; and the success of their efforts will be sure to stimulate them to increased exertions.

Maryport

Rise and Progress of The Port
(*Sea Breezes* 1927)

ACTS of Parliament of the years 1749, 1756 1791 refer to the Harbour as Ellenfoot, but in an act of 1812 the name appears as Maryport. Between the years 1791 and 1812 a change of name had been effected, and then the owners of the soil, Humphrey Senhouse, Esq., had caused the change to be made in honour of his wife, Mary – Port.

The progress of the Port from its earliest days has been largely the outcome of the wisdom and the pecuniary assistance in the development of a fishing creek into a harbour for the export of coal in the first instance and later on into a large Port used for the export of pig iron to Rotterdam, steel rails to all parts of the world, and the import of foreign iron ore from the Spanish and Mediterranean and Black Sea ports, from India and the West Coast of Africa.

The early days of the port were not without signs of future importance. Britton and Brayley, in their *Description of Cumberland*, published in 1810, mention that "Maryport," like most towns of the western coast of Cumberland, derives its origin and consequence from the coal trade. Sixty years ago the beach was occupied by only one house, called Valentia, and about half a score of miserable huts that served shelter to a few fishermen. The small hamlet from which the town arose was named Ellen, or Ellenfoot, from its situation. Wooden piers with quays have been erected on each side of the river for the convenience of the shipping, which rapidly increases. Between 90 and 100 vessels are now belonging to the port, some of which are of 250 tons burdon. They are chiefly engaged in the exportation of coals to Ireland and in the importation of timber, flax and iron from the Baltic.

Pennant, who, in 1774 published his "Tour," made mention of Maryport as "another new creation, the property of Humphrey Senhouse, Esq., and so named by him in honour of his lady. The second house was built only in 1750. Now there are about one hundred, peopled by thirteen hundred souls, all collected together by the opening of a coal trade on this estate. For the conveniency of shipping (there being seventy vessels of different sizes, from thirty to three hundred tons burden, belonging to the Harbour) are wooden piers with quays on the river Ellen, where ships lie and receive their lading."

In the olden days coal had been raised in the neighbourhood and brought down to the mouth of the River Ellen in panniers on the backs of donkeys and ponies. Later, from 1740 onwards, coal was shipped, and the records show that in 1871 twenty-two small cargoes were loaded in that year.

Jollie's *Cumberland Guide and Directory*, published in 1811, tells us that "the coal trade was the chief staple of this part of the county, and during the present war, the shipping has embarked much in the transport and timber trade. The works of an iron furnace, shipbuilding, saltworks, a pottery, a glass house, a cotton mill and extensive muslin manufactories (carried on by Messers. Bouch & Tolsen) have added much to its population."

1833-1843

Prior to the year in 1833 the port was owned and managed by the Lord of the Manor, Humphrey Senhouse, Esq. The reasons for a change are not discoverable, but in that year an Act of Parliament was obtained under which a board of trustees, for the management and control of both the town and harbour, and the first election of the board took place. The Board comprised of members elected by the ratepayers and shipowners, together with representatives of the Senhouse family, the owners of the soil.

In 1834 a drawbridge was constructed from near the Queen's Head Inn across to the Glasson side of the river. Further up the river there was a bridge used by pedestrians, pack horses and ponies for crossing the river from Paper Mill Green. Further up again there was a ford for crossing at low water. This ford was part of the highway from Carlisle to Whitehaven, which at Bank End, kept the low land adjoining the beach and by King Street made its way to Paper Mill Green and to the ford, and thence across the Bent Hills to the existing (then and now) road onwards to Workington and Whitehaven. The deepening of the Harbour as far as Paper Mill Green and beyond the ford made it necessary to stop the ford and substitute a stronger bridge across the Harbour, and this was sanctioned by an Order made by Quarter Sessions.

By 1828 the export of coal had reached 40,000 tons. The trade was an increasing one. More and larger ships were being brought into use. The river at its outlet to the sea was widened, rough quays of timber construction were built on the north side, and subsequently the same thing applied to the south side.

The then "New Dock," a tidal dock, now the basin of the Elizabeth Dock, had been constructed in 1836, but the trade increased much faster than the accommodation.

1843 – Admiralty Survey and Report

In 1843 Commander Denham, R.N., F.R.S., Marine Surveyor, by order of the Lords Commissioners of the Admiralty made a survey of the Solway Firth and the Cumberland Ports, and in his report made a number of suggestions and recommendations for the improvement of this port.

The following additions and extensions were in the years immediately following carried out to accommodate the increasing trade. The extension of the South Pier, which at the time ended near the present Inner Light House, the extension being carried out by a timber structure to assist the formation of a direct cut or a channel course to low water mark by the flow of the River Ellen, the directing force of the river at that time being spread over the strand or beach, the pierhead standing about 400 yards inside low water mark.

To secure additional berths for vessels it was recommended that a dock with gates be constructed as a continuation of the Tidal Dock (known then as the New Dock, and now as the Basin of the Elizabeth Dock), and the extension of the North Quay by the construction of a jetty as an extension, and thus formation of the new Harbour, between the old North Pier and the New Jetty.

In this report of Commander Denham there is a reference to the necessity of a harbour or port light. Up to that time a man named Currey, who had built a house on the site of the premises now known as Harbour House, used to put a lighted lamp in one of the windows of his house, and it was the only Port light.

The old method of transporting coal from the mines (panniers on the backs of donkeys and horses) had been abandoned long ago, and horses and carts had taken their place, long trains of which were constantly passing along the streets to the Harbour. A tramway had also been constructed from the Unerigg and Grasslot Collieries to the south side of the Harbour. But a greater impetus was given to the coal trade by developments of coal winning and by the construction of the Maryport and Carlisle Railway, opened for traffic at the Maryport end in 1840, followed a few years later by the construction of the Whitehaven Junction Railway.

The ever-increasing coal mining industry and other, though smaller, industries were flourishing, especially those incident to the building and equipment of sailing ships. By 1851 the population of the town was 5,698. Two years later the ships arriving at the port numbered 2,690, and the exports of coal reached 269,000 tons.

1853 – The Elizabeth Dock

By 1853 the question of better facilities became urgent. A new dock, the first floating dock in the county, was decided on. The construction of the dock was not very smooth sailing.

The act of 1853 had given the trustees unlimited borrowing powers, but there was no provision or stipulation for the repayment of the money borrowed. The promoters had a free hand for borrowing, but the limitless powers proved a vast hindrance. The pre-dock harbour mortgage debt was over £35,000. An appeal to the public for loans yielded only £6,000. That was not a large contribution towards the cost of a dock. Much dependence was placed on the surplus revenue of from £2,000 to £3,000 per annum. The work was proceeded with, but long before the prospects of a completion of the work seemed remote. Mr. and Mrs. Joseph Pocklington-Senhouse came forward and offered to provide, or obtain through friends, a named sum if the other trustees (12 in number) would do the same. A considerable sum for a small community was secured, and the work was pushed on until once more a financial crisis was reached.

The promoters were confident that if the dock was completed and opened for traffic, the trade would be so largely increased that any difficulty in raising the money needed to complete would be dispelled. Strenuous efforts were made to raise the needful capital, but were only partially successful. Appeals were made to the coal owners, but the response was not great, Mr. F. L. B. Dykes and Mr. John Harris alone responding.

In the end the Bank was approached. The money could be had conditionally on collateral security been given Mr. and Mrs. Joseph Pocklington Senhouse gave security for one-half of the amount needed. The other trustees, or some of them, became security for other financial assistance.

Eventually the Dock was completed, and opened on October 20th, 1857. It was a veritable day of rejoicing. The town was decorated for the occasion and illuminated at night.

The first ship to enter the dock was the steamer *Cumbria*, then employed as the Liverpool cargo boat, with Lowden's *Ann* in tow. The tug *Senhouse* followed, with Kerr's *Thomas* at her stern. The tug *Rambler* was next, having in tow Mirrison's *Henry*.

1857-1879

By that time the Dock at Maryport was near completion. Judged by the increase of traffic which followed the opening of the Elizabeth Dock it proved a success from the very first. Little more than four years after its opening, an agitation for more accommodation was set agoing

1878 – The Senhouse Dock

The estimated cost of the dock, including land, railways and appliances, was nearly £100,000. Borrowing powers up to £110,000 had been sanctioned, and the first sod was cut by Mrs Elizabeth Pocklington-Senhouse.

The construction of the dock proceeded apace for a time. Then difficulties were met, and in November, 1881, came a catastrophe. The Solway was lashed to fury by a south-westerly gale, the sea came rolling in amain, and in one night the sea wall, so far as it had been built, was destroyed, the site of the dock flooded, and the contractor's plant scattered topsy-turvey, the timber floating about in the bottom of the dock or being washed out to sea. The estimated cost of the damage was £70,000.

Again the anger of the elements against the project which was designed to curtail the area over which the sea held dominion was attested. Again, by storm and tempest, destruction threatened the existence of the new works, but fortunately the threat was only partially accomplished. The damage was all the same considerable.

Once more, as in the case of the earlier dock, financial aid was given from Netherhall. Mrs. Pocklington-Senhouse and her son, Mr Humphrey, gave collateral security to the Bank for a considerable loan. Later, the Bank requisitioned the advance, and the guarantors had to take over the obligation, but at last the work was completed.

Senhouse Dock and Dock Basin. Construction 1880-1884 (6 Acres)
Elizabeth Pocklington-Senhouse cut the first sod to begin the project.

The Dock, known as the Senhouse Dock, was opened for traffic on the 27th of May, 1884, one of Maryports red-letter days. In the early morning the people were approaching the town from country districts. The trains brought large crowds. The town was decorated as it had never been decorated before. There were bands of music and processions of Friendly Societies and school children. The leading citizens boarded the S.S. *Alne Holme,* from the North Quay, and she, attended by a number of other steamers and sail ships in tow, steamed out to sea and re-entered the port. Her yards were manned by men of the Royal Naval Reserve; as the steamer passed through the dock gates and the only barrier – (a blue ribbon) was broken, Mrs. Pocklington-Senhouse, on board the *Alne Holme,* declared the dock open for traffic amidst the plaudits of thousands of spectators who lined the dock sides and piers, and a solitary gun from the pierhead joined in the glad acclaim.

The leading townspeople had formed a committee to arrange for the proper celebration of the great event. A luncheon was provided, many speeches made, and the whole town joined in a great "joy" day.

In 1884, the year of the opening of the Senhouse Dock, the tonnage of imports and exports was 378,807, and the revenue £9,952. Six years later (1900) the imports and exports totalled 1,038,754 tons, and the gross revenue was £34,503. Since then the trade has fallen considerably, and for the year ending March, 1926, the imports and exports were 400,375 and the revenue £21,359.

F. Kelly

The new dock gates under construction 1883-4.

West Cumberland Times

Wednesday, May 28th, 1884.
The Inauguration of The
Senhouse Dock, Maryport

THE completion of the important work which has been in progress at Maryport during the past four years was celebrated yesterday with appropriate ceremony. The town was gay with streaming colours and long processions; the crowded streets rang with music; there were feastings and games and all other holiday accessories. The weather arrangements were also the very best that could have been made. The broad Solway lay smiling, with unruffled aspect, under the steady gaze of the sun from a cloudless sky. Several times the encroaching Solway, stirred by storm and tempest, has interrupted the progress of the work of making the dock; but yesterday, as if sorry for its previous rude behaviour, it was as calm as a penitent child.

The good ship *Alne Holme*, with her jubilant freight, glided smoothly over its tranquil bosom, watched by tens of thousands from the shore, crowding the wharves and piers, the walls and embankments, the windows of the Maryport habitations and every accessible point of vantage. The shoreward view from the Solway was one that would impress itself on the memories of all those on board the steamer. All the faces in the vast, diversified crowds seemed to be turned expectingly towards the approaching vessel; and when she steamed within the dock gates, amidst the waving banners and extended hands, successive cheers went up into the welkin, high above the clang of musical instruments and the crashing of artillery.

The arrangement of the day's proceedings evinced skilful generalship on the part of those to whom the elaborate task was committed. The celebrations were of an impressive and effective character throughout, and designed on a liberal scale. In the following columns we have endeavoured as to have made a complete record of the events of the day as the short time at our disposal would admit. The present issue is also embellished with a pictorial view of the town and its harbour and docks, the new Senhouse Dock occupying its position in the foreground of the picture, nearest to the sea. We also give portraits of Mrs. Senhouse, of Netherhall, Maryport, the venerable lady of the manor, who kindly undertook the important ceremony of opening the dock; Mr. H. P. Senhouse, of Hames Hall, Cockermouth, the chairman of the Maryport Town and Harbour Trust, and Mr. E. Tyson, who is likewise prominently connected to the town, and has given substantial testimony of his interest in the town's affairs, especially in

The opening of the Senhouse Dock 27th May, 1884. The vessel The Alne Holme *(Owners Hine Bros.)
of Maryport, is just about to cut the fine ribbon with her bows as she approaches the dock entrance.
Lady Senhouse on board the ship with her guests then declared the dock open, a memorable day for the town.*

relation to the progress of the new dock. Preceding our reports of yesterday's celebrations we offer, with other information on matters of general interest, a brief history of the town of Maryport and of the work undertaken by its inhabitants. The inauguration of the Senhouse Dock is certainly a momentous event in the chronicles of the district. It will mark an important era in the advancement of the commerce of Maryport.

The construction of the Maryport and Carlisle Railway, and subsequently, of the Elizabeth Dock were both works of incalculable value to Maryport, and largely instrumental in establishing it in the foreward position it occupies among the Cumberland ports, But the Senhouse Dock, with its more ample area and greater depth of water, may be regarded as the crowning achievement in providing facilities for the carrying trade of Maryport.

This consummation has not been brought about without a vast expenditure of money. Two hundred thousand pounds, with, perhaps, another score of thousands to be added, implies a considerable annual charge upon the revenues of the harbour. From strangers, who had not previously seen the dock, we heard expressions of surprise, yesterday, that so much money had been sunk into its construction. To their cursory view it appeared merely an exaggerated tank. They would have obtained a fuller idea of the vast labour involved in the undertaking had they been able to observe its progress from the time the first gang of excavators began the work of scooping out the immense cavity, which subsequent titanic labours reduced to its present shape. The money might have served to build a town of a thousand substantial houses, with a decent church and school; but in that case the work would have mostly been above the surface, rising prominent to the view. The architecture of the wet dock, however is on a different system to that of the street. The ponderous masonry of the dock walls and of its extensive environments are in great part concealed. Further on some figures will be found from which an idea may be gathered of the prodigious extent of the undertaking and the solid character of the work. It is made to last ; and centuries after the final ship-load of coal or iron has left the coast, and the British argosies are banished from the seas, its massive walls will endure as a monument to the enterprise of the present generation of Maryport Cumbrians.

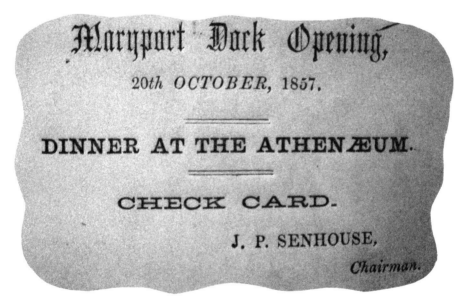

Dinner at Atheneum.

The Ports of West Cumberland

Sea Breezes March 1936

(*Editor's Note*: In view of the frequency with which the ports of Cumberland and their industries have been discussed in *Sea Breezes*, the following brief review of their Economic History will doubtless be appreciated by "Sea Breezers" whose interests lie in that particular direction.)

———————

THE economic development of the ports of West Cumberland dates from the seventeenth century, and is very intimately linked with the coalfield which stretches along the coast for about fourteen miles from Maryport to Barrow mouth, one and a half miles south-west of Whitehaven.

Amongst the first shipments of coal were some from Workington to Ireland in 1604. The Workington district did not, however, make much progress owing, it is said, to mutual jealousy between the numerous freeholders who worked the pits and the excessive rates demanded by the lord of the manor. Progress was made nevertheless at Whitehaven, and about 1620 Sir Christopher Lowther commenced to work coal for sale and export, and in order to further the latter, he converted the little creek into a harbour by building a small pier. Sir John Lowther, his son, exhibited such skill that by 1680 – Whitehaven had a large share in the Dublin coal trade.

By the year 1680 the Fletcher family of Moresby, Lords of the manor of Distington, had achieved some success with a colliery, the shipments from Parton, less than two miles to the north, came into competition with Whitehaven coal in Dublin. Parton however, had a short life, for in 1796 a great storm washed away the pier and ended the attempt to make it into a port.

In the early eighteenth century, profiting by the example of Whitehaven, The Curwen family were exploiting the coal seams with enough efficiecy to make Workington a port of some importance. Harrington, some two miles south of Workington, was made into a port in 1760 by the influence of Henry Curwen, whilst in 1781 twenty-two small cargoes of coal were shipped from Ellenfoot – shortly afterwards called Maryport. In this year, 1781, over 200,000 tons of coal were shipped from the Cumbrian ports and half of this was from Whitehaven.

Although the Lowther family had developed Whitehaven purely as a port for exporting coal to Ireland, Dr. P. Ford has shown how it enjoyed, in the mid-eighteenth century, a short period of "coloniel" prosperity. Tobacco was imported from Virginia in considerable quantities, but declined under the pressure of Glasgow competition, and then "the wealth of the tobacco trade, which itself had risen on the port facilities for the Irish coal traffic, was turned back into the coal trade and industry."

The state of affairs at the beginning of the nineteenth century can be seen from the following table:

Ports of Cumberland Shipping and Tonnage. 1810

Port.	Shipping.	Tonnage.
Whitehaven	188	20,312
Workington	134	18,911
Maryport	101	13,580
Harrington	42	4,960

Not only was Whitehaven the chief port of Cumberland, but according to a parliamentary return issued in 1828 it was then the sixth port the Kingdom, being only preceded only by London, Newcastle, Liverpool, Sunderland, and Hull.

The latter half of the nineteenth century was a period of rapid development. With the construction of the railways in 1845, and later, the transport of coal to the ports increased very greatly and the expansion was reflected in the need for increased shipping accommodation. Previous to 1857, tidal basins were used, but that year saw the opening at Maryport of the first wet dock in Cumberland. This was a successful venture, and soon Maryport was the leading coal exporting port, leaving Whitehaven far behind. After exporting 225,435 tons of coal in 1856, by 1865 this was more than doubled, and what were probably the maximum coal shipments from any Cumberland port took place in 1867 when 476,162 tons of coal were shipped from Maryport.

At Workington a similar expansion of coastal trade had proved more than the limited accommodation of the harbour could handle, and in 1865 the Lonsdale Dock was opened. If Workington hoped to have an increase in coal shipments similar to that of Maryport they were disappointed, for after the "70s" the coal shipments declined, owing to the demand of the local iron industry which was then beginning.

As quickly as the coal exports had increased just as quickly did they decrease. There were compensations however. With the opening in 1870 of the Maryport Hematite Works and the Solway Iron Works, iron ore was imported and pig iron exported. For this latter traffic large steamships were used, the days of sailing-ships had passed, and the larger vessels necessitated better and more adequate accommodation than the small coasters. This was met by the construction at Maryport in 1884 of another and larger dock called the Senhouse Dock, after the chief landed family of the port. Whitehaven, too, followed the example of Maryport, and a wet dock was started in 1875, and although eclipsed by its more northerly rival as a coal exporting port it nevertheless had the unique distinction of adding to its coal trade both an export and an import trade in iron ore. By 1892, considerable quantities of iron ore from the Cleator Moor district were shipped to South Wales, and this continued until about 1898. The decline of local ore shipments was marked by an increase in the imports of Bilbao ore, which was not the sole prerogative of Whitehaven, for in 1899, 67,168 tons were imported at Whitehaven, 218, 524 tons at Workington, and 522,896 tons at Maryport.

The developments in the shipping trade in the nineteenth century were accompanied by great activity in shipbuilding. Between 1788 and 1865 one Whitehaven firm alone, Brocklebank's, had built 152 wooden vessels, the largest being 1,302 tons, whilst five other firms each built thirty or more vessels. It is interesting to notice that Whitehaven can claim to have established, by one of her sons, the oldest shipping line in Great Britain, namely, the Brocklebank Line (now established with the Cunard Line). Although Whitehaven was most certainly the chief centre for the building of wooden ships, at Maryport (where Thomas Henry Ismay was born, who was responsible for the foundation of the White Star Line), and Workington, there shipbuilding yards, and the number of ship builders must have been considerable. When the industry died out in the "70s", not only was it the building of ships which finished, but allied trades and occupations also declined, such as ships' carpenters, ships' painters, riggers, block-makers, spar-makers, sail-makers, rope-makers, and ships' chandlers. As these ports had no large estuaries to be deepened, steel shipbuilding did not take place of the former industry, and now only one small yard exists at Workington.

In the period immediately preceding the war Maryport was easily the leading port, both for the total value of its trade and also for coal shipments to Ireland. Unlike the other ports the trade was balanced, coal being the chief export and iron ore the chief import, to supply the needs of the iron works at Maryport itself, and also in part, those of Workington. The dock at Maryport was capable of accommodating vessels of 5,000 to 6,000 tons, that of Whitehaven vessels of about 3,000 tons, whilst Workington and Harrington were only available for coasting vessels of about 1,500 tons. The relatively small imports at Whitehaven consisted essentially of timber for the mines, and iron ore from Spain, whilst the exports consisted of coal for Ireland. At Workington the imports were chiefly cargoes of ore for the local furnaces and some coal exported.

Any study of the post war economic history of these ports makes it clear that 1927 was a highly and outstanding and important year. On the 30th June, 1927, there was opened at Workington the Prince of Wales Dock, being the former Lonsdale Dock, enlarged at the cost of about one million pounds. This dock was built essentially to meet the needs of the United Steel Companies for the importing of foreign ore (Hematite from North Africa – Manganese Ore from Mysore, and Zinter ore from Hamburg), and the export of their steel rails and sleepers made at their Moss Bay Works, Workington. The largest vessel to use the dock is the *Delambre* (registered tonnage 14,000 tons), which entered for a part cargo of steel rails for Brazil.

Whilst the dock has been of inestimable value to Workington, and has made it the leading port, it has been disastrous to Maryport. No ore is now imported through Maryport, because the local works were closed shortly after the war, and the Workington trade has been lost entirely. In addition, a colliery which exported through Maryport, its nearest port, has, since 1930, been exporting

Maryport – Photo 1904.

through Workington Dock, the reason being that the United Steel Companies, Ltd., control both the colliery and the dock. Several collieries north of the port have closed because of the exhaustion of their best coal seams. The result of the withdrawal of trade is reflected in the condition of the town where more than fifty per cent. Of the insured population is unemployed.

Harrington has suffered even more than Maryport, in fact that the harbour has been closed and has became silted up, whilst large breaches are evident in the breakwaters, so that apparently it has ended its serviceable days.

Whitehaven has not been unduly influenced, for its hinterland is most probably the most limited of all the Cumbrian ports, only the pits in the immediate vicinity of the town using the harbour. The coal trade, however, suffer because of the imposition (in July 1932) by the Irish Free State Government of a tarrif of 5s. per ton on imported coal. As this was removed early in 1935, the outlook is brighter, and if harbour improvements could be affected the local colliery company claim that they have also a continental market for coal.

Such, then is in brief the economic history of the ports of West Cumberland, but before taking leave of them, a few further remarks may be not out of place.

It is evident that the ports owed their growth to the working of a coastal coalfield which was in proximity to Ireland, denuded of coal. Shipbuilding, accompanied the increased coal exporting trade, but died out, to be replaced by an iron and steel trade, which is now wholly centred upon Workington. The people of West Cumberland, therefore, depend for their very exsistence on the basic industries – with their varied and fluctuating fortunes.

The ports are characterised by an amazingly small "mineralised" hinterland.

As the industries grew they had to keep their "faces" turned seaward, for the inland region is sparsely populated, and land communication is difficult because of the double barrier formed by the Cumbrian Dome and the northern Pennines. Of the 80,500 people on the West Cumberland coalfield, 70 per cent. Are in the trinity of ports; Workington being the largest, with 29,000 people since the incorporation of Harrington in 1934.

Finally, it is interesting to recall the fluctuating fortunes of these ports. W. G. Collingwood, in his *Lakes Counties*, writes, "these little harbours have cut one another's throats" – and even at the end of the 18th century, this started when Parton ceased to function as a port. Whitehaven held pride of place until 1857, when Maryport became the premier port after the opening of the Elizabeth Dock, and now it is the turn of Workington. With dock facilities unequalled by its neighbours, the port at the mouth of the Derwent is now the the chief port of Cumberland. But in consequence, Harrington Harbour has been closed down and Maryport is passing through a period of trial. Thus one is forced to ask whether there is room in such a short stretch as fourteen miles for three competing ports, or whether one large and flourishing up-to-date seaport would be more beneficial?

By T. H. Bainbridge, M.Sc., Workington.
From – *Sea Breezes*, March 1936.

Construction workers on new dock 1880.

The Wanderers

I wonder what they think about, and how their lives are spent?
The crowd that fills the city street, their faces so intent.
Had I but power to tell them of the wonders of the sea,
Of ships, and distant countries, would they hearken unto me?

I would tell them of the river, how the bellboy ringing low,
Seemed to chime across the waters from a fairy tower below;
And the city in the distance weaves a halo in the night;
Where the lightship through the darkness, throws a path of golden light.

The hilltops fade and vanish, and the ship wherein we sail
Is all the world we've ever known: the earth's an idle tale.
For the sea mists stalked the waters: like ghosts they writhed and swirled;
And we floated on a sea of cloud far out beyond the world.

The sun goes down in anger, and the air is filled with spray,
We hear the sea pack howling in the blackness for their prey.
Our vessel throbs and quivers, battling fiercely for her life,
And we feel a sense of power and the joy of savage strife.

Cool and fresh the dawn at breaking, when the mists of night unfold,
Show the hills of Spain before us, purple mantles fringed with gold,
Cold grey skies we left behind us. Through a sapphire lake we run,
Past the islands like brown lizards basking in the tropic sun.

Once again we see the city where the toilers never cease;
And the contrast lends a savour to the idle lands and peace.
Here the people miss the purpose, waste the gifts that nature lent.
I wonder what they think about, and how their lives are spent?

T.J.C.B.

Maryport Shipbuilding

AS Maryport grew as a town along with it grew its shipbuilding industry, which also paved the way for other industries connected with the same, timber yards, ships chandlers etc. In 1752 one of the first residents of the town Mr John Bell, fitted out a vessel named the *Centurion*, most probably the first ship of note to be built, this was across from Mote Hill on the Glasson side of the river.

The first shipbuilding yard in Maryport was situated in Strand Street, it was the first major yard of the town and this was opened by Mr William Wood, who came from Whitehaven, this was in the month of January 1765. In that same year William Wood launched his first ship, she was a brigantine of 106 tons – the *Sally*. The Wood family ran the Strand Street yard for some 97 years, building over one hundred ships. In 1811, the yard was operating under Adam Wood, on the 19th of October of that year the yard launched the *Helena*, she was the largest ship built in Maryport to date, a vessel of 270 tons. Kelsick Wood built the towns first steamer, she was the 113 ton the *Cheshire Witch*, launched in March 1837. The last ship to be launched in Woods shipyard was a brigantine called the *Flimby*, she was 290 tons, the yard at this time was operating under Mr. Wilton Wood.

Mr John Peat was another shipbuilder of the town who built over some forty vessels, the Brigantine – *Thompson*, was launched in 1784, at this particular time the shipbuilding industry was prospering, the town was a busy place, when John Peat launched the *John And Bella* in April of 1875 there were eight other ships on the stocks.

Peats yard was noted for it unusual method of launching its ships, they were launched broadside because of the narrowness of the river Ellen, which at its broadest is only 60 feet, on the day of a launch great crowds would gather to watch this spectacle, and no doubt some would return home rather wet and bedraggled. The first ever broadside launch took place at Peats yard in December 1837, the ship was called the *Airey*. Mr John Peat died in 1840, he was 90 years of age.

The most renowned and well known shipbuilders of Maryport were the Ritson family. Mr. John Ritson, who at one time had worked as a manager in the Peat shipyard began to build ships in his own right. In the 1820s, the 218 ton *Mary* was launched. In 1828 John's two sons Robert and William joined the firm which grew quite rapidly, taking over Peat's yard. John Ritson died in the year 1844, and his son William in 1866, Robert continued the family firm, eventually bringing in his own sons into the business.

In the 1880s Ritson's began to build steel vessels, they were launching ships of some 2,000 tons broadside into the River Ellen, which was quite a day for the spectators, who would come from miles around to view these historic launches. The largest ship built by the firm was 2,100 tons. The first iron ship built was the *Ellenbank*. 1,426 tons net register, she was a fully rigged vessel. Several of Ritson's ships became quite famous. The last ship to be built by Ritson family was the *Acanthus*, which was a steamer. Ritsons shipyard launched over 80 ships, the last was in 1902 when the firm ceased to operate due to the deaths of the partners.

Mr. William Walker took over the shipyard between 1902 and 1911, over which time twelve vessels were built. When William Walker retired, the yard finally became the Maryport Shipbuilding & Repair Co. It was this firm that carried out the last broadside launch, the vessel being the *S.S. Rhennas*, this was in the month of November, 1913. The last launch carried out in the conventional manner was that of the *S.S. Silverburn*, on the 8th of August 1914.

Maryport's last boardside launch the SS Rhenass, *April 1914. The last vessel launched was the* Silverburn *on the 10th August 1914. This launch was in the conventional manner.*

Maryport Ship Launches
Article which settles a controversy

SOME time ago a note in "Maryport Things in General" raised a controversy in the town regarding when the last Maryport shipyard broadside launch took place. Many people relying upon memory and basing their time check on the date of their first baby, or marriage, plumped for 1913. It seemed to be the most popular year. In order to get the accurate facts, the aid of Dr. J. W. Crerar was sought, he in turn went to great pains, with the result that anyone who keeps this article should have an accurate record of "first and last ships" of several types and builders.

Before going further, acknowledgments are due to Mr. Stewart Rees, the recorder of the Liverpool Nautical Research Society; to Mr. Dan Young, of Netherton, whose son was the manager of the shipyard at Maryport for the last firm to build ships there (R. Jobson and Co. Ltd., West Hartlepool, trading under the name of the Maryport Shipbuilding and Repair Co. Ltd.). Without Mr. Stewart Rees's aid the article would have been impossible, without Mr. Dan Young there would have remained an "iff" in the last broadside launch.

Broadside launching was practised in Maryport for 77 years and two months. At Netherhall there is a painting by William Brown showing the broadside launch of the *Airey*, and dated December. Most, probably the date the picture was completed, for from Mr. Stewart Rees states the information that the *Airey* was the first broadside launch at Maryport in the stocks in February, 1837, and was a barque of 354 tons, built by John Peat & Co., and owned by Nicholson, Liverpool.

The reason why she was so launched goes back three years earlier to 1834 when on February 20, the harbour master was ordered to prepare the quays of the support of a drawbridge. On November 13th, 1834, tolls for carts over the bridge were fixed and in December of that year the old footbridge was revived. Dr. Crerar's records show conclusively that the construction of the drawbridge (the first harbour bridge) made necessary the adoption of broadside launching.

Three photographs

More recent records show that the *Rhenass*, a small steamer of 256 tons gross, was launched in April, 1914. That she was a broadside launch is placed beyond doubt by a series of three photographs, they are the property of Mrs. Wilfrid Robley, and show in turn, the *Rhenass* on the stocks, being launched broadside, and floating proudly in the river Ellen. The late Mr. John Robley was manager for Jobsons as stated, but they built two ships, and the *Rhenass* was not the last.

According to the *Whitehaven News* of August 13th, 1914 (Thursday), the small steamer *Silverburn*, was launched the previous Saturday – (August 8th, four days after the outbreak of the Great War) viewed by a small number of people in spite of the inclement weather, and in tow for Glasgow to have her engines fitted.

The Airey
The first broadside launch at Maryport, in February 1837, A barque of 354 tons.
Built by John Peat & Co.

Significantly the "News" makes no mention of the type of launch, a fact in itself which indicates that the *Silverburn* was not launched broadside, for such a happening was invariably mentioned in a report. However, proof is better than surmise and Mr. Dan Young of Netherton, supplied the proof. He worked on both these ships and re-called with certainty that one was a broadside and one was an end on slip launch, more than that he would not say, but no more was necessary for the photograph shows the – *Rhenass* being launched broadside.

The last launch

Maryport's last launch broadside was therefore the *Rhenass,* in April, 1914, almost 80 years after the first launch of that type, the last launch, which attracted little attention because of the outbreak of war and the bad weather on that Saturday morning, was the *Silverburn,* an end launch in August 1914.

Maryport's proudest shipbuilding days, are, however, the days of the sailing ships, a run through them is interesting. The last wooden ship built by Ritson's was the *Southerfield,* launched in 1881.

For details of the first of Ritson's iron ships launched in Maryport one need go no farther than Captain James George, still living in the town. It was the *Ellenbank*, a full-rigged, three masted ship launched in 1885 and rigged in the Senhouse dock by Messrs. John and Sam Monkhouse. Captain. George served the first three years of his apprenticeship in the *Ellenbank*, and completed his articles in the ship *Kinkora* – The *Ellenbank*, which was of 1,426 tons net register, left Maryport on October 31st 1885, in tow for Penarth to load a cargo for San Francisco. She sailed from Cardiff on November 25th that year and reached San Francisco after a passage of 163 days. Her Captain was Hugh McKenzie, of Maryport. Captain John Briscoe, of Maryport, was master of the *Ellenbank* on her second voyage before she was sold to Liverpool owners in 1888. The *Kinkora*, the second iron ship to be launched broadside and of 1,999 registered tons, left the slipway in 1888, was also rigged in the Senhouse dock by the Monkhouse firm, and was owned by Iredale and Porter, Belfast.

The two proudest vessels

The two proudest vessels built in Maryport were both Ritson vessels, they were launched respectively 50 and 60 years ago, and Mrs. J Crellin, John Street, and one or two others, have been able to show me some very good framed photographs of them. Both of them were four masted barques. The *Peter Iredale* had a gross tonnage of 2,075 (1,994 net R.T.), was $287^1/2$ feet long, and had a 39 foot beam and $23^1/2$ foot-draught. Her hull was of steel and iron. The *Auchencairn* was very similar with a gross tonnage of 2,040 (1,295 net R.T.), and dimensions $287^3/4$ feet x $46^1/4$ feet by $23^1/2$ feet. she was therefore, a few inches longer and had a foot more beam though lesser tonnage than the *Peter Iredale*.

Both were very fine vessels, and late as September 1939, Dr. Crerar had an interesting letter indicating the fate of one of them. Mr. George Brown, manager of the Hoboken yard for the Bethlehem Steel Co. U.S.A. wrote of a visit on holiday to the mouth of the Columbia River, dividing the U.S.A. states of Oregan and Washington West. There his "attention was directed to a bowsprit of a ship which was sticking out of the sand. Imagine my surprise when I looked and saw the name *Peter Iredale*' on the remains of the ship. If my memory serves me right this ship was built in Maryport." Mr Brown is the – brother-in-law of Mr. R. Williams, the Maryport surveyor, and will now be playing an important part in the war shipbuilding plan of the U.S.A.

The *Auchencairn* was not only one of the biggest but one of the best known Maryport ships, In records of her builders (Ritsons) it is set down that under the late Captain William Nelson "She used to trade between Australia and the United Kingdom with the regularity of an Atlantic Liner, taking 93 days from leaving Melbourne until sighted off Land's End.

The Rhenass
The last broadside launch at Maryport, a small steamer of 256 tons. April 1914.
Built by R. Jobson & Co. Ltd.

Ships on the stocks, Maryport shipyard, November 19th, 1906.

Sold to the Germans

The fate of the *Auchencairn* is more obscure, Ritson's believe she was sold to the Germans, as were most of their sailing ships. One of the reasons was that legislation introduced early in this century made it difficult for them to compete in normal trade under the British flag. That, however, was about 1905-6, with the right Hon. Lloyd George largely responsible. Already before that time steam was ousting sail and the yard had passed accordingly to Mr. William Walker.

Ritsons did build steamships. Probably that is why the photograph of the *Point Clear* is so common. She happened to be a steamer and was launched in February, 1901. The other reason is that the photographer got an exceptionally good negative which makes an excellent postcard print, showing the name clearly as she struck the water broadside.

In August 1902 Ritsons launched their last Maryport-built vessel, a steam vessel, the *Lycidas,* and in the same year Mr. William Walker took over the yard. For a time it was busy. One photograph shows six small ships on the stocks and the first of these to be launched was the *Haller* in 1905. Mr. Walker built 11 ships altogether, and the last two were the *Endcliffe,* in January 1911, an end wise slip launch, and the *Zeitieh* in April 1911, a broadside launch. The Maryport Shipbuilding and Repair Co., Ltd., previously mentioned was an offshoot of Jobson and Co., Ltd., West Hartlepool, took over the yard in January 1913, and held it until February 1918. Their only two ships were the *Rhenass* and the *Silverburn.*

Jack Marlin

Now at the window, side by side,
  We sit and take our ease,
And watch the ebb and flow of tide
  That sweetens all the seas.

His face is in the twilight glow,
  His teeth a pipe between –
A sailor of the years ago,
  An old man grey and lean.

He knew the Western waterways
  Before the whirling screw;
The clippers of the sailing days,
  In all their pride he knew.

Jack Marlin's voice is harsh and shrill,
*   But as he hoarsely sings,*
I see the grand old vessels fill
*   Their white, outspreading wings.*

I hear his long dead messmates round
*   A rusty capstan go;*
I hear the songs of "Homeward Bound,"
*   The song of "Lowland's Low."*

I hear the cotton chanteys ring,
*   And, out across the bars,*
I see the Black-ball flyers fling
*   Their topmasts to the stars.*

The Indi'man she tacks and wears
*   O'er heaving miles of foam;*
The Bristol humbly bears
*   Her owner's cargoes home.*

The riding lamps glint through the rain
*   Where in there roadsteds lie*
The timid hulls of trade again –
*   As in the nights gone by.*

Aye, in the night their rain – wet spars
*   Loom high and strange, I ween,*
When out beyond the crooning bars,
*   The seabirds call unseen.*

The light has faded from the west
*   And o'er a shadowed sea,*
With black wings folded on her breast,
*   Night broods – and mystery.*

Jack Marlin, with the rising moon
*   Is singing, hoarse and low,*
Strange words to some forgotten tune
*   Of fifty years ago!*

E. J. Brady

The launch of the SS Lycidas, *576 ton steamer.*
The last vessel launched by Ritsons of Maryport in 1902.

SS Lycidas.

An Eminent Victorian

In his book, *Eminent Victorians*, Lytton Strachey found no space for shipowners; so here is Mr. Clement Jones' effort to portray the character of "Baccy Ismay". Amongst the shipowners of his period he was the classic example, and it is believed that Mr. Clement Jones' portrayal is, in turn, a little classic that does justice to the subject and stands favourable comparison with the other remarkable characters who peopled the Victorian era. This extract is taken from the book, *Pioneer Shipowners*.

YEARS ago a Cambridge don said to me; "The odd thing about this university is that it is always run by one individual; at the moment it's run by Shipley of Christ's." And that is the odd thing about many other places and institutions besides Cambridge. It is the inevitable result of competition. It is true of practically every profession that there is apt to be one outstanding personality; and it is certainly true of the shipping business.

It could, I think, be said without fear of contradiction, that during the last decade of the 19th century Thomas Henry Ismay occupied the chief place among British shipowners. Indeed, of all the "eminent Victorian" shipowners of his day Ismay was not only the most eminent but the most Victorian, by reason of the dates of his birth and death. Thus, had he lived but two years longer, he would have been in very truth the complete Victorian.

Dean Inge, in the introduction to a recent book on the post-Victorians, has pointed out the difficulty of classifying as Victorian those whose lives overlapped into Edwardian times, and also of describing as post-Victorians those who did their best work before 1901. "The habit," he writes, "of dividing history into epochs, each with its label, is convenient but misleading. The business of the historian is to carve the past at the joints." In the case of many of the pioneer British steamship owners the flesh was entirely between the joints of 1837 and 1901, but the spirit was definitely Elizabethan. This was specially true of Thomas Ismay. All the qualities that we are taught to regard as Elizabethan were to be found in him throughout his whole life.

As a boy he carved models of boats with his first penknife; he stood on the shore of his native Cumberland, looking out to sea, and dreaming of his future fleet; he went to school, and then took to smoking in the manner of Sir Walter Raleigh; he was known to his schoolfellows as "Baccy Ismay." His schooling finished at the age of 16, he left home for Liverpool. There he served his time as an apprentice to a firm of shipbrokers, waiting impatiently for the day when he could run his own ships. Before long his dream came true – partnership; ownership; sailing ships; steamships; the Atlantic; finer and faster ships; success. Then the last act – now a merchant prince, he gives liberally; he entertains Royalty; all in the Elizabethan pattern.

In order to get a clear view of Thomas Henry Ismay's career it is well, I think, to trace and mount these Elizabethan steps one by one. Home at Maryport – Schooldays – Liverpool – Apprenticeship – Promotion – Partnership – Profits – Prosperity – Position – Royalty. The steps were many and the upward path was steep.

Thomas Henry Ismay

His father and grandfather lived at Maryport, in Cumberland. Maryport is to-day a town of some importance, but at the end of the 18th century its existence had only just started. Thomas Ismay's grandfather, Henry Ismay, was born at Maryport in the year 1777. Now it so happens that in the same year there was published what is still in many ways the best and most readable history of Cumberland, compiled by Joseph Nicholson and Richard Burn.

In this work we read that "in 1747 the number of families in Maryport was certified at 64. But a harbour having been made at the mouth of the River Ellen and a town there built named Maryport, this number of families is greatly increased. There are at present (in 1777) belonging to the said port between 70 and 80 sail of shipping, from 30 to 250 tons burden". Such was the place where the father of Thomas Ismay carried on his work of shipbuilding. Perhaps Joseph Ismay's chief claim to fame may be that he was the father of Thomas.

The education provided locally in 1890 was not up to the standard required by a successful shipbuilder for his son, and therefore the young Thomas was sent to Croft House School, at Brampton near Carlisle. One of his contemporaries there has left a record there of Ismay's schooldays. The account was written in 1899. "Fifty years ago", he writes, "Thomas Henry Ismay was a pupil at Croft House under the late Mr Coulthard".

Survivors will remember well the dark-complexioned lad with, dark piercing eyes, whose hobby was the seafaring life, and who never seemed so happy as when fashioning a miniature sailing vessel with a pocket knife out of a block of wood, rigging it with masts and sails and then sailing it on the pond at Irthington. "We learn from the same source that he took part in all games" but anything affecting the sailing of ships touched him in a tender place and awakened those instincts which were destined to make his name famous throughout the world."

Ismay finished his education at Croft House, taking the general course of the school, which was regarded as a very good course and far ahead of the general notions of education in those days. Ismay left school in 1853 at the age of 16 and went straight into business in Liverpool, where he served an apprenticeship with Messrs. Imrie and Tomlinson, shipowners and shipbrokers. He must be regarded at the time of his apprenticeship as the architect of his own fortunes, for, although his father carried on with some success the business of a shipowner at Maryport, he came to Liverpool having little capital except his own natural and acquired qualities.

After completing his indentures he widened his experience by travel, sailing round Cape Horn and visiting the ports of Chile, Peru, and other places on the West Coast of America. Returning to Liverpool he started business on his own account; and in 1867, when but 30 years of age, he took the first of many bold steps in his career as a shipowner by acquiring the name and flag of the White Star Line of Australian clippers.

Thus were joined together the names of Thomas Henry Ismay and the White Star Line – a union that was to prove of such a lasting benefit to the interests of British shipping. The history of the White Star Line takes us back to the old style of clipper ships; it includes the transition from these relatively small ships to the magnificent sailing clippers which carried Her Majesty's Australian mails; and it includes the modern steamers for whose construction, as we shall see, Ismay was to become responsible.

In 1867, after Ismay had taken over the White Star flag, he took another step forward by introducing iron ships instead of wooden vessels formerly employed in the Australian trade.

But the great event in the history of the White Star flag came two years later, in 1869, when Ismay deeming the moment ripe for the introduction into the

Liverpool and New York trade of a high-class passenger service, induced some friends to help him in the formation of the Oceanic Steam Navigation Co. Ismay was then joined in the management by William Imire, of the late firm of Imire Tomlinson & Co. The firm now became Ismay, Imrie & Co. It was an association in which Ismay devoted himself to the development of the steamship department, while Imire took the direction of the sailing ships.

The project of establishing a new company was well planned. Ismay had the vision to see that finality in the Atlantic trade was far from having been reached in 1870. He perceived, indeed not only that great changes were ahead, but that fortune waited upon initiative. With that policy he began and in that policy he continued unto his life's end.

Thoroughly acquainted with the construction and management of ships and with a remarkable power of organization and method, he introduced a new style of steamer, more economical than any yet in use, but swift and graceful. This vessel, the first Oceanic, was built by Messrs Harland & Wolf, of Belfast. The points of departure on the part of the new company may be thus summarised. First, by increasing the length of their vessels in proportion to the breadth they enlarged the cargo capacity without adding to expenses; secondly, they increased the engine power to ensure greater steadiness; thirdly, they introduced the midships staterooms and salon.

The change to midships was so universally appreciated that the White Star Line at once leapt to a foremost place in the Atlantic enterprise. Ismay was, in truth, the inventor of luxurious ocean travel. When the first Oceanic was launched in 1870 she was the object of adverse criticism, but experience indicated her suitability for the trade for which she was built. She was built for safety first and speed second.

During the 1870s and 1880s the White Star Line rapidly developed in popularity. One of the earlier of the ships to excite notice for her speed was the *Brittanic*, which made her first trip to New York in 1874. The *Majestic* and *Teutonic* marked a great advance, and at the close of Ismay's life in 1899 the second Oceanic showed still greater progress.

It was not, however, only upon the conveyance of passengers in the Atlantic trade that Ismay concentrated his energy. Steamers were specially built for the cattle and cargo traffic in the Atlantic. In addition, Ismay controlled a fleet of steamers running between London and New Zealand, and a fleet, similar in character to the White Star Line, which, under the name of the Occidental and Oriental Steamship Co., maintained a regular service between Hong Kong, Japan and San Francisco.

So shrewd a man as Ismay naturally did not fail to see the great future of the trade between this country and Australia and New Zealand. He greatly developed it by running a fleet of steamers specially fitted with refrigerators and other appointments necessary for the traffic. It might have been supposed that Ismay would not find time to join the boards of other companies; yet he was also a director of the L.N.-W.R. Company, a director of the Royal Insurance Company,

Ismay was born in a small house in Whillans Yard, Wood Street, Maryport. The family moved from here to Ropery House, Ellenbourgh Place where he grew up as a boy. This photograph is dated 1905.

Ropery House 2003.

chairman of the Liverpool and London Steamship Protection Association, and one of the founders of the Sea Insurance Company.

Again, with all these occupations, such a man might surely have answered "Pray have me excused" when calls were made upon his time for public service. Yet no such answer came from the lips of Thomas Ismay. Over and over again he put his business affairs on one side in order to do some service for the State by working on a Royal Commission or a Departmental Committee. He was in great request.

In politics he was recognised as a staunch Liberal-Unionist, though he refused to stand for Parliament. He was a J.P. and a D.L. of the county in which he lived, and in due course High Sheriff.

In 1877-1878, when the Russo-Turkish War seemed likely to involve this country in hostilities, Ismay offered the steamers of the White Star fleet to the Government for the use of transports or cruisers, as occurred during the Great War, As the Spithead Navel Review in 1897, on the occasion of Queen Victoria's Jubilee, this Victorian shipowner sent his White Star steamer *Tuetonic*, armed as a crusier with 16 guns, to participate in the naval display, and show that mercantile cruisers were not myths.

If his time for private enterprise and public service seemed to have no closing hours, neither did his generosity appear to know any stopping place. He was one of the founders of the training ship *Indefatigable*, and a liberal supporter of the Liverpool Seamen's Orphan Institution. And in addition to these more notable benefactions he was forever giving endless small sums and doing endless little "In remembrance acts of kindness and of love". In a city famous for the charity of its leading men, Ismay was a prince of givers.

Young men of to-day in shipping offices may be inclined, after hearing about Ismay's amazing career, to question: "How did he do it?"

The question still seems unanswered, but happily Ismay's own answer has come down to us in the pages of "Fair play", published shortly after his death. Asked to what he attributed his success, Ismay said he always kept two principles in sight; first, whenever you have a good thing, remember not to be to greedy, but let someone else have a bit; and the other was never let a weak man out of your trade to make room for a strong one. A wise housewife does not give away all her cooking recipes, even to her best friend, and I cannot help thinking that Ismay had more than two recipes in his cookery-book. For the rest, perhaps the best answer can be found in "the Elizabethan spirit" of which he had so large a portion.

The Fall of a Once Great Star
Book review – 1967

STRANGE though it may seem to some members of the older generation, there are many today who cannot remember the existence of the White Star Line as a separate entity. Reflecting however that more than a quarter of a century has elapsed since that great Liverpool Shipping Company, the name of which was synonymous with the North Atlantic, merged with the equally famous Cunard Steam-Ship Co. Ltd., it is perhaps not so surprising that personal memories of the White Star Line are becoming fewer.

Yet at the turn of the century the Oceanic Steam Navigation Co. Ltd., to give the White Star Line its official title, was one of the most eminent and successful steamship companies in the world. Although writers have chronicled the histories of the world's great shipowners, there has up to now been a serious deficiency in the ranks of maritime literature in that no one has attempted a detailed history of the White Star Line and the men who guided its fortunes.

The appearance of **The Ismay Line,** by Wilton J. Oldham (*The Journal of Commerce*, 17 James Street, Liverpool, price 30s.), means for the first time the story of how the White Star Line grew from a small sailing fleet in the Australian trade into one of the greatest names in the history of the North Atlantic, has become available to the student of maritime history.

The story of the White Star Line is insolubly connected with the careers of the founder Thomas Henry Ismay, and of his son, J. Bruce Ismay who was chairman at the time of the *Titanic* disaster in April 1912. Through his friendship with Mrs. J. Bruce Ismay the author has been able to examine all relevant family papers and also draw off Mrs. Ismay's personal reminiscences. Thus it has been possible to describe the growth of the undertaking from the diaries and letters of the Ismay family through four glittering decades in the struggle for supremacy in speed and later "comfort" on the North Atlantic.

The first chapter includes a genealogical tree tracing the family from Thomas Henry Ismay's father – Henry Ismay, born 1777 – to the surviving branches. Early chapters also contain abstracts of the engineers' log of the first voyage of the *Republic* in 1872 but it is in the appendices to the book that Mr. J. Oldham deserves special praise for he not only include a fully detailed fleet list of the company's ships, both sail and steam, but also quotes the original rules and regulations "for Safe and Efficient Navigation of the Company's Steam-ships". J. Bruce Ismay's New York voyages are also listed from the *Celtic* in 1873 to May 4th, 1912 the time he returned to the U.K. in the *Adriatic* after the *Titanic* disaster and the much criticised inquiry instituted by the United States Senate.

Bruce Ismay.

Thomas Henry Ismay was born in Maryport in 1837. Destined to become one of the great Victorian shipowners, he was in business on his own account by the time he was 20 and in 1867 he bought the White Star Line of sailing ships. When he died in 1889 he was a millionaire; had been asked to stand for Parliament, had been offered a baronetcy, built a mansion for himself and his family at Thurston, Wirral in 1884 at a cost of £53,000, received the freedom of the City of Belfast and entertained some of the most prominent people alive during the Victorian era, Including Queen Victoria herself, the Prince of Wales (later Edward VII) and the German Emperor.

Eldest son of T. H. Ismay was J. Bruce Ismay, a very different personality from that of his father, but it was with his name that the "big ship" policy of the White Star Line was primarily associated. He was on board the *Titanic*, latest and largest ship of the line, when she collided with an iceberg and sank while on her maiden voyage from Southampton to New York in April, 1912 with the loss of over 1,500 lives. He was saved in the last lifeboat to leave the starboard side of the doomed liner and was bitterly attacked by certain sections of the press in Britain and the United States, as they held him largely responsible for the disaster; they also severely criticised his personal behaviour that night. It is perfectly true to say that the *Titanic* disaster ruined him.

The author is not alone in the belief that J. Bruce Ismay was one of the most misunderstood and misjudged characters of the early part of the century and it is to his credit that by dint of much careful research he has been able to present the facts as they really were and to disprove the merciless campaign of verification and hate stirred up against Bruce Ismay by, in particular the American Press.

After the *Titanic* disaster, the White Star Line was never the same again. The fortunes of the International Mercantile Marine Company, of which it had become part in 1902, declined after the First World War and in 1926 the ordinary share capital of the Oceanic Steam Navigation Co. Ltd was bought by Lord Kyslant, chairman of the Royal Mail Steam Packet group. A new company, White Star Line, Ltd., was formed in January 1927, but further success was not to be. The great Royal Mail group crashed in financial ruins in 1932 and after the tangled wreckage had been sorted out there was little future for the White Star Line. The reason for its merger with Cunard in 1934 are so well-known that they need not be repeated here and thus there passed away a great shipping company – some believe the greatest ever to sail the North Atlantic.

There are in all 18 pages of half-tone illustrations amply covering both sail and steam fleets, family groups and individual portraits and the homes of T. H. Ismay and of his son. Of these the most grandiose was the fabulous Dawpool House designed for T. H. Ismay by Norman Shaw who was responsible for the present New Scotland Yard Building in London and for the White Star head office in James Street, Liverpool, now the headquarters of the Pacific Steam Navigation Company.

Dawpool House was put up for sale after T. H. Ismay's death in November 1899; his widow had continued to live in the mansion but on her death it was

The ill fated Titanic.

offered to each member of the family in turn but declined. After the sale of fittings the vast hall was demolished and stone from it used to build three smaller houses which today occupy the site.

The inclusion of a combined subject/personal index and separate index of ships names (in two parts, White Star and ships owned by other companies) make the book a detailed, and well presented addition to the literature of the Western Ocean.

There springs to mind Whitman's lines

When lilacs last in the dooryard bloom'd,
And the great star early dropped in the Western sky in the night,
I mourn'd, and yet shall mourn ever returning spring.

C.J.M.C.

Sixty Years Back

Reminiscences of 77-year-old Henry Hands, a grandson of
John Hands who at the age of 14 years,
Was a powder monkey aboard the "Orion", under
Lord Nelson, at the Battle of Trafalgar in the year 1805.
(*Sea Breezes* 1939)

AS I watch the *Queen Mary* coming up New York Harbour, my thoughts run back sixty years, when I was an apprentice in the White Star barque *Esmeralda* of Liverpool. She was 730 tons register, and as trim a little vessel as ever sailed the seas. She was flush on deck fore and aft, and in bad weather the captain got as wet as anyone else. The *Esmeralda* was built in Birkenhead in 1861, and like others of her type, her usual run was to Valpariso, then home with saltpetre from some port up north. I was in the *Esmeralda* 4 years and 8 months with the same skipper – Captain Jonathan L. Park, who hailed from Maryport in Cumberland. During that time she made three voyages around the Horn to Chile and Peru, and one voyage to Newcastle, N.S.W., going from there with coal to Callao, and back home with wheat from Talcahuano, in Conception Bay.

Captain Park was a sailor from the old school, he loved his ship. A very careful man, he nursed her along in light winds, so that she made very good passages. In all that time I was in her only one vessel passed her in fair weather, that was a French barque called the *Marie*, of St. Malo. In heavy weather, off Cape Horn, of course it was another story. One of my fellow apprentices, William Lowcock, of Burslem, Staffordshire, was shipmate with me the whole of the time, the last voyage as second mate.

I first joined the *Esmeralda* in Glasgow, in June, 1876. We took out coal to Coquimbo, Chile, and made passage in 74 days. I was a little over 15 years old. It was tough going in those days for a first voyager, and I do confess many times I cried with the cold hanging on to the ropes. Although it was winter time off the Horn, we got around the corner easily – so I was told. After discharging our cargo, we sailed away in ballast to the Columbia river, arriving at Astoria, at the mouth of the river, on Christmas day. It did not stop snowing or raining until we sailed away in ballast on New Year's Day, 1877, bound for Talcahuano, Chile. The big freight we expected to get at Portland did not materialise. During the week we were in Astoria several incidents took place that were worth recording. One night I fell overboard and all kind of things might have happened, as the current runs very swiftly there. One day the Captain sent the carpenter, Lowcock and

51

myself to a sawmill to get some lumber. We started to tow it to the ship, but the current swept us nearly out to the bar, so we cut the towline and let the lumber go out to sea. My first impression of the United States was not altogether cheerful.

We arrived in Conception Bay after a passage of 74 days, and loaded wheat at Pinco, a small village. There was just a sandy beach not a wharf of any kind. All the cargo was brought in Bullock carts, dumped on the sand, and then carried on the backs of men wading in the water and dropped into lighters. A very slow process. We arrived at Falmouth and the *Esmeralda* was ordered to Bristol to discharge.

After a vacation of a fortnight in Shrewsbury, my birthplace, I was told to report to the ship at Cardiff. We left there with a cargo of "patent fuel" for Inquiqe. At that time this famous nitrate port belonged to Peru, but Chile took it from her a year or two later. After discharging we went to Pisagua, a small port a little north, to load. We had a long stay there – four months. A terrific earthquake occurred one night, and the natives, fearing a repetition of a tidal wave, which took place a few years before, fled into the hills. No tidal wave came, but the surf was so bad that no cargo was worked for two months. It has always been a mystery to me how the people existed during that time, for all communication was cut off from the coastwise steamers that brought food and water. Pisagua was the most desolate place imaginable, being all rocks and sand and high mountains at the back of the town.

I could tell many stories of how the captains of various ships in the harbour spent their time, but principal diversions were boat sailing, fishing outside the harbour, and card-playing at night. We boat boys hardly knew what a night's sleep was. Lowcock and I gained quite a reputation as boatmen, for nearly every ship's boat but ours was smashed on the rocks in an effort to make a landing. One night we nearly met with disaster in trying to land a Scotch navel engineer, his wife and two children and a servant.

They had disembarked from the P. S. N. Company's mailboat and were put on the *Esmeralda* till the surf went down a bit, but Captain Park had the utmost confidence in his boys and said we could land them all right. In the darkness backing in stern first, a big wave landed us on a rock ; the boat went over and filled. The next wave lifted her off. Somehow we got her back to the ship, full of water. The captain was with us to share the escapade. We put our "guests" ashore at daylight next day. We were scared, for the women and children screamed unmercifully.

Finally we got away from Pisagua. Several ships sent their crews to help us weigh anchor, which was some job after being in the mud for some four months. We had good weather on the whole to Queenstown, and were sent to Dunkirk, France, to discharge the cargo. The captain went over to England to bring his wife to the ship, so Lowcock and I took care of her in his absence, for everyone else had left. From Dunkirk we sailed to South Shields, to load railroad iron and machinery for Newcastle, N.S.W.

We left the Tyne on a nice autumn day, but we were ten days beating to the Downs. In spite of having such a heavy cargo and the crates of machinery breaking adrift frequently, we reached Newcastle in good shape after a passage of 112 days. Some of the fine ships lying near us were the *Drumpark*, also the – *Steelfield*, *Cutty Sark*, and the American ships the *Olustee* and *Edward May*. Our crew all deserted, and we sent to Sydney for another. Men were scarce and wages high. We boys (there were four of us on this trip) spent several pleasant evenings at the home of a Mr. Cowan, an engineer who was interested in a mission on Bullock Island. Mrs. Cowan was very kind to us.

After a small-sized mutiny by the shanghaied sailors, we finally sailed for Valparaiso with coal in November, 1878. We ran into a storm the first night out, and then found that of the eight men we had shipped, only three were sailors, the others being sheep farmers or landsmen. One man never left his bunk until we reached Valparaiso, 42 days later. He claimed to have been injured the first night out. He was sent to hospital on arrival. Years afterward I heard that he was Britain's "No 1 bad man", whom the police had been trying to find for a long time, as a gangster and murderer. That was the worst trip I remember – continued bad weather and only a few who could go aloft or steer.

In Valparaiso we learned that Chile and Peru were at war. We went north with the coal, but were not allowed to enter Iquique or Pisagua, so we went to Callao, and sold the coal to the Peruvians, and got away quick. The day after we left, the Chilean fleet battered away at the forts of Callao. We went south, picked up a cargo of wheat at Talcahuano and sailed for home, making a quick passage to Liverpool of 75 days.

My fourth and last voyage in the *Esmeralda* was from Liverpool to Valparaiso with general cargo. If my memory serves me right, nothing very exiting occurred this trip. We had heavy weather of the Horn and lost 100 feet of the bulwarks. In Valparaiso things were very unsettled, as the war with Peru was still going on. Our second mate Mr. Cunningham, left to go mate of the *Advancement*. My fellow apprentice, William Lowcock, was examined by the British council and two shipmasters and was signed on as second mate of the *Esmeralda*. I missed his companionship much, as we were together for such a long time. Some years afterwards he was he was master of the *Explorer*, and on his first voyage as captain was washed off the poop while running before a gale, off the Horn. He was picked up around the main pumps, badly hurt. He died a few years afterwards as a result of his injury.

The last year of my five-year apprenticeship was in the ship *Ireby*, on her maiden voyage from Liverpool to San Francisco. Her tonnage was 1,426, she was not, but was heavily rigged and had an iron standing jibboom. The *Ireby* was commanded by Captain Thomas P. Thompson. He came from the White Star "yacht" *Grace Gibson*, a full-rigged ship of about 400 tons. We took out a general cargo. We had six apprentices. I was the eldest, and the captain held me responsible for the other five. This got me in no end of trouble.

The captain, knowing he had a stiff ship and new gear, carried on tremendously, and she was over on her beam ends off the Horn. She righted when the foresail and the topsails blew away. Forty-eight hours later we blew away another suit of sails. We sailed through the Straits of Le Maire, a new experience for me. The *Esmeralda* never attempted it while I was in her. We reached San Francisco in 144 days. We stayed there six weeks and then went on to Vallejo and loaded a full load of flour for Liverpool. While there President Garfield was shot. There was much excitement and indignation. San Francisco was a gay town in those days. Shanghaing was in its prime, and several of our men were victims. On the way home, in the Pacific, near the equator, four of us boys rowed the captain to the little barque *River Avon*, bound to Liverpool from Portland, Oregan. We pulled from 7.00 a.m. until noon before we caught up with her. They gave us some dinner and squared yards to help us reach our ship, which we did about 5 o'clock, all fagged out after the long pull. The reason for this unusual jaunt was that the carpenter had lost nearly all his tools while in San Francisco, and the Old Man went to buy some. We reached Liverpool on January 22nd, 1882, after a passage of 142 days.

Letters from Old Shipmates

Christmas and New Year was made happier for me by the receipt of two letters from shipmates of over forty years ago, both of whom were apprentices with me in the White Star Line.

The Christmas mail brought me one from Captain Harry Rhode, who served his time in the ship *Dawpool*. I was in the barque *Esmeralda* of the same line. We met in New York in the early part of 1893. I saw him last on January 31st, 1897. Captain Rhode was then in command of the steamer *Croft*, of Dundee. For many years he was in the ship chandlery business in Genoa, Italy. The firms name was Davidson and Rhode. His son succeeded him in the firm a few years ago. He is now retired, and lives in Italy. We have corresponded at least once a year ever since 1897. He is a good sailor and equally a good business man and as true as steel.

The New Year mail brought a long ten-page letter from Captain Inman Sealby. He, too is retired, and lives in New Jersey, U.S.A. Captain Sealby and I were apprentices together on the barque *Esmeralda*, 730 tons, on a voyage from Newcastle-On-Tyne to Newcastle, N.S.W. from there to Valparaiso, up the coast to Callao and back to Talcahuano, where we loaded for Liverpool. The voyage occupied fifteen months. Captain Sealby has had an adventurous career as commander of White Star steamers in the Far East and Atlantic trade. He commanded the White Star liner *Republic* when she was sunk by the *Florida* off Nantucket in 1909. During the war he was sent to command an interned German liner at Honolulu, and with her carried stores and troops to France. We have met many times since our boyhood days in "Sail", and delight to talk about the old days at sea. Since his retirement, the captain has frequently lectured before the New Jersey Historical Society and other and other organisations; his principal lectures being "Men of the Sea", "China", "Reminiscences of the West Coast – Chile and Peru". It is one of the joys of life to have been associated as an apprentice boy in half-deck with two such men as these.

Henry Hands,
Sea Breezes May 1936.

Ah! what pleasant visions haunt me
As I gaze upon the sea!
All the old romantic legends,
All my dreams come back to me.

– Longfellow.

The Pier Heads, Maryport 1936.

Dinner to Old White Star Men in New York

Submitted by Henry Hands N.Y.

A QUINTET of former White Star people sat in a quiet corner of the dining – room on the roof garden of the Hotel Mcalpin, in New York at noon of September 4th, 1936. They were luncheon guests of Captain Inman Sealby, who sailed for London at four o'clock the same afternoon on the *American Banker*.

The happy party swapped yarns of adventures afloat and ashore for nearly three hours. Old scenes were recalled of boxhauling the yards on a windjammer in the doldrums off the Equator, to go goose-winging the mainsail amid snow and ice off Cape Horn. Pleasanter scenes of life on the ocean wave were related, too. The *Swift* and beautiful *Queen Mary* was discussed also by these old timers, all having been in the White Star Line in the early days.

Those at the gathering were:
Captain Inman Sealby, who served his apprenticeship in White Star Ships. He made his first deep-water voyage to Australia and the West Coast of South America in the barque *Esmeralda,* a vessel of 730 tons, in 1878-79. Other ships of the same Company he sailed in were the *Aminta* and the famous *Dawpool*. After going into steam his promotion was rapid, and he was reported to be the youngest captain in the White Star Line. Among the vessels he commanded in the San Francisco, Honolulu and Hong Kong trade were the *Coptic, Corinthic* and the first *Oceanic*. When the United States annexed the Phillipine Islands in 1908, Captain Sealby, in the *Coptic*, took the official papers to Honolulu. There was great rejoicing, and the captain was tendered a testimonial dinner and given the freedom of the city. In February, 1912, Captain Sealby commanded the *Republic*. On a voyage from Boston to Genoa, with 1,700 passengers (mostly returning Italians), and a large amount of specie, which was to be used in paying off Uncle Sam's sailors of the White Fleet, which had been sent around the world by President Theodore Roosevelt, his ship was sunk by the Italian steamer *Florida*. Several people were killed by the impact of the two vessels, but the rest were taken off by the *Baltic,* under Captain Ransom. During the World War he commanded other vessels.

Another of the party was Mr. Williams, a special writer on the *New York Times*, who sailed the following day on the *Paris*, to represent his paper at the Geneva Conference. He is an old friend of the captain's, and sailed with him as an officer

The Republic.
Commanded by Capt Inman Sealby.

on the China run. As a recorder of nautical affairs, he is not excelled in newspaperdom.

The third was Jack Binns. He arrived in New York a few days before on the *Georgic,* after spending the summer in Europe with his wife and family. Binns became internationally known as the man who sent the first S.O.S. call for help at sea when it was desperately needed. He was the wireless operator under Captain Sealby on the *Republic,* whose urgent call brought the *Baltic, Lucania* and other ships to the rescue. Jack Binns was for ten years a reporter on the New York *Tribune.* He is now in the experimental department of the Radio Corporation of America, as a technical engineer. His work is chiefly with airplanes.

Fourth of the quintet was Winton Sealby, a younger brother of the captain. He has resided in New York for many years, and until recently he was connected with the White Star Line in the main office here.

The last in the group at this dinner was the writer, Henry Hands. He served a five-year apprenticeship with the White Star Line – 1876-81. He made four voyages to Australia and Chile and Peru in the barque *Esmeralda,* and one in the ship *Ireby,* from Liverpool to San Francisco and return, 142 and 144 days respectively. Captain Sealby made his first voyage to sea in 1878, and was a fellow apprentice with Hands. This voyage occupied fifteen months, which took

Sealby Coat of Arms.
A noted family in the maritime annals
of Maryport, Cumberland.

us from South Shields to Newcastle, N.S.W., thence to Valparaiso and Callao, and back to Liverpool. We were in those South American ports together during the exiting times of the war between Chile and Peru. I gave up the sea years ago. My last voyage to sea was as second mate in the *Kestrel*, Captain Faulkner, of Windsor, N.S., to Demerara and Trinidad. For twenty years I worked on the Brooklyn *Eagle*. It is 58 years since Captain Inman Sealby and I sailed the seas together, but we have been friends and have kept in touch with one another all these years.

The Sealby family is noted for many years in the maritime annals of **Maryport, Cumberland.**

I have passed the 75 year mark, and I am strong and hearty, and hope to meet these "men of the sea" of windjammer days again in New York at some future time.

> *In dreams the fleets of childhood*
> *Sail back a thousand years,*
> *To coasts of strange old fancies,*
> *And strangely sweet old fears;*
> *And, bound for fair Atlantis*
> *From out the port of Chance,*
> *For poet, child and woman,*
> *Still sails the ship Romance.*
>
> *E. J. Brady.*

The Holme Line of Maryport

An account by a descendant of the founder of the once – well-known Hine Brother's company of Maryport whose sailing vessels figured prominently in the Australian trade in the last decades of the 19th century.

by Alfred Hine

(*Sea Breezes* 1959)

HINE Brothers of Maryport would seem to have begun business about 1873 through the enterprise of Wilfrid Hine who the previous year was in business at 14, South Castle Street, Liverpool having trade connections with R. Nicholson and Company. At this time Hine jointly owned at least four sailing vessels; the *Alne, Glenfalloch, John Norman* and *Cereal*, a barque of 298 net tons, built in 1859 by Dennison of Sunderland. She never joined the Hine Brother's fleet as she was burned at sea in 4 deg. 30 min. S. 27 deg. 45 min. W. on September 28th, 1872. Wilfrid and my grandfather, Alfred, formed the firm of Hine Bros., which operated from Maryport until 1911, their fleet of ships eventually becoming known as the Holme line.

The ship the *Myrtle Holme* was one of a number of fast clippers which sailed in the Australian trade, shown (below) as she was in 1898 rigged as a barque. Built in 1875 by Bartram and Company of Sunderland, she was originally a ship and appears so in an illustration in *Sea Breezes* of June 1927.

Lloyd's Register of 1878 indicates an alteration to her rig to barque and so she remained to the end of her career. Her master was evidently a "driver" and inclined to crack on whenever possible and on one occasion is reputed to have nearly laid his ship on her beam ends. I wonder if this is why they changed her rig.

There was another ship built by the same firm in 1875, the *Castle Holme*, and she is shown altered to a barque in Lloyd's register of 1881. The *Myrtle Holme* under the name of *Glint* survived 1915 when torpedoed, and the *Castle Holme* until 1926. She was renamed *Ester* and then *Ternan* or *Tornan* sailing under the Norwegian, Swedish and Danish flags. It is interesting to compare the dimensions of the *Myrtle Holme* and *Castle Holme* with those of the *Cutty Sark*.

Cutty Sark (1869)   212 feet x 36 feet x 21 feet, 921 net reg. tons.
Castle Holme (1875)   214 feet x 34^1/2 feet x 21 feet., 996 net reg. tons.
Myrtle Holme (1875)   211 feet x 33 feet x 20 feet., 902 net reg. tons.

Two other smart barques were the *Eden Holme*, 786 tons, built by Bartram and Company and the *Briar Holme*, 894 tons, built by J. L. Thompson of Sunderland; this firm built a number of "Holme" steamers in later years. The *Briar Holme* was wrecked in 1904 off Tasmania and her loss is described in Lubbock's "Colonial Clippers" the *Eden Holme* was wrecked in 1907 on the Hebe Reef.

One of the best known ships in the Tasmanian wool trade, the *Briar Holme* shared with her sisters the reputation of being among the smartest and best-run vessels in the business. Frequent references to the "smart little Holmes" are to be found in many old issues of *Sea Breezes* for they made fast passages rarely being more than 80 days out and usually about 90 home. The photograph of her reproduced in connection with this article was lent to the author by her builders J. L. Thompson and Sons Ltd. who also possess a fine model of the ship. In *Sea Breezes* for September 1925 there appears on the following paragraph:

> "The finest vessel I have ever been in was the *Briar Holme*; she had heavy carved work from stem to stern, all teak wood with mottoes over the boat skids such as 'A place for everything and everything in its place', or another, 'waste not, want not', another 'The sea is His and He made it, and his hands prepared the dry land'."

The tragic loss of the *Briar Holme* is described in the *Sea Breezes*, May 1926. Under the command of Capt. J. H. Rich, who was making his last voyage before retiring, she was very much overdue at Hobart towards the end of November 1904. After weeks of anxiety she was posted missing on January 18th, 1905. Late in January wreckage was discovered on the south-west of Tasmania and identified as belonging to the *Briar Holme*. Two Government search parties were unsuccessful but eventually the fishing vessel the *Brittania* on February 13th, 1905, found Oscar Larsen, the sole survivor of the barque's company.

The Loughrigg Holme *in Heavy Seas.*
Built 1891 – 2,069 tons.

The Ardmore.
Pictured in the Solway Firth.
Built 1872.

He had been leading an arduous existence, endeavouring on several occasions to penetrate the bush in order to reach civilisation, but without success, He was living off stores from the wreck. Larsen related how the *Briar Holme*, due to adverse winds, had had a slow passage to the Cape of Good Hope but then made good time towards Tasmania. On November 5th, 1904, when 107 days out, she was hove – to in thick and heavy weather when she struck a submerged reef and soon broke up. On October 26th, 1905 a tablet was dedicated in St. Paul's Church, Dock Street, London, to the memory of her crew.

Another pair, the *Abbey Holme* and *Hazel Holme*, mentioned in past numbers of *Sea Breezes*, were also barques but considerably smaller than the *Castle* and the *Myrtle Holme*. The *Hazel Holme* was built in 1870 as the barque *King Arthur* and sold to Hine Bros., in the seventies, a wood vessel, she was of 422 gross tons. The *Horatio* was a venerable barque of 336 tons, built at Workington in 1824 and was appearing in Hine's list in 1887, She was sold to Horatio Battle of Valparaiso in 1887.

After running aground once in her career somewhere near Punta Arenas when homeward bound with a cargo of nitrate, the *Abbey Holme* met her fate in home waters. During a strong north-easterly gale in April 1890 she was being towed out of the Tyne when off South Shields the tow rope parted and before the tug could do anything she was driven ashore on the inside part of Shields pier. It seems she came to rest on an even keel and the crew were able to reach the pier by lowering themselves from the rigging. The ship was fully loaded with coal and due to the terrific pounding of the seas she soon went to pieces.

The steamer the *Rydal Holme*, 1,255 tons, built in1889 by J. Blumer and Company of Sunderland with triple-expansion engines by Amos and Smith of

Hull. To commemorate Queen Victoria's Diamond jubilee in 1897, she led a squadron of merchantmen through the lines of the fleet. In 1914 she was bought by the Admiralty and sunk as a blockship.

Of two small steamers listed the *Henry Scholefield* was the first to be built, in 1872 by J. L. Thompson and Sons. She was rated as a two masted schooner as was the *Florence Richards* built the following year. The propelling machinery of both vessels seem to have been identical and was constructed by the firm of John Dickinson of Sunderland. Each was designed to steam at eight knots. The first *Ivy Holme* was a steamer of 98 net tons built by J. L. Thompson and sons in 1881. She was lost on her maiden voyage round the North of Scotland but there was no loss of life. The crew were all picked up by a trawler and taken to Stornaway.

The Alne Holme *in Senhouse Dock.*
Built 1876 – 1,036 tons.

There appear to have been about 26 steamers in lists of Hine's fleet, the largest being the *Isel Holme*, 2,426 tons built in 1889 by J. L. Thompson, with triple expansion engines by Geo. Clarke and Company of Sunderland. The smallest, illustrated in *Sea Breezes* for November 1956, was the *Elizabeth and Ann*, 41 tons, built in 1875 by Dodgin of Newcastle, with engines by Wardhaugh and Bulmer, also of Newcastle. She was built of wood. The *Hazel Holme* and *Abbey Holme* again appear in the list but this time as steamers. In 1876 there were 15 vessels in Hine's list, of which 14 were sailing vessels, two ships, eight barques, one schooner (*Tom Roberts*), two brigantines and one brig. The remaining vessel was the "screw schooner" *Florence Richards* 667 tons, built by Thompson.

The fleet seems to have been largest in about 1883 when 23 vessels were listed, of which 12 were sailing vessels, including 10 barques, the brigantine *Clara* which was built in Novia Scotia in 1865 and the schooner *Tom Roberts*, built at Milford in 1838. The other veteran, the *Horatio* (barque) was also still running. The *Castle*

Holme was the largest sailing vessel and the *Fern Holme,* 1,715 tons, the largest of the steamers. For some years the size of the fleet seemed to have altered little, old ships being replaced by new steamers, such as the *Derwent Holme, Forest Holme, Loughrigg Holme, Nether Holme,* and *Rydal Holme,* between 1890 and 1892.

There were 16 vessels in 1892, five of the larger sailing vessels still remaining, and in 1906 there were nine ships only; the smallest was the barque *Eden Holme* and the largest the steel steamer *Isel Holme.*

The West Cumberland Iron and Steel Trade may be forgotten by all but a few, but many tons of railway lines were carried all over the world in Hine's ships, out of Maryport, including the first consignment for the Canadian Pacific Railway.

Although these ships were small by present-day standards and the company they served Lilliputian with the great shipping concerns of our time, they were all part of the great tradition of merchant ships and seamen that is such a vital part of our national heritage. The tragic loss of the *Pamir* served as a reminder of the hazards of life in a sailing vessel, hazards which were a constant anxiety in times when a ship might be away for two or three years on end, covering thousands of miles of ocean, including the frequent rounding of Cape Horn when the only navigational aids were the faithful magnetic compass, sextant, log and chronometer.

The Myrtle Holme *loading wool for the home market. The beautiful staying of her masts, squared yards with the upper topsail yards hoisted to improve appearance, indicate a smart ship. But that was expected in the Holmes. Built 1875 – 945 tons.*

Nor was superb seamanship confined to the men of sailing vessels, for it is recorded that when the steamer *West Cumberland,* loaded with steel rails from Maryport, lost her screw in mid-Atlantic, her master, Capt. George Brown rigged a jury mast on her funnel and sailed her into Halifax, Nova Scotia.

For much of this information, I am indebted to Mr. W. Robinson, of Silloth whose father and uncle held managerial positions with Hine Bros., to the National Maritime Museum, Greenwich, for allowing me to consult their set of Lloyd's Registers and to Mr. A. L. Bland of the Worlds Ship Society.

The Eden Holme.
Built 1875 – 827 tons.

FLEET LIST
Sailing vessels

Name	Year Built	Gross Tons	Remarks
Abbey Holme (barque)	1886	534	Wrecked at South Shields April 8th 1890 through parting tow rope while on passage. Leith-Middlesbrough.
Aikshaw (barque)	1875	596	Wrecked near Antofagasta, December 1891, through being caught in a strong current and heavy swell, light winds and no anchorage.
Aline (barque)	1867	474	Wrecked September 13th, 1880 at Maldanado, Uruguay.

Name	Year Built	Gross Tons	Remarks
Briar Holme (barque)	1876	921	Wrecked November 5th, 1904 near Port Davey, Tasmania, on passage London-Hobart; one Survivor.
Castle Holme (ship-barque)	1875	1, 042	Sold 1908 to A. H. Mysen, Fredrikstad, Norway, re-sold 1912 to H. Jacobson Fredrikstad and renamed *Ester*. Re-sold to V. Muller, Copenhagen, 1916, as *Ternen*. Bought by E. Fosberg, Kariskrona, Sweden in 1922 and renamed *Tarnan*. Wrecked December 18, 1924 off Torelior on passage London-Baltic.
Clara (brigantine)	1865	145	Sold to W. Shelton, Swansea, in 1884. Owned by B. Sheffield, Swansea, 1889. Dismantled as a coal hulk, 1891.
Eden Holme (barque)	1875	827	Wrecked on Holm reef passage London-Hobart and Launceston, January 7th, 1907.
Glastry (brig)	1861	167	Bought by Hine 1876 from G. Shaddick, Dublin. Sold in 1878 to J. Davidson of Maryport.
Glenfalloch (brig)	1861	462	Condemned 1883, but sold to Chile as *Natalia*.
Hazel Holme (barque)	1870	427	Wood barque built as *King Arthur*. Bought by Hine's about 1875. Re-sold In 1887 to H. Battle and Co of Valpariso. Wrecked June 1898.
Horatio (brig-barque)	1824	348	Built as brig (279 tons).
John Norman (ship-barque)	1855	513	Built as a ship but later cut down to barque rig. Abandoned leaking June 21st, 1872 while on passage to Cape Verde Is, Lota 18 miles off Bahia.
Maggie Gross (brigantine)	1869	185	Owned in 1874 by J. Burgess, Swansea. Sold 1879 to S. Morrison, Swansea.

The Derwent Holme.
Pictured in the Solway Firth.
Built 1888 – 2,107 tons.

Name	Year Built	Gross Tons	Remarks
Myrtle Holme (ship barque)	1875	945	Sold to Arendal (Norway) owners 1908, renamed *Glint*. Sunk by submarine in North Sea, while on passage to Ellesmere Port-Gaspe in ballast, September, 4th, 1915.
Robert Hine (barque)	1868	327	Sold 1885 to J. Bevan. Liverpool. Wrecked at Imbituba (Brazil) August 19th, 1891.
Tom Roberts (schooner)	1838	122	Sold to W. Walker, Milford, 1884. Wrecked November 16th, 1887, near Peel, Isle Of Man, on passage Belfast-Workington.

Steamers

Name	Year Built	Gross Tons	Remarks
Abbey Holme	1899	3, 365	Sold 1908 to de Vap. Charge Francais; renamed *Rigel*. Sold for scrap 1927.
Alne Holme	1876	1, 036	Wrecked May 5th, 1895, off (Burriana), Spain after collision with steamer *Ambrose*.
Ardmore	1872		Owned by Hines, Sold 1898 to Glen & Company. Stranded in Pentland Firth, August 20th, 1899. Total loss.

Name	Year Built	Gross Tons	Remarks
Bavington	1873		Wrecked at Maryport, September 1883.
Dent Holme	1883	1,221	Lost in collision with steamer *Lake Champlain* in Gulf of the St. Lawrence while on passage – Montreal-Sydney, Nova Scotia. July 6th, 1885.
Derwent Holme	1888	2,107	Ex-*Crest*. Sold 1901 to Cie. Nat. Belge de Trans, Mar., renamed *Flanders*. Foundered off Molene-(France) 1911.
Earl of Carrick	1875	258	Wrecked at Oban. September 1878.
Eizabeth and Ann	1875	84	Bought from W. H. Poole and Co, Newcastle in 1883. sold 1890 to R. Mason, not in Lloyd's Register.
Esk Holme	1877	925	Wrecked off Lavernock Point, January 31st 1892 on passage Newport, Mon-Valencia.

The Nether Holme.
Built 1888 – 1,969 tons.

Name	Year Built	Gross Tons	Remarks
Fern Holme	1883	2,610	Wrecked in Holyroad Bay, Newfoundland, July 9th 1888, on Passage Montreal-London.
Forest Holme	1890	2,407	Sold November 1911; Last ship in Hines fleet. Resold February 1912 to L. Macarthy, Newcastle, name retained. Again sold December 1913 to Greece as *Kardamila.* Passed to Uruguay in 1916 as *Begona No.* 4. Sold to Rees Jones and Co. in 1917 as *Camphill.* Torpedoed and sunk June 26th, 1917, West of Fastnet.
Glen Holme	1894	826	Ex-*Margaret Banks* of London. Bought 1882. Lost in collision in sound of Islay with steamer *C.P.A. Koch.*
Greta Holme	1894	2,626	Sold by auction to D. Kydonifes and renamed *Antonios,* 1911. Lost with all hands at Scilly, 1912.

The Dent Holme.
Leaving St. John's Harbour Newfoundland, Canada 1884.
Built 1883 – 1,221 tons.

Maryport Cemetry, Headstone to Mr. Alfred Hine (Ship owner) of Parkhill, Maryport (The Holme Line).
Died September 14th, 1902. Aged 61 years.

Name	Year Built	Gross Tons	Remarks
Hazel Holme	1900	3,097	Sold before being completed to Charlton and Thompson as *Hughenden*. Foundered in Bay of Biscay on passage Symrna-Dublin. December 21st, 1911.
Isel Holme	1899	3,741	Sold November 1907 to Nautilus Steam Shipping Company and Renamed *Myrtle Branch*. Torpedoed and sunk 9 miles N.E. by E. of Innistrahull, April 1918.
Henry Schoefield	1872	963	Wrecked at Nethertown on Passage London Whitehaven. December 24th, 1881.
Ivy Holme	1881	170	Foundered of Butt of Lewis, May 5th, 1881, on passage. Sunderland to Dublin.

Name	Year Built	Gross Tons	Remarks
Ivy Holme	1883	237	Sold to Spain 1894 became *Chindor*. Resold 1903 and became *Kontzesi*. Wrecked January 11th, 1929 Ondarroa, passage Zumayo-Santander.
Loughrigg Holme	1891	2,069	Stranded at Bari, April 2nd, 1906. Refloated and broken up at Palmero.
Maitland	1872	660	Sunk in collision off Ushant, January 1880.
Nether Holme	1888	1,969	Wrecked off Pembrokeshire November 3rd, 1907. Refloated and scrapped at Milford, March 1908.
Ovington	1873	697	Lost in collision with steamer *Queen Victoria* on passage Glasgow-Hamburg December 29th, 1929.
Rydal Holme	1889	1,931	Sold in 1900 to the Rydal Shipping Company and she retained her name. Was sold to Bailey and Leetham, Hull. In 1902 becoming *Ronda* retained same name. Bought by the the Admiralty 1914 was sunk as a blockship.
San Domingo	1874	1,087	She was bought in 1889 from H. Bucknall and Sons, Newcastle. Sold to Sweden in 1899, becoming *Blenda*. Mined and sunk off Hango on passage Viborg-Hull, November 21st, 1920.
Thos. Vaughan	1871	645	First owned by C. Muller, Middlesborough; bought by Hines in 1877. Missing off Pembrokeshire coast, January 1882.
West Cumberland	1879	1, 387	Stranded October 1881; later refloated on passage – Cartagena-Mostyn. Lost in collision with barque *Nuncio*, N.W. of Cape Finisterre, June 11th, 1890.

The Castle Holme.
Built 1875 – 1,042 tons.

The Glenfalloch.
John Saul Commander of Maryport.
Built 1861 – 462 tons.

Ships' Figureheads

and wood carving

AS a young boy myself I always held a deep fascination for ships and the sea, especially the sailing ships of the 17th and 18th centuries, rather than the steam driven vessels that followed and took over from sail. The sailing ship painted a picture of adventure, the discovery of new lands, piracy on the high seas, and buried treasure.

Myself and a school friend who lived just around the corner from me on Lawson Street in Maryport, with a penknife or a scouts knife we would carve and fashion small ships out of softwood, we would then fix masts and bowsprit to them out of bamboo cane, sails made out of cloth, or a strong waterproof type of greased paper, the type our mothers used in the kitchen for cooking or roasting meats.

When our vessels were ready for launching, with boyhood pride we would transport them to the allotments on Selby Terrace on the banks of the River Ellen, we climbed over the railings and over the allotments to the rivers edge, and after a small ceremony we proudly launched our ships into the river, we would climb back as fast as we could over the railings, and then run like the wind down to the bridge at the end of Selby Terrace, which adjoins Station Street, and wait with great expectation and excitement for our ships to arrive, with the hope that it would our own ship that arrived first.

They always did arrive, but not always the way we had planned or anticipated. There was the odd occasion when they would arrive bow first, which we would look upon with pride, toast ourselves in boyhood fashion on the excellent shipbuilding that we had achieved, and watch our small proud vessels carry on downstream on there way to the sea, and wishing them well on their journey into the unknown, but nine times out of ten, they would arrive either spinning like a top, or upside down, on these regular occasions it was back to the drawing board for the young shipbuilders to reflect and to re-design.

While attending school my best and favourite subjects were art and history, towards the end of my schooling, my parents wanted me to study and to take up art, and eventually attend art college, but at that time, and being rather strong willed, and with the Rock-N-Roll era just around the corner, I'm afraid art fell by the wayside, which I now look upon after all these years with a feeling of regret.

As I have previously mentioned, ships and the sea have always held a fascination to me, this is most probably due to my family on the maternal side having connections with seafaring, and also due to being born and raised in a seafaring community. This now brings us to the subject on the art of wood-carving, and to one man in particular, who carried out this art with great expertise, at a time when Maryport was in its glory and known all over for its shipbuilding, and the quality of the vessels turned out and launched in the town.

Firstly, the carving on the bows or prow of a ship can be traced back to the days of the ancient Egyptians, as far back as 3000 B.C. they would carve the head of a bird or animal which had been made holy, its eyes pronounced in bright colours, as if the eyes were guiding the vessel on journey to its destination.

Human beings and wild animals would at times be sacrificed, their heads would then be attached to the bow, or on the end of the bowsprit of the vessel.

The ancient Greeks adorned their vessels with the carved heads of charging beasts, such as the wild boar or a rams head, or maybe the carved head of a majestic horse with its mane flying in the wind. This type of figurehead was also used by the Romans, likewise the rams head.

In the era of the Vikings, these warrior adventurers had a long curved stem at the fore of their longships, to which would be carved the images of a serpent, dragon, or sea snake, or other ferocious looking carvings to add to their warlike image. So through the centuries the craft of wood carving on sea going vessels has continued into the modern era, even today, if a replica ship of a bygone age is reproduced it will carry a figurehead on its bows.

A ship was recognisable by its figurehead, a ship without a figurehead was a ship with no face. The figurehead of the ship was the spirit of the vessel, its identification.

I refer now to a gentleman who followed this trade in Maryport in the 1840s onward, when shipbuilding was at its height in the town.

J.D.W.

Mr James Brooker
Ships figurehead and ornamental wood carver
Past Master of a Vanished Craft
by J. W. Crerar. J.P., M.B., F.R.C.S.Ed.

Mr. A. C. Wardle's very interesting article, *Ship' Figureheads*, in *Sea Breezes* and the subsequent letter of Mr. Daniel Hay, supply the motif of this account of **James Brooker,** a celebrated craftsman in the art of ship-carving who received his training in Liverpool.

On December 21st. 1828, he was apprenticed by his father, William, to Archibald Robertson, ship carver and block maker, of Liverpool. William was himself a shipwright or carver in that city. On the completion of his apprenticeship James Brooker went to Maryport, Cumberland, where extensive shipbuilding was being carried out by the old-established firm of Wood and Sons, and by the newer firm of Ritson and Company.

It has not been possible to determine the precise year in which Brooker began his work in Maryport, which had no local newspaper prior to October, 1841 when the *Maryport Locomotive.* under the editorship Mr. Robert Adair, first saw the light, and ended its brief career in February 1844. owing to the embargo of the Stamp Office on all unstamped newspapers. There was then no local news sheet until 1853, when Robert Adair launched his *"Maryport Advertiser"* This parenthesis is needed to account for the fact that it is only by inference, but an inference so strong as almost to be a demonstration, that James Brooker can be identified as the carver of the figurehead be described.

It is certain that Brooker was working in Maryport before 1840 as "Brooker, of Maryport" is named as the carver of the figureheads of the *Warlock* (330 tons), of the *Syren* (314 tons), launched respectively on January 20th and September 14th, 1840, and the *Enchantress* (284 tons), launched on February 22nd, 1841. (Mr. D. Hay). In the *Maryport Locomotive.* February 4th, 1842. "Our townsman, Mr James Brooker" is named as the carver of the figurehead – "a striking likeness of the original" of the *George Bucham* (385 tons). built by Ritson & Company. "Brooker of Maryport" was the carver of the *Saneta Bega* (265 tons), in 1844 (Mr. Wardle). In the directories of Mannix & Whellan (1847) and of Slater (1848), James Brooker is

The figurehead of the Mary Ann Johnston.

described as "Ship and ornamental carver" of Eaglesfield Street, Maryport. On February 7th, 1848. Ritson & Company launched the *Mary Ann Johnston* (377 tons) for Captain. Fawcett Johnston, a cousin of Robert and William Ritson the builders but unfortunately the *Cumberland Pacquet.* February 15th, 1848, in its report of the launch, while stating that the vessel was named "in compliment to the sister of Captain. Johnston." makes no mention of the figurehead, and therefore no absolute proof can be adduced that James Brooker was the carver of her figurehead.

However it is recorded that, in addition to the vessels already named, he was the carver of the figurehead etc, of the *Robert Barbour* (330 tons), built by Kelsick Wood & Sons, in 1851, and of the *Martaban* (778 tons), built by the Brocklebanks of Whitehaven, in 1852. (Mr. Stewart Rees). Apart from any vessels built by K. Wood & Sons, he is recorded as the carver of figureheads of the following vessels built by Ritson & Company: the *Nottingham* (303 tons) in 1853, the *John Currey* (852 tons) and in 1854 the *Ann Pitcairn Sharp* (339 tons) – "an exquisite specimen of wood carving by Mr. James Brooker" – in 1855, and the

Aladdin (867 tons) in 1856. The inference that he was the carver of the figurehead of the *Mary Ann Johnston*, at the very least, is justifiable.

The Mary Ann Johnston *(three masted barque – 361 tons). With the tug* Rambler *alongside.*
Built by Ritson & Co. Maryport 1848. Owner Capt. Fawcett Johnston. Maryport registered in 1862.
Owner Capt. W. Coglin. He was also the master of the vessel.
She was wrecked at Barbados on February 28th 1878.

On this assumption a series of happy chances provided an interesting specimen of his work. a painting of the *Mary Ann Johnston* in the possession of the descendants of Robert Ritson clearly demonstrates the figurehead, and the actual figurehead is still in the grounds of the house which was occupied by Captain Fawcett Johnston until his death in 1890, and now owned by Miss M. E. Williamson, who kindly took the photograph. The *Mary Ann Johnston* was commanded by her owner from 1848 to 1857, and thereafter was owned by Robert Ritson and others. She was wrecked at Barbados on February 28th, 1878.

The photograph demonstrates the gracefulness of the figurehead but for the disproportionate massiveness of the arms. However, the explanation of the bulkiness of these was given to me by an old sailor, Joseph Monaghan, who was close on 91 years of age, died in March 1946. He stated that he sailed before the mast in the *Mary Ann Johnston* and that the arms were removed on getting to sea and were screwed on again on making a landfall.

Another example of the work of James Brooker, this time indubitably beyond cavil or question, remains to this day to testify to his skill. On the stone lintel of the house he built in Eaglesfield Street in 1842 he carved a reproduction of the "Lion of Lucerne." This bas-relief was shown to his grandson, Mr. J. Gorton Brooker of Calcutta, on September, 15th, 1944. It may be permissible to mention that the "Lion of Lucerne" is a colossal carving in the living rock at Lake Lucerne wrought by the swiss sculptor Ahorn in 1821, after a model of the great Danish sculptor – Thorwaldsen to commemorate the heroism of the Swiss guards of Louis XVI in 1792 – "Helvetorium – Fidei ac Virtuti." This reference is not alien to the main subject of this paper as Thorwaldsen in his youth was brought up by his father, an exponent of the art, as a carver of ship's figureheads. At the Great Exhibition of 1851 James Brooker was awarded a medal, now in the possession of his grandson.

In or about 1856 – John Adair's *Maryport Directory* does not include the name of any Brooker – James Brooker migrated to Sunderland. In an advertisement in Kelly's *Post Office Directory* (1858) James Brooker, Crowtree Road, Sunderland, describes himself as "Ship and Ornamental Carver and Sculptor in General," and makes mention of the Exhibition medal in 1851 and of certain testimonials. He died there on March 13th 1860.

In a tribute to his memory in the *Maryport Advertiser* Robert Adair wrote of "The celebrated wood carver . . . the beautiful creations of his chisel which once graced all the vessels built here." It is over 80 years since this master craftsman died; an appreciative article in *Sea Breezes* would probably be welcomed in the Elysian Fields.

I make grateful acknowledgment to Messrs. W. Stewart Rees. Daniel Hay, J. Gorton Brooker, Robert Hope, Brian Adair, Miss M. E. Williamson, and the Ritson family, for much of the material is based.

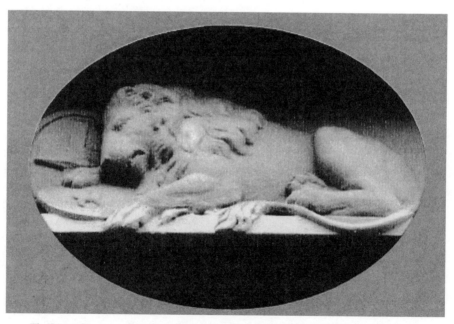

*The Lion of Lucerne, by James Brooker. sculpted in stone, above the lintel of the door of the house he built in 1842, at Lower Eaglesfield Street Maryport.
Photo May 2003.*

SHIP LAUNCH
1842

On Saturday the 20th, a splendid new vessel was launched from the ship-building yard of Messrs. R. Ritson & Co., called the *Nottingham*, burthen per register 550 tons. She has a figurehead of Robin Hood carved by Mr James Brooker, in his usual excellent style. The hill in front of the yard was crowded with spectators; and, as she left her cradle and glided gracefully and "like a thing of life" into her destined element, she was greeted by vociferous and hearty cheering, betokening a sympathy, and uttered as a benediction on one about to be committed to the storms and perils of the deep. This vessel is built for Mr. Huthwaite, and is intended for the Australian trade, to be commanded by Captain Ball. She is pronounced by critics in navel architecture, to be a happy combination of symetry of mould with sailing and carrying qualities; and in fact second to none which have been turned out by the same distinguished firm.

The bow of the Clipper Ship adorned with fine carved figurehead.

It is more than likely that James Brooker launched his profession in Maryport well before 1842. It is recorded that he took out a grant on a plot of land in the town in 1842, this being at lower Eaglesfield Street adjoining to Church Street. He there built his house and workshop, his house in Eaglesfield Street, and his workshop just around the corner in Church Street.

In 1838 the Ritson shipyard launched a barque named the *Blair* (330 tons), the figurehead and the taffrail had been carved by James Brooker. So it would seem without doubt that James Brooker was applying his craft in Maryport well before the year 1842.

In 1851 Brooker applied his carving skills for Mr. Charles Lamport of Workington, to a vessel named the *Dinapore* (780 tons), the largest ship built in Cumberland to date. This was carried out at short notice, but the finished article was highly praised for the workmanship, he carved two full length figures, which represented the images of Venus and Adonis, which was executed beautifully by the hands of this master craftsman.

The name of Brooker was now spreading to different parts of the country, other yards required his skills, he carved quite a number of ships for the firm of Laings of Sunderland. The well known local firm of Brocklebanks of Whitehaven required his skills, even though they employed one man for almost fifty years, Mr. John Askew.

For some reason James Brooker closed down his workshop on the 14th of December 1853. He then moved to Glasgow to start up in business there, most probably with the thought that the trees would bear more fruit in a much larger and busier environment where he could apply his trade. On his arrival he announced himself thus by way of advert.

𝕵𝖆𝖒𝖊𝖘 𝕭𝖗𝖔𝖔𝖐𝖊𝖗

Begs to announce to the Shipbuilders of the Clyde and its Vicinity, that he has commenced

SHIP AND ORNAMENTAL CARVING
IN EVERY VARIETY,
AT
109 HYDEPARK STREET

And having been in business in Cumberland for twenty years, hopes, by quality of Work and punctuality, to merit a share of the Public patronage.

The following are a few of the numerous Testimonials J.B. has received:

"Maryport, 21st July, 1846.

"We have much pleasure in certifying that we have for many years employed Mr James Brooker in Carving Figureheads and Sterns, and all other Carved Work belonging to Vessels, and that we consider him inferior to none, but superior to most in that Art. We feel confident that he will give satisfaction to those who may employ him.

"K. WOOD & SONS, Shipbuilders."

Respecting the launching of a new Vessel the 'Lord Hardinge,' the Editor thus writes: "She has a finely-executed and elaborately-defined full-length portrait of that gallant soldier and wise statesman, in the full uniform of a field-marshal, and having all his newly-acquired badges of honour conspienously set forth as a figure-head. Also a beautiful medallion of the gallant General cut in the stern carvings with other appropriate devices. We understand that the representation of the great warrior is a very striking one. It is in our opinion. As fine a piece of workmanship as ever we saw from the chisel of that eminent carver Mr. Brooker of Maryport." **(*From the* Whitehaven Herald, *May 16th, 1846.*)**

James Brooker moved from Glasgow after less than one year, most probably because there were more than enough well-established men in the same field, and to a stranger arriving, however good the quality of his work, it takes some time to get known and accepted in new surroundings.

He then moved to Sunderland where he was quite well-accepted, again carving for the firm of Laing, plus others. Even after leaving the coast of Cumberland he still was in demand there, receiving orders to which he loyally gave attention. Readers will note in the above advert, which he placed in the local newspapers on his arrival in Glasgow, that he stated he had been in Cumberland for twenty years. In his days an apprenticeship would start at an early age 12 years or so, on the completion of a five year apprenticeship, he would be qualified at his trade at the age of 17 or 18 years, and apparently he moved to Maryport shortly after the completion of his training, so one must assume that James Brooker began to apply his skills in Maryport much earlier than was thought, also leaving a little later than we are led to believe by previous accounts, as Dr. Crerar points out in his article.

Listed in the book of *British Figurehead and Carvers*, it is stated that in the Maritime Museum in Gothenburg in Sweden there is an unknown figurehead signed "J. Brooker M'Pt" which has removable arms and weapons, a feature commonly found on top figureheads where projecting parts could be lost or damaged at sea. There were apparently very few carvers who signed their figureheads. So the figurehead in the museum at Gothenburg suggests it was carved at Maryport before 1853, or possibly Sunderland.

Most probably the last creation carried out by the hands and tools of this fine craftsman, was the vessel the *Mary Lee* (465 tons in 1859), built by Ritson of Maryport.

This chapter is ended on rather a sad note regarding Mr. Brooker. It was early in the year 1860, we find him penniless, also in bad health and an affected mind. Sadly he was admitted to the workhouse, and then into an asylum, where he died on the 13th March 1860, as a result of injuries inflicted upon him by the keeper.

Maybe, if he had stayed where he had made his name, fame, customers and friends, he would have been a much happier person, enjoying a longer and fuller life, and to enjoy the fruits of his God given talent, he was well-respected in Maryport and treated as a son of the town.

Ship's Figurehead

The carving of the Lion Of Lucerne, which he sculpted some 165 years ago above the door of his home in Maryport, serves as a tribute and a memorial to the man himself, a remembrance of his time spent in the town,

(Footnote: He had a son William Brooker, who was also a wood carver, who also turned out work for the firm of Laing of Sunderland. William was also a merchant seaman, and it was this profession which he favoured to follow.

J.D.W.

Lines Written after a Storm

BY AN APPRENTICE ABOARD THE *MYRTLE HOLME*

If all the ships were gathered, to pick the best alone,
The one that would excel them all would be the "Myrtle Holme"
For she's a well-built clipper, and, for for beauty and for grace,
I do not think her equal you could find in any place.

The "Myrtle" hails from Maryport, as does her Captain too,
Her apprentices are English lads, a mixture is her crew,
Her Chief Mate was a Cornishman, from England's sunny south,
Where ships bound home for orders call – a port they call Falmouth.

Twas on Sunday evening, on the 29th of June,
That Mr – Baker our Chief Mate, regretted met his doom:
He was a true kind officer, so full of joy and mirth,
We little thought his moments were so limited on earth.

Twas in the second dog watch, with starboard watch below,
The gale blew hard as night approached more fiercely did blow:
And as the seas rolled up astern with loud and angry roar,
We saw the mate upon the poop, as oft we'd done before.

With arms around each back – stay firmly braced, he took his stand,
P'raps thinking of his wife and children, or of his native land;
And as that sea swept o'er our barque. yards crashed and canvas tore,
Our gallant ship to starboard heeled, we thought to rise no more.

Our Captain stood, lashed to the boom, where he could give command,
And cheered each seaman as they cried, Our ship can never stand;
His coolness and encouragement brought hope to every breast,
And God our Heavenly Father. spared, and all our efforts blest.

"But where's Mr. Baker, where's the Mate?" the Captain anxious cries,
His name is called by all on board, no answering voice replies,
That sea that thundered o'er our decks had borne him to his grave;
No more he'll see his wife or friends; God took, 'twas He that gave.

Maryport Pier

THE subject of our engraving is a scene but to often visible on our coasts, and by no means peculiar to Maryport. The storm is evidently exhausting it fury upon the pier and lighthouse in vain, they are destined to sustain the shock of many such rude assaults, and to afford the shelter and warning to mariners so requisite in the hour of Ocean's rage. The coast of Cumberland is at all times of the year rough and inhospitable to the sailor: but at the equinoxes, especially the autumnal one, its dangers are more imminent; and the trading vessels in the Solway Firth and the Irish Channel, are exposed to serious risk. Owing to the numerous shoals and sand-banks lying at various points, the navigation is at all times intricate; and even to those best acquainted with its peculiarities, the passage from Ireland is frequently attended with greater hazard than many longer voyages.

The Town of Maryport is the subject of another view, and in the notice accompanying it will be found such particulars as we could glean in connection with this small but bustling port. The pier itself, though well adapted for the

The Fury of the Storm.
Maryport Pier and Lighthouse, from an engraving.

purposes of illustration, is not a subject upon which we can profitably occupy the reader's attention; we shall therefore, avail ourselves of the opportunity thus afforded us to say a few words upon one of the finest of the English Lakes, situated within a few miles of Maryport, and a visit to which is a favourite excursion with its inhabitants and visitors. It is to the far-famed Derwent Water that we allude. It occupies a beautiful valley, surrounded by romantic mountains, its shores and islands, covered with luxurious wood, and towards Keswick its northern extremity opening to a spacious and fertile plain. The mountains on the eastern side of the lake are finely broken, in some places presenting precipices mingled with copse-wood and verdure; the chasms of rock discharging a great many streams in beautiful falls. The mountains on the western side of Derwent Water are more regular in their forms, generally verdant, and adorned with a profusion of wood near the water's edge. At the southern extremity of the lake, three miles from the town, is Lowdore waterfall, the height of which is said to be not less than 200 feet. It is a very considerable stream, rushing through an immense chasm, and bounding over huge blocks of stone, with which the channel is filled. Near the fall is Gowder Crag and Shepherd's Crag, constituting one of the finest scenes amongst the lakes.

Robert Ritson,
Maryport Shipbuilder 1810-1877.

The manor of Derwentwater belonged to a family which derived their name from it. In the reign of Henry VI, the heiress of Sir John De Derwentwater married Sir Nicholas Radcliffe, of Dilston in Northumberland, whose descendant Sir Francis Radcliffe, was created by King James II. Earl of Derwentwater, &c. James, the second earl, having been engaged in the rebellion of 1715, was beheaded on Tower-hill; and the Derwentwater estates, becoming forfeited to the Crown, were granted to Greenwich Hospital, by act of Parliament. Lord's Island, in the lake, was the residence of the earls.

The beautiful scenery of Derwent Water, said to be about ten miles in circumference, has often been described, St. Herbert's Island is named from a hermitage dedicated to that saint. Vicar's Island formerly belonged to Fountain's Abbey. Rampsholm, a small island, is covered in wood. The fish in greatest estimation in the lake is a sort of salmon trout. The celebrated mountain Skiddaw, in this vicinity, is said to be about 3,036 feet in height, extends to several townships; that part which is in Crossthwaite parish is within the township of Under Skiddaw and Crossthwaite, and comprises the manor of Brundholm.The mountain is of easy access; and standing in some measure detached, the view from the summit, particularly to the north and west, is not intercepted by other mountains: it comprehends the principal part of the county, including the coast from St. Bees Head to the head of the Solway Firth, with its several bays and promontories, the Isle of Man, and a considerable portion of the southern part of Scotland. The summit of Ingleborough-hill, in Yorkshire, may be seen over the range of hills bounding the head of Ullswater; and a glimpse of the sea near Lancaster is obtained through the gap in Dunmail Raise. Derwent Water and Bassenthwaite lake are the only lakes seen, and but one of these from the summit. The views from the neighbouring mountains may exceed in grandeur the view from the summit of this, but in no other ascent are the prospects equalled, which unfold themselves when overlooking the lake and vale of Keswick, with Borrowdale and Newlands mountains.

Shipping Brow, Maryport 1915.

Re – the *Mary Moore*

Sea Breezes June, 1930

IN the February issue of the journal it is interesting to learn that Captain R. L. Sealby and Captain J. W. Millican have both sailed in the pretty little barque the *Mary Moore*. I might say that my late brother was also mate of her in the latter part of her career, when she was in the inter-Colonial trade, and, I think, owned by her master Captain Robilliard, if I am not mistaken. In the eighties, she was owned by Mr. Norman who hailed from Maryport, and commanded by Captain J. Briscoe from the same town. In the nineties she hailed from London, owned by Maddox & Co., and presumably sailed by her owner, Captain Maddox.

In 1901, we find her sailing out of Sydney, N.S.W., in the interi-Colonial trade, under the command of Captain Wood, and owned by G. L. Robertson of that city, who was the owner of many other renowned old clippers in their old age.

The *Mary Moore* was a stately little ship and traded between Australia and New Zealand and *vice-versa* for some years, and was pretty well looked after and kept right up to the end, which came in 1908, when, owing to the keen competition of steam, she was like many other old but good vessels, driven out of the trade, and was then sold for a hulk and was taken to either Freemantle or Albany and did duty there for a few years, and some years ago she was towed round to Melbourne and no doubt will finish her days there. I had a letter from a friend in Melbourne recently, who informs me that he thinks her end is not far off.

P. S. – I hope Captain Millican will be good enough to let us have an account of his apprenticeship in her, etc., or anything he might write, and his experiences in past issues were appreciated by all readers I am sure, quite as much as I appreciated them myself.

Mr. George Irvine

More about – *Mary Moore*

In your June number I read with interest the list of "Hulks of Melbourne," many of them known to me over forty years ago. One, the *Mary Moore*, brought back a whiff of old times, as I have often wondered what her last years had been. I joined her in 1884 – my first trip as second mate from Garston to Valparaiso and Caleta Olivia, and back to Liverpool. She was a beautiful little composite barque of 564 tons, hailing from Maryport, Captain J. G. Briscoe (a native of the same port) in command. (He passed away on the 12th inst., aged 79, at Newcastle N.S.W.), I had just finished my time in the ship *Houghton Tower*, 1,500 tons, of Liverpool, and I remember how small everything, especially the skysail, was to me after the big ship. A picture, and any story of her career, would be interesting to many old-timers like myself.

I would also like to know the ending of the ship *Houghton Tower*, barque *Norseman*, of Liverpool, and barque *Phillip Nelson*, once of Maryport. I was mate in her in 1886. She had a reputation of being haunted, and never made a voyage without a death. On the voyage I made in her the captain, who was owner, died in Valparaiso, and an **A.B.**, who was also a bit of a pug, died on the passage out. He had been badly knocked about in a fight to a finish – bare knuckles, five pounds a side just before sailing. She was sold to the Norwegians on the homeward passage. I saw her once again in 1896 at Townsville, can any old hand recall her and her ghostly reputation – very real to her crew in my time, also her final end.

Since I first received a copy of your interesting little magazine from my brother, Captain Inman Sealby, it has been eagerly anticipated by myself and many other old-timers, to whom it has been like a breath of the past; may it have a long and breezy life.

Capt. R. L. Sealby

King's Son, Queen's Son, Girl of Belted Earl

The sailor sings as his ship takes wings
And makes for the deep blue ocean.
He feels the call that has held in thrall
And responds to true emotion.

He does not disdain to remember the Dane
Who taught him to love the water;
And likes to recall that great day of all
When we welcomed a Sea King's daughter.

Now the years are sped, and we see instead
A meeting of York – his house all in order –
With a bright bonny bride to stand by his side
Whose house will be South of the Border.

It is pleasant to think as time goes by
That a match may be made without e' er a sigh,
And that England may count with a smiling face
On the strengthening bonds of the British race.

F.E.H.

The Foreign Sailor's Grave

Note: The following story is a true one, and refers to the grave of an unknown sailor in the little churchyard at Llandwrog, an old-world village near Caernarvon, North Wales.

IT lies in a secluded corner of a little Welsh churchyard – the foreign sailor's grave – close within the shelter of a crumbling moss-grown wall, where sunbeams seldom penetrate and where all is steeped in soft brooding shadow. At the head of the narrow, grassy mound, a rude stone cross, erected years and years before, with a date its only epitaph – 1857. But perhaps in all the world there is no more hallowed spot than that little green acre down by the Cambrian sea.

The dead are never lonely there, for the little graveyard lies just between the church and the village school. All day long the muffled prattle of children's voices breaks upon the sweet, soft air. In the dewy freshness of summer mornings, above those silent hearts, their old Welsh songs and hymns arise upon the stillness. In the glory of noontide the sound of their joyous playtime is as the touch of a warm, kindly, living hand upon the cold brows of the sleepers 'neath the green and the flowers. At night, when all else is still, the sobbing murmur of the sea, borne up across the darkened meadowland, breathes its eternal requiem o'er the dead.

Little feet in clogs, in days gone by, often crunched along the gravel path to stop at the foreign sailor's grave. Little hot hands have thrown flowers down upon it, scores of times, and youthful voices have been wont to repeat over and over again the story of the strange alien seaman who lies buried in that sacred shade.

Given up by the sea

The story is told even now at farmhouse firesides along the countryside. One wild March morning, far back in the misted years, a farmer was carting sand from the beach. Away along the foaming fringe of the rolling breakers he saw a dark object mauled by their cruel sportive play. When he reached the spot, the body of a man clad in sodden sailor's clothes was washed up on the glistening sands, the body of an olive-skinned, swarthy fellow, the sea spume in his thick black hair, tiny gold rings in his ears, as was the fashion then among Mediterranean seamen.

The castaway was presumed to have been one of the crew of some ship that had foundered some weeks before on the storm-racked Caernarvonshire coast. He was buried namelessly, by a Welsh country folk, who ever lay their dead to rest with reverence most wonderfully kind. They made enquires, the good vicar and the squire of the parish. In those days, however, the Consular service was slow moving and inefficient, so that the matter lapsed and with the years lost its interest.

In his Southern homeland, on some golden Valencian shoreway, did some woman, with child in her arms perhaps, wait long? – looking out upon a blue rippling sea that seemed always to mock the grief in her haggard eyes. Or, in some dark tenement house near the waterways of old Genoa, some aged, trembling mother, telling her beads in the soft bronze dusk of the Italian night, did she start and listen for his step on the mouldering stairs? – years and years after all hope had fled.

Who shall say that somewhere – somewhere – kind hearts have not mourned him – that lonely mariner sleeping so serenely there in the shade.

G. Bruce Thomas (April 1929).

Longevity of Cumberland People

Date of Death	Name and Residence	Age
1664 – May 5th	John Dand, of Waverbridge.	108
1685 – ?	Mrs. Margaret Dykes, Dearham	106
1761 – May 19th	Thomas Fearon, of Tallentire, Bridekirk	112
1713 – Mar 20th	Margaret Santon, of Cockermouth	103
1717 – Feb 2nd	Jane Hodgson, widow, Harrington	114
1726 – Jan 19th	William Sibson, of Hayton, Aspatria	107
1765 – Mar 7th	Thomas Holliday, Aspatria	101
1771 – July 23rd	George Mc.Farland, Wigton	103
1772 – Aug 20th	William Nicholson, Aspatria	100
1778 – ?	Jane Wood, Buttermere	106
1786 – Nov 4th	Sarah Nixon, widow, Hesket	107
1790 – Nov 19th	Joseph Peel, Mariner, Maryport	106
1793 – June 20th	John Milliken, tinker, Maryport	112

His epitaph is as follows; "Joseph Peel, born at Bank-End Feb 2, 1684; he lived in the rein of eight princes, viz., King Charles 11., William 111., Queen Mary, Queen Anne, and three King Georges; aged 106 years and 10 months, and was buried November. 19, 1790." Annos c vi. natus, toterrim vixit Josephus Peel; ita'ferebat duo quae maxima putaoetur opera, pauperatatem and senectutem, ut eis poene delectari videretur." There is a portrait of this old sailor at Netherhall, the seat of Humphrey Senhouse, Esq., with one of whose ancestors he lived as a servant when a boy. He went to sea at 17, and was in the voyage with Captain Stradling, when Alexander Selkirk was left at Juan Fernandez in 1704. He had acquired a small estate, but in his old age reduced to poverty by his children. He dined at Netherhall on his one-hundredth birthday, which he had previously ascertained by examining the register. This poor man died in consequence of a remarkable accident – of bruises which he received by a fall from a horse, having being startled and annoyed by the claws of a cat, which Joseph Peel had been employed to carry some miles in a basket.

Reminiscences of Maryport

January, 1873. – A father and son, the son's daughter, and this daughter's son (all descendants from one stock of a well known Maryport Family) the last of whom – Mr. Joseph Sanderson – is now living, averaged 93 years each, their total ages amounting to 372 years.

Joseph Peel, aged 106.

(Footnote: The painting of the above Mr. Joseph Peel is now housed and on display in the Maritime Museum in Maryport).

The Voyage of The *Hannah*

Introduction

AS one coming of seafaring stock – my father was lost at sea in the brig *Dove*, of Maryport, in 1859 – and who has been so much entertained and refreshed in memory by reading that excellent magazine the *Sea Breezes*, I venture to submit the following story as told to *The News*, a local paper, of 14th April, 1888, by my old friend Captain Mounsey, long since departed. It relates to the voyage of the barque – *Hannah*, of Maryport, when engaged in taking emigrants to America in 1847, and provides matter for thought and comparison. Think of the difference between the miserable emigrants of 1847 and those of 1928. Think also of the *Hannah,* devoid of all the amenities, and compare her with the palatial and magestic liners of the P.S.N. Co. They afford hospital accommodation as well as medical and nursing skill, and annually transport thousands of emigrants, in luxury and comfort, with speed and safety, over intervening oceans, in a few days as compared with the weeks of agony and suspense inseperable from those early ships. All this wonderful improvement has taken place within the lifetime of myself and a few others still living.

The Narrative
TOLD BY CAPTAIN MOUNSEY, OF MARYPORT

The following narrative, as told to our Special Commissioner, by Captain Mounsey, of Maryport, will probably be read with interest.

Yes! I can tell you something about that remarkable voyage of the *Hannah*, although there are several others in Maryport who could tell you quite as much, if not a little more.

My old friend Mulcaster, for instance, could give you a rare yarn about it, and he would be sure to tell you the truth.

However, I will do my best. The *Hannah,* you must understand, was a barque and carried 580 tons deadweight. She belonged to Mr. Henry Shaw of Maryport, and was the largest ship that sailed from here at that time. Of course, times have altered since then. There was no Senhouse Dock; in fact, the Elizabeth Dock had not been built then, and the *Hannah* was regarded a pretty big craft.

We sailed away from Maryport on the 15th of April in the year 1847. Carrie Shaw (son of the owner) was captain, John Ormondy was mate, and I was second. There was fourteen of us all told, and most of us belonged to Maryport.

You remember the Irish famine, of course. No! Well, but you know there was a famine in Ireland in 1847. The distress, I suppose, was truly awful. The Government was sending a whole heap of half-starved Irish people out to the

Colonies and various places. The *Hannah* was one of the ships chosen by the Government for this purpose. We had 150 tons of coal by way of ballast, and at Sligo we 390 of the Irish emigrants.

Of all the poor distressed beings I ever saw those beat the lot, gaunt and weak, some of them only half clothed. Starvation was written on their faces. How we managed to pack 390 in is more than I can say. I am sure that the *Hannah* would not be allowed to carry more than 80 passengers nowadays at the very outside, but we did pack them in, although it was a close fit I can assure you. Men, women and children were all crowded together in open bunks like herrings in a box or pigs in a sty.

No doubt they tried to be as decent as they could, but you can imagine how much decency there was with people crowded together in this way. Well, fever broke out on board before we left Sligo, and we had to bury two before we weighed anchor. No doubt it would have been better to have stayed until the ship had been disinfected, but we had our orders and off we had to go.

If we had had a fair voyage the passengers would have suffered enough, but we had not gone more than three hundred miles when it began to blow great guns. Before and since I have been in many a gale but I think this capped them all.

The poor emigrants were in a fearful plight. Most of them were sea sick, and many of the men and women were as helpless as the children they brought with them. We could hear their shrieks above the howling of the wind and the roar of the waves.

A number of them went down on their knees and shrieked for mercy, some calling upon God and others upon the crew to save them. Those who could keep their feet wanted to go on deck. This would never have done, so we just fastened them below, then they made more noise than before, although we could not hear them so well. Of course we felt sorry for them, but what could we do? We had our work cut out to save the ship.

The mainmast went by the board, and at one time it looked very much as though we were going to the bottom. Three days elapsed before the storm abated, and it was not until then that we could properly attend to the passengers.

I don't think I ever knew what real misery was until I went below after that storm abated. The emigrants looked bad enough when they first came on board, but they looked fifty times worse now. They had a fearful time of it. During the height of the storm, one side of the bunks had given way and all the poor beggars were thrown together in a heap. The stench was awful, and to hear the children crying and the women moaning was just one of those things one never wants to experience a second time. Of course, we did what we could for them, but it was not much; we had enough to do on deck.

As I have said, the main mast was gone, and there was no help for it but to return to England to repair damages. We should have gone back to Sligo but the wind was against us, and so we went on to Maryport.

The natives were surprised to see us back again so soon, I can tell you. The

Hannah looked very different to what she did when she sailed away a few weeks before, but she was well known in Maryport and was recognised afar off.

Timely hospitality from citizens

The people came down to the shore to meet us. They were, if possible, more anxious to get the news in those days than they are now, and all they wanted to know what the *Hannah* had returned for. Our dilapidated appearance told them a great deal. The people who had relatives among the crew were anxious to know if their friends were safe.

Fortunately we could soon satisfy them on that score. It leaked out, however, that we had fever on board and the authorities wanted us to go into quarantine a mile or two off land.

I do not remember much about this part of the business, but I know there was a rare fight about it. Eventually we were allowed to land such of our passengers who wished to come ashore. As you may imagine they had had enough of the ship for a time, and were glad enough to get on to dry land. I must say the Maryport people were very kind to the storm-beaten emigrants. I cannot mention names, for just now I do not remember anyone in particular. All I know is the poor people were very kindly treated by the townspeople of Maryport.

Of course, some of the inhabitants were afraid of the fever. On the other hand, some went fearlessly among the sick emigrants and did their best for them. There was a tallow chandler's shop, where Mr. Bell, the hairdresser, now lives. Some of the inhabitants established a soup kitchen there, and the poor emigrants were supplied with many a good meal. Many of them were accommodated in the old watch-house close to where the lime-hurry now stands. Altogether we were in Maryport about three weeks, whilst our ship was being repaired and cleaned at Wood's Yard.

Once bitten; twice shy

Most of the emigrants had altered their minds about going abroad. The storm and the sea-sickness had knocked the notion out of them. Those who could find means to take them back to their homes in Ireland did so, and went back. Four of the crew had enough of it and refused to go out again. I forgot to tell you that whilst we were waiting at Maryport, the fever asserted itself and eight of the passengers died, they were buried I believe in St. Mary's Churchyard.

What with one thing and another we had only 300 passengers on board when we re-started from Maryport. As we went out people stood on the shore and cheered. They little knew how many were going out to meet their doom.

We had not left Maryport many days before fever again broke out. I cannot describe the horrors of that voyage. I was growing accustomed to death and danger, but I shall never forget the scenes that we witnessed on board the *Hannah*.

Although we had so many emigrants on board we had no doctor. That was the worst of it. The captain did the best he could with his medicine chest, but what we wanted was a medical man. As I have told you, the people were all huddled together in bunks. We did not know any of them by name, we simply called them by the number of their bunks. Every morning we called upon the head of each family to come forward for provisions, and those who were well enough were not slow in doing so.

Those who were able to do so cooked their food on stoves we had rigged up on deck. There was many a squabble at cooking time, as all wanted a first turn. There would have been more quarrelling, only twelve of the best-behaved men among the emigrants had sworn in to preserve order. I must say they did their duty well.

Unpalatable duties amid heartrending scenes

The fever still kept on raging and getting worse. We could not save the sick, do what we could. Sometimes as many as three or four of the emigrants died within twenty-four hours. It was a singular thing, but most of them (no matter how they had been all day) kept alive until midnight and then died. Of course, we had to throw the bodies overboard. We sewed them up in hammocks with lumps of coal at one end to make them sink. At first the buriel service was read over them, but as the funerals grew more numerous I am afraid we omitted a part of it if not the whole of this ceremony.

I tell you some of these scenes we saw were heartrending. The strangest thing of all that was when a man, woman or child died their friends left on board did not care to part with their bodies. The task of taking the bodies on deck and committing them to the deep always fell to the lot of the crew. In this respect we could get no assistance from the passengers. When a death occurred they concealed it from us for as long as possible.

They crowded round the body as it lay in the bunk and tried to persuade us that the dead man was asleep. Then what a scene there was when we insisted on taking the body away for the sake of the living. If they had all been swimming in the waves with only one lifebuoy between them they could not have stuck to the buoy closer than they did to those dead bodies. The women shrieked, and the children screamed, and the groans of the men when they saw the bodies of their dear ones taken away were loud and deep. What could we do? We were bound to get rid of them as soon as possible.

From bad, to worse: A well-earned "Tot."

I do not say violence was actually used, but sometimes we were almost obliged to be violent in order to do our duty. Aye, man, it was a fearful time. A death nearly every day, and sometimes three or four. The sharks followed in our wake almost from first to last. An undertaker ashore keeps his eye well open when he thinks there is going to be a funeral, but a shark beats an undertaker hollow. It was almost as bad for the crew as it was for the passengers. Three of us (Nicholas Finlinson, Thomas Mullin, and Henry Bell) succumbed to fever and had to be thrown overboard the same as the rest of them. Before it was all over we were pretty well worn out. The Captain gave each one of us half a pint of rum every day, and I can tell you we wanted it. Of course, most of us got pretty well accustomed to the funerals before the voyage was over.

One of the crew, however (he was not very old then), was always terribly frightened at night. Knowing this, one of his mates determined to give him a greater fright than ever. So one night he put a sheet over his head and approached that part of deck where the timid sailor was doing duty. If you had seen that man's face when he saw the sailor with the sheet over his head you would never have forgotten it. I never shall. He did not shout, he was too frightened for that, he simply retreated as fast as the supposed ghost advanced. I am sure he would have jumped over the side if the man with the sheet (thinking the joke had gone far enough) had not made himself known.

Well our destination was St. John, New Brunswick, we landed our fever-stricken passengers on an island thirty miles away. We really had "a ship full of fever," and the authorities would never have allowed us to land at St. John in our then state. We stayed on the island under canvas for about a month. The ship having been cleansed, we went into St. John and thus ended one of the most unpleasant voyages I ever had. By the time we got to St. John many of the passengers had pulled themselves together, but I and some other members of the crew had to remain behind in hospital.

Thomas Carey, Maryport.
(Sea Breezes 1929)

Entering Port. The Barque Dun Crag – *May 1883.*

Obituary

THE following is a reprint from an obituary card which was submitted some time ago by Captain James Nelson, Oxton, Cheshire. Although 55 years have passed over their heads since young Graham met with his tragic end, there may be some *Sea Breezers* still going who may recall the circumstances of the fate of this young seaman.

Headstone in Maryport Cemetry in memory of Edward Wilson who was drowned at Canton, November 9th 1863, aged 23 years. William Wilson, second son of John Graham and nephew to the above Edward Wilson who was lost at sea, he fell from the top gallant yard of the ship Young America on her passage from San Francisco to New York. January 14th 1876.

William Wilson Graham,

Second son of William Wilson Graham,

Of Maryport.

Aged 18 years.

He joined the ship *Young America* in December last at San Francisco for New York. On the 14th January, he was on duty on the top gallant yard, when he was observed to lean forward and fall, coming in contact with the main yard, and then struck the side of the ship and went overboard. It was thought life was extinct before he reached the water, the distance of the fall being 150 feet Wood Street, April 17th, 1876.

Pitcairn Island in 1899

Visit by a Cumbrian

ON January 12th, 1899, the ship *General Roberts,* T. C. Fearon, Master, sighted Pitcairn Island on her passage from Newcastle, Australia, to San Francisco, and Mrs. Fearon sent the following account of her visit to her home in Cockermouth:

We came up to the island in the early morning, and soon saw two boats putting off to the ship. We were some miles away, but they were soon alongside, and asked permission to come on board. The men were fine specimens – strong, healthy, muscular, and very happy-looking. They brought several kinds of fruit and vegetables, slabs of orange wood, and cocoanuts, hand-painted (floral devices) little handbags worked with wools, men's hats, etc. The bags and hats were all made from the leaves of a palm, dried in the sun, then cut to the required width and plaited; they do several kinds of plaiting. All the things, with the exception of the hats bear some allusion to Pitcairn.

Two islanders leave home

The decks were soon something like a rummage sale, as the Islanders were ripe for barter. Some of the things I got I paid for with English money, by request, as they find a little money useful to buy from some ships who prefer money than the exchange. Last year more than thirty ships called at the Island, and ours was the fifth this year, so they did not go short of anything in the way of food. I bought some chickens at one shilling each.

Two great grandsons of Fletcher Christian were anxious to return to California (one of them had married a Californian girl), so the captain agreed to take them. As they had to return to the Island for their things, I went with them. We went in the fine boat presented to Pitcairn by her Majesty the Queen, which is named *Queen Victoria.* I distinguished myself by being sick en route, but was all right when we set foot on terra firma. We landed in Bounty Bay, and a very rocky coast it is. They have a very narrow channel to pass through to the shore; any ship getting on to these rocks would be no more good, so it is not safe to go too near, as there is no anchorage.

As soon as we landed we were escorted by the President (McCoy) to his house, the path being steep, And in one part hewn out of solid rock. The island is clothed with tropical verdure, and the lovely flowers, ferns, etc, were a treat to see. Fruit and vegetables grow in abundance, oranges, lemons, water melons, pineapples, bananas, cocoanuts, and rose apples, are some of the fruits we received. Irish potatoes were scarce, but very good.

Music – Loving people

Plenty of sweet potatoes they brought, and they were splendid, fine and fine and floury. There were also pumpkins and yams. Tomatoes were only in the green stage, but I got quite a stock, and ate them as they ripened. What a treat this was in the middle of a long sea passage.

I received quite an ovation, and the women were delighted to see me. The women are strong and healthy-looking, some of them very well built, modest and unaffected. Poor things, they were poorly clad, but seemed quite happy about it. Shoes are not in use, consequently the feet of all are fairly large. I just wished I had a few webs of cotton prints, but I gave them all I could spare. The men fare better, they can always get clothing from sailors, but few have more than one lady on board, and depend mostly on passing ships for wearables.

A link with Cumberland

We visited Thursday October Christian, grandson of Fletcher Christian (leader of the Mutiny of the *Bounty*). He is quite an old man. He seemed pleased when I told him my birthplace and home were so near to Moorland Close. He asked if any of the Christian family lived in the neighbourhood, and I told him there were not, so far as I knew, though I believed a family called Fletcher were descendants, but how far removed I could not say. They said Mr. Curwen of Workington Hall was a descendant, and told me that when one of the islanders was in England Mr. Curwen wrote to him to go and see him, but he could not go at the time, as he was by a ship, trying the life of a sailor. I saw the man on board, but had very little time to talk to him. There was a large framed photograph of Moorland close hanging in the church, it looked quite home-like.

My time on the island was too short, not more than three hours, but I thoroughly enjoyed the visit. I could have found plenty to see for several days. I suppose there are some lovely places. I believe the island is $2^1/_2$ miles long and one mile broad, and six miles in circumference. Highest point about 1,000 feet, population between 140 and 150, and as usual, the females are in the majority.

Each man has a plot of ground given him to work and make the most of, and on occasion they all work for the public good. There are no wages, money is not in circulation, and everybody is on an equality. It is the realisation of the Socialists' dream. They had a family of four named Smith who came to reside among them from California about a year ago. The daughter was pining to get back to California. I felt sorry for her; she is a bonny girl, just out of her teens.

There is good fishing off the island, white, red and deep-sea cod, at a depth of 140 fathoms. All the fishing is done in canoes built built by themselves. They can all swim – men, women and children. Sharks abound in plenty, but they have never been known to touch a single native. Weddings and funerals are conducted by the President, who also preaches and conducts the service every alternate Sabbath during his term in office.

There are two or three fine springs on the island which never run dry. Public houses are conspicuous by there absence. The school is managed by Rosa Young, who, they tell me, is self-taught, and the writer on the latest book on Pitcairn. I was sorry I did not see her. The Islanders have quite an American accent, but when I asked one of the girls whether they called themselves American, she gave an emphatic, "No we are English."

We had a few of the females on board just before sailing. It was a sight to see the crowd that trooped down to the boat landing to see us off, and telling us to be sure to come again soon, and bring plenty of letters. After hearing of Pitcairn and the Mutiny of the *Bounty* from my childhood, you can imagine what a treat it was to have the opportunity of actually visiting the island I had heard so much about. We eventually reached San Francisco, and landed our passengers, and so ends the story.

Rounding Cape Horn.

"Missing"

Briar Holme's One Survivor

T HE story which appeared in the March number of *Sea Breezes*, entitled "Days in *Myrtle Holme*", from the pen of Captain Millican, recalls the dire fate which overtook her sister ship the *Briar Holme*.

We, in the *Isel Holme*, arrived at Maryport towards the end of November, 1904, and were grieved to learn that our fleet companion was very much overdue on her passage to Hobart. Needless to say, there was grave anxiety in port, among relatives of her crew and others, for the safety of a vessel noted over long years for her regular passages.

The *Briar Holme*, a clipper barque and a unit of Messrs, Hine Bros.' fleet, was 894 tons register, and built at Sunderland in 1876 by Messrs. J. L. Thompson & Sons. She was under the command of Captain J. H. Rich, with a crew of 18, and sailed from London on 21st July, 1904, for Tasmanian ports.

Posted at Lloyds

The *Briar Holme* was admitted to be one of the finest examples of the ship-builders' art when turned over to her owners (her model won a prize at the Paris Exhibition), whilst Captain Rich, a veteran commander of the Holme Line, was making his last voyage preparatory to retiring.

The weeks dragged into months, but still no tidings of the vessel's arrival in Tasmania reached the anxious relatives and friends of those on board. The experts, one by one, despaired of her safety. Finally all hope was abandoned, and on the 18th of January, 1905, the *Briar Holme* was posted missing at Lloyds.

Even then a lone survivor was leading, and had led for nearly three months, a Robinson Crusoe-like existence on the wild west coast of Tasmania, and was destined to do so for some weeks longer. It was in late January that information reached Hobart of wreckage having been discovered on the south-west coast of the island, which was identified as belonging to the *Briar Holme*.

In response to considerable public pressure the Government of Tasmania sent out two expeditions – by water – to search for possible survivors, but they both proved futile. It was left for the fishing vessel *Britannia* – then operating off Port Davey – to discover, on the 13th February, 1905, what proved to be the sole survivor of the *Briar Holme*, In the person of Oscar Larsen, an able seaman.

How the end came

From Larsen it was learned that the ill-fated barque, whilst hove to in thick weather with a terrific sea running, had struck a submerged reef shortly before midnight on the 5th November, 1904, when 107 days out from London. The vessel pounded heavily, and almost immediately the high seas carried the Lifeboats overboard.

The crew took to the rigging, but it was not long before the ship began to open up and, the masts going by the board, the men were hurled into the angry breakers. Not so Larsen, however. He, after long and severe buffeting, was finally cast ashore and, dragging himself clear of the treacherous backwash, found at daybreak that he, bleeding and torn, was the only one left of all the crew.

Owing to adverse winds the *Briar Holme* had made a tedious passage from the Channel to the Meridian of the Cape of Good Hope, but from the latter point she made good time, running her Easting down in the roaring forties among the brave west winds. All hands had been, therefore, aware of their proximity to Tasmania, so Larsen soon decided and rightly, that he was treading the mainland, and hoped soon to be rescued.

The cargo of the *Briar Holme* consisted of London general, consequently Larsen found plenty of food among the wreckage which he retrieved. After several attempts to reach civilisation by inland routes, during which he suffered some intense hardships, he had to eventually abandon the idea owing to the desolate nature of the region.

The smart little Briar Holme *which met her end in such tragic circumstances. Pictured here lying at Port Chalmers.*

A fitting memorial

It was while Larsen was absent on these excursions that the rescue party arrived on each occasion and, finding no trace of survivors, concluded there were none. The shipwrecked mariner had almost reached the point of desperation when the *Britannia* appeared and rescued him from a dismal plight.

Even a dull imagination can conjure up the delight with which Larsen met the hardy fishermen. His rescuers speedily set sail for Hobart, some 150 miles distant. En route a steamer overhauled them and, learning of the rescue, made it known directly on arrival at Hobart, with the result that large crowds were waiting to welcome the *Brittania* and the solitary survivor of a tragic shipwreck.

The rescue of Larsen was soon flashed to the ship's owner at Maryport and the world at large. With its receipt all hope in the anxious hearts of those waiting and watching fearfully for news of their dear ones among the crew was dispelled.

It is fitting that the memory of this gallant barque, which was a regular London trader for nearly thirty years, and those who perished with her, should be perpetuated in in St. Paul's, Church, Dock Street, London, where so many of "those who go down to the sea in ships" have worshipped.

To this end a memorial tablet was dedicated on the 26th October, 1905, by the Right Reverend Bishop Taylor-Smith, and reads:

**To the Glory of God and in Memory of
the following Officers and men of the Barque**

"Briar Holme."

**which was lost near Port Davey, Tasmania, on 5th Nov., 1904,
with all hands, save one.**

This Tablet is erected by the boarders of the Sailors' home.

**John H. Rich, Master.
Robert Disney, Mate; Ernest Jas. Millet, 2nd Mate.
John Pollard, Victor Anderson, W. Miller, A. Rydberg,
Phillip Canivet, Alex.Coull, Wm. Dobie, M. Friersen,
George Tarbet.**

**Apprentices :
Edward Sadler, Phillip Dulling, Ernest Cecil Blake,
Rd. A. C. Saunders, Wm. Arnold, James A. F. Howell.**

"Until the day break."

G. A. Cockell
Maryport

Brier Holme wreck
Marine Court enquiry.
Evidence not conclusive.   Hobart. Monday.

A marine court enquiry was held today respecting the wreck of the Barque Briar Holme. The evidence was that all hands had been lost with the exception of Oscar Larsen, and he being in his bunk at the time of the grounding was unable to say whether blame was attachable to anybody.

The explosives on board consisted of 85 cases of gunpowder, 75 cases of cartridges and one case of primers. The primers exploded blowing the after deck out, killing the Captain, first mate, second mate and nine seamen. All the others were drowned within 20 yards of the shore, only one body being washed ashore.

For over three months, Oscar Larsen, the sole survivor of the ships company remained in the bush near the coast, and and although search parties were sent out they failed to find him. Nearly a fortnight ago Larsen was found by fishermen near Low Rocky Point, a few miles from where the vessel was wrecked, and then he related the story of the loss of the vessel.

Larsen is a Norwegian and it is stated that he intends to return to his native country as soon as he can get a passage.

Oscar Larsen, sole survivor.

*There are heroes of whom
we have never heard,
Their names lost in history,
Brave men who answered the
call of the sea
And its depths was their destiny.*

J.D.W.

Headstone to Captain George Albert Cockell and his wife Jessie. Also to Captain James Ritchie and his wife Hannah. Maryport Cemetery.

City Chatter

The Romance of Maryport
Carlisle Journal and Patriot
April 5th, 1935
By CIVIS

FORTY or fifty years ago Maryport was probably the most attractive place in Cumberland to inspire the spirit of adventure. Going down Shipping Brow, at the side of the harbour, all the wonderful sights and smells there were for an enterprising small boy – fishing smacks with one or two of the crew busy tarring or painting or sail-mending – a small barque setting off for Ireland with coal from the Ellenborough collieries getting into the sea-way, the main-sail hoisted. Ship-builders hard at work in Ritson's Yard. Traffic across the old wooden bridge from the ship's merchants carrying the stores for a voyage, probably for one of the Messrs. Hine Bros. steamers – the whole port was a magic place for adventure.

———————

Messrs. Hine Bros. were a power in the land, or rather, on the sea in those days. The *Myrtle Holme* and the *Briar Holme* were crack sailing ships held in happy remembrance by many old-seafarers in Maryport. Then whilst they were still in commission the less romantic steamers came into being, sailing very likely to Italy with coal, and grain. How many Maryport lads served their time to the sea, either as ships officers or engineers in this famous shipping line?

———————

The Hines lived in what were called The Mansions, at the top of Camp Road – two large houses set in one big garden. Mr. Wilfred Hine, the elder brother, became a Liberal Unionist in politics. but the younger brother. Mr. Alfred Hine, lived and died a liberal. One of his sons went down as an engineer officer on a battleship at Jutland, after serving as superintendent of the line.

———————

Going further back one may recall that Lord Lister, the famous surgeon, found a wife in Maryport. Sir Francis Laking, Court Physician, was, I think, born in the town, and so was Mr. Thomas Ismay, who founded the White Star Line, under romantic circumstances. He went to Liverpool to improve his fortune, and became ships husband to a vessel sailed by Captain Bruce. Falling in love with the Captains daughter, he found that her father only agreed to marrige on the condition that he became the owner of a ship. This he did, and after running one or two ships he bought the name of the White Star Line, hitherto attached to a line of sailing ships which became the famous Company. Thomas Henry Ismay never forgot the town of Maryport, and his charities during his lifetime, offered to the old folk in his native place were manifold.

Then there was the Addison family. Mr. Addison was the engineer to the Maryport and Carlisle Railway, and lived at Moat Hill, which was the Dower House of the Senhouses. Miss Addison survived her sister by some years.

The head of the Senhouse family is, of course, the Lord of the Manor of Maryport. They have held a distinguished position for centuries past. The name was well-known in Carlisle in ancient days, and representatives of the family have been Prior, Bishop, and Recorder at various times. Mrs. Senhouse, grandmother of Colonel Senhouse, ruled supreme until the eighty's of last century. To Maryport folk she held a position almost akin to that of the Queen. Her son, Mr. Humphrey Pocklington Senhouse, followed on and took his share in the county affairs, and was a gentleman of high standing. One of his sisters married Lord Scarsdale, and was the mother of Lord Curzon. Another married Sir Wilfrid Lawson. His eldest son was killed in boyhood, and so in turn Colonel Guy Pocklington-Senhouse lived at Netherhall, as his forebears have done for centuries, and where he still holds benevolent sway.

There were many old sea-captains who, after sailing the seven seas, settled down in their native place, and were often drawn into telling their tales of the Horn, the Equator, and the happenings and adventures of their ships. Captain Ritchie, Captain Rich, Captain Brown, Captain Turney, who once underwent the ordeal of walking the plank; Captain Cuthbertson, who settled at Birkby outside the town, and Captain Nelson, are names which readily occur to one.

Then there was Mr. Robert Adair, the bookseller, with whom William Wordsworth held frequent conversations. His shop is still carried on in Senhouse Street by his descendants. Mr. Temple's Italian warehouse in the High Street, was a well-known shopping centre. The small boy taken by his mother on shopping expeditions always looked forward to a few sweets given to him on such occasions.

Robert Adair, book seller of Maryport.
April 1802-October 1889.

Mr. John Hamilton, grocer, in Senhouse Street, was another old tradesman. His brother, Mr. R. H. Hamilton, also in the business was Secretary to the Liberal Association, Mr. Hardy, in Crosby Street, had his bootmaker's shop there. His son became a chemist later on, and took to public affairs, for which he had a natural gift. Mr. John Dixon, the chemist, portly and dignified, was adviser-in-chief on small ailments as well as worldly affairs to many anxious parents. He was a devout Churchman. A large cross was once presented to the Church for use in processions. Mr. Dixon always rose and walked out of the church, as a protest against high church observances when the cross was used ceremoniously.

Mr. John Cockton had his chemist's shop opposite the old Post Office in High Street. He was a relative of Mr. Thomas Ismay, and took a keen interest in the Tug Company, and in various other undertakings. He died a rich man, and left his business to Mr. Skelton, who was his chief assistant for some years. Mr. John Cockton was a church-warden at St. Mary's for almost 50 years.

The Rev. Mr. Sampson was vicar at Maryport for 20 years, and when the new Trinity Baptist Church was opened a scathing criticism was published in one of the local newspapers, which resulted in a libel action and heavy damages. The writer turned out to be one of the Sampson family. This created a great scandal at the time, and a general subject for conversation over the tea cups at the friendly little tea parties of those days.

In later years a new Vicar came to the church, and the two curates resigned. One was an elderly man and the other a deacon. The elderly Curate preached his farewell sermon from the text "Abide ye here with the ass, while I and the lad go yonder." This was another subject for discussion over the tea cups as well may be imagined, and more so, as the Curate wrote to the local paper to say that no allusion to anyone was instanced.

Mr. Thomas Carey, fortunately still with us, had his business in John Street, from which he retired more than forty years ago.

Dr. Crerar was a great figure in Maryport in his day he wore a large moustache and a long beard in the old-ashioned way, and was very alert and zealous in his profession, and equally at the call of patients, whether rich or poor. His son Dr. John Crerar. who had a brilliant career at the University, came to Maryport to carry on the practice after his father's death. He and his brothers have distinguished themselves in various spheres.

Dr. Clarke. senior, started practising quite forty years ago, I should think. Dr. Proud was another doctor about that time, and carried on his practice from the corner house, where Senhouse Street and Curzon Street meet.

Part – II
The Romance of Maryport
Friday, April 26th, 1935

Old residents of Maryport will remember Mr. J. B. Mason, the banker, the father of Colonel. Dan Mason, of Workington. He was a man of whose advice was much sought, and was one of the outstanding men of the town.

Another of the Maryport residents of forty or fifty years ago was Mr. John Hewitson, the solicitor. He was the only solicitor of that time, except the famous old firm of Messrs. Tyson and Hobson. The latter firm had close association with the old Maryport and Carlisle Railway.

Then there was Dr. Little, Captain of the Cricket Club, even after he became very portly in build. He was a very keen sportsman and a good shot.

Mr. Hobson lived in High Street close to Mote Hill. He had a large family. Mr. William Hobson, the present respected clerk to the Magistrates, was the eldest son, and succeeded to the whole practice, which he still carries on, though he now lives at beautiful Woodhall Cockermouth

---

Mr. John Maugham was another Maryportian, who made his mark on the old town. After serving his apprenticeship in the old-fashioned way to the City and District Bank, he went into the brewing business, and was the Managing Director of the old Maryport Brewery. His charming wife and he lived at Hayborough. He had a son who entered the law, and his daughters, of whom one is now a Justice of the Peace, live at Kirkborough.

Miss Porter, who, I think, lives at Keswick now, conducted a Girls' School for many a long year, to which the daughters of well-known Maryport people were sent almost automatically. Ladies now in their seventies were certainly pupils there, and the teaching must have been exceedingly good – judging by the results.

A well known tradesman in Maryport was Mirehouse Wilson, the ironmonger, whose place of business was in Wood Street. He was a man of determined character, very ready to give an expression of opinion on most subjects, backed by sound common sense. One of the old-fashioned, hard working tradesmen.

Another old family in Maryport were the Eaglesfields. Mr. Charles Eaglesfield was an architect in practice there almost a hundred years ago, and was succeeded by his son with the same name, who married Miss Hine, of the shipping family. Mr. Charles Eaglesfield, junior, a clever architect, was a man of the greatest affability and kindness. He loved children, and was a great success at the parties at Christmas time, when he often played Santa Claus to the great delight of the children.

A well-known person who is Maryport born is Sir James Crerar, who made a name for himself in India, and was knighted for his services in that Empire. He is a younger brother of Dr. Crerar. Another brother is Dr. Charles Crerar, of Silloth, and another was Mr. Alfred Crerar, solicitor.

Another shop that will not be forgotten is that of Miss Nelty, opposite St. Mary's Church, which was filled with all the good things of life, as a small boy looks at it. Currant cakes and buns, home-made toffee, sweets in mysterious jars, and at fashionable gatherings Miss Nelty's three-halfpenny buns could be detected with half a glance by the experienced visitor.

There was a great stir in Maryport at the end of the last century when Mr. Eliot. the pastor of the Baptist Church, resigned his charge in order to qualify for Holy Orders in the English Church. Two, if not three, of his sons went to Carlisle Grammar School, and two of them are well-known now as clergymen. One, the Rev. Canon William Eliot, is, I think, Vicar of Leeds, and a leading rotarian; the other, the Rev. Spencer Eliot, is a Vicar and an outstanding preacher in Lancashire.

Reference should be made to Mr. Symington's Academy, which was a sort of complementary school to Miss Porter's School for Girls. Mr. Symington was previously an assistant master at Blair Lodge, a school well-known in Scotland in those days. He was a strict disciplinarian, and his annual prize-giving was quite an event. Parents attended to hear their boys perform by song or recitation. Pleasant speeches were made, and the whole affair carried off in the old fashioned way. When the Christmas holidays approached the boys all got to school early one morning and locked the door to keep the master out. He always fussed in the same way year after year and was finally let in when the boys presented him with a Christmas present, and asked for their holidays.

Of the larger business firms the Maryport Iron Works were for some years run by the Messrs. Gilmour, of Glasgow, until disaster began to overwhelm isolated ironworks such as these. The Gilmour sons were among the "bright lads of the town" and were great acquisitions at the dances, shooting parties, and the like.

Mr. Walker's engineering works was a well-known business situated near the

Docks. The main business was that of the repairing of ships and of ships' engines. One of the Walkers married a Japanese wife, and lived in the big red house at Netherton. He was the first Englishman to settle in Japan. He brought his wife and family to England, but did not stay long, and went back, called by the glamour of the East.

No reference to Maryport is complete without naming the Brows. Here the townsfolk took their walks abroad and the children went off on their picnics. It has, and has always been, the most popular walk in the town. There are few that can rival it in beauty. In the evening with the Solway Firth below, and across the water the beautiful coast of Scotland. Often the sun sets brilliantly over the sea and hills, and the colour and the panorama are something to be remembered.

Other names of old days keep coming back to one. Mr. Quintin Moore, the ship chandler; Mr. Benson. grocer and ship stores merchant, on Shipping Brow; Barber Bell, whose place furnished all – or – nearly all – of the town's gossip; Mr. J. Robley, the station master, and famous Rugby full-back; Mr. W. E. Fisher, keen business man and famous footballer. too, who died a few years ago; Mr. Joe Thomlinson, the spirit merchant; the Campbell family, who were all-pervading; the late Mr. Tom Ritson of Ridgemount;

Mrs. John Ritson, who was so greatly admired in her youth; the late Mr. Hugh Carr, general manager of the Maryport and Carlisle Railway, and his successor Mr. Blain. What a jumble of names, but all good Maryport folks, staunch and true.

The Rev. J. A. Richards, now Vicar of Wetheral, was for some years Vicar of Maryport, and as Maryport took him to its heart so he took Maryport. He was very popular with all classes. I noted his reference in the *Carlisle Journal* to the late Mr. John Dixon and to Joseph Vevers with great interest. One of my recollections of the latter is his pride in what he called his *"goon and waand."*

Canon Code was Vicar of Maryport before his preferment. The Rev. R. A. Davenport was Curate there, and in charge more particularly of Christ Church. Mr. H. K. Campbell and Mr. E. G. Eaglesfield are both natives of Maryport ; so is Mr. Moore, the motor engineer in Fisher Street. Miss Dixon, the science mistress at the Girls' High School, also. There are many more – almost sufficient to form a Maryport society to help the old town on a bit should the need arise.

Adventures in the *Robert Hine*

Among the Patagonions

Having read and enjoyed the stories of life at sea appearing in *Sea Breezes* from time to time, I have pleasure enclosing the following story told by my late father, the late Captain George Brown, of Maryport, who sailed the *Robert Hine,* one of the early vessels of Messrs. Hine Brothers' fleet, relative to his experiences among the Patagonions while in that vessel.

Wilfrid J Brown

ONE fine day early in the year 1873, we left Liverpool bound for Valpariso with general cargo,in the *Robert Hine,* of Maryport. She was a wooden barque of 329 tons nett, built at Sunderland in 1868, under the command of the writer, who was accompanied by his wife.

Through Nassau Straits

All went well until we were within 100 miles of the Straits of Le Maire when we encountered a violent south-west gale. About midnight a heavy sea struck the vessel and carried away nearly all her bulwarks, rails and stanchions on the starboard side, also started the decks and waterways, damaged the crew's quarters and flooded the cabin.

At daybreak the fore-rigging carried away, and we found the vessel was leaking badly. Therefore I decided to run for Port Stanley, in the Falkland Islands, to have my vessel repaired, as she was not in a fit condition to proceed round Cape Horn. In due time we arrived at the best harbour I have ever visited.

Whilst the repairs were going on, which occupied six weeks, we had a very pleasant time among the residents, numbering about 150, mostly Scotsman, there not being more than half a dozen women in the community. Incidentally, I was commissioned by many of the men to bring them each a wife should I visit their port again.

Repairs completed, we resumed our voyage under favourable conditions but, meantime, I had decided to avoid the treacherous Horn by going through Nassau Straits. That way, however, lay another danger.

Ready for 'em

Having heard and read so much about the Patagonion savages I resolved to take no risk of them boarding my ship, so I gave orders for the cannon, all guns and

The Robert Hine.
Wooden Barque 329 tons net. Built Sunderland 1868.

revolvers to be got ready, whilst the carpenter sharpened all his axes, adzes and other cutting instruments, and the cook was instructed to make provision for having plenty of boiling water handy when it might be required.

Mrs. Brown, who was keenly interested in all these precautionary measures, suggested that the empty pickle and preserve bottles, of which there was a quantity in the storeroom, should be got up and broken. Ready for spreading on the decks should the natives attack us. I thought this an excellent plan, and acted accordingly.

We were bowling along nicely when the barometer began to fall rapidly and the weather to the southward looked bad. This was about two o'clock in the afternoon, so I made for Good Success Bay to shelter there until the impeding gale moderated. We anchored four hours later and remained for three nights and two days.

While approaching the bay we saw a small fore and aft schooner, flying British colours, already at anchor. Fearing she might be a pirate, I gave orders for all weapons to be loaded ready for action.

We had been kept guessing for a couple of hours when a small boat came alongside with four men from the schooner. The men were decidedly foreign looking, so I warned them to keep at a distance. They replied that they were missionaries.

While still dubious of their credentials, I considered the ship's company could hold them if necessary, so asked them to come on board. I then learned they were from Port Stanley, bound for the Beagle-Channel Mission Station, and that their schooner was the *Allen Gardner No. 3*, loaded with stores and fresh provisions, consisting of beef, mutton, geese and rabbits, among other things.

A Bit of Exploring

Before dark our visitors returned to their own ship after promising to bring us some of the tasty viands already mentioned. The following morning they did so, and brought a very acceptable variety which lasted several days. On enquiring the cost I was told it was a free gift.

In return, I offered to let them have whatever clothing they required for themselves, their wives and families at cost price. (I had invested in this clothing as a speculation at the beginning of the voyage.) They were pleased to accept my offer and purchased largely of my stock, but, like myself, they had no money, so gave me an order on a gentleman in Liverpool, of whom I was to receive payment.

They then asked me to accompany them on shore as they were anxious to learn for themselves what the natives were like. The information which had reached them was to the effect that the people were very wild and treacherous, indeed perfect savages. How much truth there was in this, the sequel will show.

I agreed to join them, providing they did not object to my taking "two bulldogs" with me. They looked about and asked where I kept the bulldogs. I produced two revolvers which they said I could take provided they were used in self-defence.

Very Primitive people

We set off in the schooner's boat and approached within a hundred yards of the shore. From that distance the missionaries hailed the natives in a language they knew, and received, from one of the tribe, a reply in the same tongue. The knowledge that at least one man could understand them was very pleasing to the missionaries.

As to landing, the prospect was not very inviting, as the people all appeared to be painted ready for war. Not one of them had a stitch of clothing on, men, women and children were all quite naked, although it was freezing. On receiving an assurance that it was quite safe to land, we did and immediately the natives came crowding around us.

They began by taking hold of our clothes, shaking them vigorously, first our coats and then every article we had on. I asked the missionary the meaning of this, and he said the natives desired possession of our clothes. As we were shivering with cold this was, of course, out of the question.

After this they sat round their fires, first one then another going close to the burning sticks to get warm. These people had no places of shelter whatever, neither houses or huts, there only comfort was a wood fire and, what appeared very strange to me, they always sat on that side of the fire where the wind was blowing towards them. I asked the reason of this and was told if they were sheltered by the land it would be draughty and they would be more liable to take cold.

Once I struck a match to light my pipe, and in an instant they were all around me, amazed by the sight, they had never seen a match before, and when I gave them one or two their delight was very great. For a box of matches they gave me a bow and arrow.

I continued to barter until I had secured all their weapons, which were placed in the boat so as to be out of reach. The missionaries gave the natives some beef and a couple of geese and some rabbits, whilst I gave them salt beef and ship's bread or hard tack, as sailors call it.

They already possessed a large oval pan salved from the beach, but up to the time of our visit no use had been found for it. One of the missionaries now told them to fill it with water and promised to show them how to cook the meat, etc. He put some meat in the pan, but it had not been in there long before they pulled it out and ate it.

So delighted were they that more was put in the pan with some shell, fish a goose, and two rabbits – these latter were put in as they were, feathers fur and all – and in the same way they were eaten, for all that remained of the feast were a few shells.

After the banquet was over we took three of the natives on board the *Robert Hine* to show them over the ship. I went into the cabin followed by my visitors. Almost the first thing the leading native saw was a reflection of himself in the mirror on the stern-post casing. The shock to him was tremendous; he made a flying leap nearly through the skylight, and, dropping on the floor, fainted right away. His friends would not venture near him, the cause of his plight being incomprehensible to them, and they stood bewildered. After we brought the fellow round they became reassured and then the fun began. First one and then another would have a peep at the mirror and give a jump backwards, which was repeated several times. The missionaries then explained the mysteries to the one who acted as interpreter and so satisfied them all as to the identity of the "other fellows".

The sailors took them through their quarters, and when they reappeared they were decked out in all old clothes belonging to the crew. They were pleased with their costumes and their pleasure was amusing to watch. It was in a happy frame of mind that they returned to the shore.

Skins like leather

Next morning we paid the natives another visit, when we found three of the women arrayed in the sailors' old clothes, and we were told they would go the rounds, different persons wearing them each day until they were finished.

About noon we set off to climb one of the mountains in order to view the surrounding country. The ascent was difficult owing to the steep sides being covered with small trees and shrubs. It was nearly dark when we got back to the beach and a ragged-looking lot we were, our clothes being very much torn. I took particular notice of our native guide, but could see that he had not a single scratch upon him!

With the prospect of sailing on the morrow I bid my newly-found friends adieu. The morning broke fair and both vessels sailed together, keeping company for about eight hours, after which we parted, the *Allan Gardner* making for Beagle Channel and the *Robert Hine* for Nassau Straits once again.

When we reached False Cape Horn we found it was blowing hard so had to run back and anchor in Orange Bay, we lay there for three days and nights in a splendid anchorage, sheltered from all winds. During the first day we saw several natives roaming about on shore but none afterwards. On the second day we landed and cut about twenty fine spars, of which there was a large quantity available.

Tragic end of the *San Rafael*

When the gale abated we resumed our voyage and passed safely through the Straits and out into the broad Pacific. We made a fine passage of fourteen days to Valparaiso and so circumvented the stormy Horn where ships have often been battering about for six weeks in their attempts to round it.

As usual, the captains and officers of vessels in port were interested in the new arrival and made enquires as to passage, etc. On learning of my Patagonian experiences they were anxious to know all about the anchorages I used, and what I thought about the natives, in event of being shipwrecked in that region. I replied that, although I should not care to be cast amongst them, yet I would prefer landing rather than keep to sea in an open boat.

One man I remember especially he was mate of the *Peckforton Castle,* and on arrival at Liverpool he was given command of the *San Rafael* of that port. He sailed in October, 1874, with a cargo of coal for Valparaiso and was accompanied by his wife. On New Year's Day, 1875, after rounding Cape Horn, the ship was found to be on fire and had to be abandoned.

The Captain, his wife and part of the crew were in one boat, the officers and remainder of the crew in the other two boats. The officers kept to the sea, and after being tossed about for twenty-seven days were eventually picked up.

It transpired subsequently that the captain and his companions landed on a small island off the mainland, where they hoped to attract the attention of a passing vessel. No help arrived, and after enduring dreadful hardships all perished of starvation.

The natives on the mainland saw the fires on the island but were afraid to go near. When the fires ceased they went there and found the bodies of Captain and Mrs. McAdams and the crew of the boat. Returning to the mainland they walked over 100 miles to the Mission Station and reported the calamity. The *Allen Gardner* was sent to the island and the bodies were reverently buried. The diary of Captain McAdams was then found from which the dreadful fate of himself and his companions was learned.

With reference to the Missionary schooner mentioned in this story, she was called the *Allen Gardner* after two previous missionary ships of the same name, so to perpetuate the memory of the first missionary to the Patagonians, who, along with his companions, died of starvation in the early days owing to the the non-arrival of the ship carrying their stores.

Disaster also overtook the *Allen Gardner No.* 2 as, running aground in Beagle Channel, the whole of her passengers and crew – with one exception were cruelly murdered by the savages of that locality, who then set fire to the ship.

Captain George Brown
(Maryport)

Maryport Harbour 1837 from a Lithograph.

Placid *Hazel Holme*
Peaceful Days and Good Voyages

IN May, 1877, I joined the barque *Hazel Holme,* as mate at Swansea. Where she was loading a cargo of rails for Rockhampton, Queensland. Of 405 tons register she belonged to Messers. Hine Bros, Of Maryport, who had built just a year or two before a lovely quartette of Clipper vessels, which became so well known in the Australian trade. I refer to the *Briar Holme, Castle Holme, Eden Holme, and Myrtle Holme.* These with the *Robert Hine, Abbey Holme,* and *Hazel Holme,* made up the crack vessels in the Holme Line fleet of sailers.

Bad For The Temper

After loading we were delayed about a week, owing to a dispute over the cargo. In the end we sailed, having taken on board a beam scale and weights with which to weigh it out. Nothing of note happened on the passage if we leave out the thought and anxiety of having to go all through the cargo at least twice a day watching the wedges and toms. This was indeed a serious business, especially in running our Easting down, and we were all glad when we dropped anchor in Keppel Bay.

It was a very awkward job weighing every rail before it left the hold, and in the awful heat of the place we got a foretaste of what is supposed to be the experience of the unregenerate. However, we survived it, and after discharge, loaded wool for London. This was my first visit to Australia, and as for Rockhampton I had never heard the name until I joined the *Hazel Holme.* Here we experienced the full wonderful hospitality of the people, and everyone was made so comfortable that it was a hard matter to leave as heart – whole as one entered it. To myself this port this port remains the first milestone on life's journey. Being a young man of 23 years, it was natural that I should fall to the charms of one of the many charming girls of the place, and it makes me rather proud of my good judgment to be able to say, after 50 years' close acquaintance, she is as charming as ever. I would have said more if that were possible.

Quick promotion

We sailed on 20th December and it was a slow passage to Cape Horn, much light winds and fine weather. On February 6th in 54 deg. S. Lat. and 80 deg. W. Long., we saw one small piece of ice just awash, but big enough to have done some damage if we had hit it. Soon after rounding the Horn the captain complained of not feeling up to the mark, but no one thought of it being serious; but on 1st March, in 28 deg. S. Lat. And 25 deg. W. Long., he succumbed to what we diagnosed as an apoplectic fit. This sad event cast a gloom on all the crew and upon myself, who had the double pressure of a sudden responsibility cast upon my young shoulders, beside the sorrow of our loss.

The second mate was a bit older in years and experience than I, and our first question was the appointment of a man to take his place. The four apprentices were all first-voyagers, as was also the carpenter; it then remained only for one of us to choose one of the crew. Three of them had joined in Swansea and made the voyage, but one had deserted in Rockhampton, been caught about a week before sailing, and kept in gaol until we left, when he was put on board by the police. He was an excellent sailor but just a bit troublesome on the passage out, and wasn't much improved by having to come home with us against his will. Still he was the best seaman, so calling all hands aft I said a few words about our loss, and bluntly told them I had selected him as second mate.

This was a bit of a surprise to all and had a bit of an electric effect upon the man himself. He stepped in front of the men and asked if there were any objections. As none were raised he continued, "Now, men any complaints you have on passage tell me, and I will tell the chief officer and he will report to the captain". So then I heard the title applied to me for the first time.

Ship ready – ticket to get

Reaching London we berthed In the West India Dock. I went up to the city and found the agents were Messers. Devitt and Moore, who entered the ship and got everything in readiness for paying off the crew. In due course Captain Robinson came on board and the condition of the ship seemed to please him, which was satisfactory to me. Then later the owner came and made enquiries as to the death of the captain, and having said a few kind words to me, promised that if I passed my examination he would give me command.

Words fail to express what I felt at this promise. I at 24, and looking but 19, with barely ten years' experience, to have command! But I daren't let the thought run away with me for there was that small fly in the ointment, my certificate still to get. Moreover, time was getting on, and I could not be released until she was discharged, dry-docked and in her loading berth for her next voyage to Yokohama. I had passed for second and first mate in Liverpool, so felt I must go there again for my master's certificate. After two weeks' coaching I made up my mind to put in my papers, but I had the damping assurance of Captain Coggle that I would fail – and the further bogle of the rest of the school that Captain Mcnab was taking seamanship that week. However, I carried out my intentions and it came off O.K. The first part in navigation was quickly over and the rest of the papers were easy. Then came the orals, and Captain John who was very good, considering his reputation. Anyway, one left his room satisfied that one knew something about a ship.

Bank End Farm. Maryport's oldest building built 1716.
Photo May 2002.

Appeal of the ship

Having secured my master's certificate, I had just a few days at home and then the final interview with the owner, who was, as I always found after many years' service under him, most kind and considerate. Among other things he said that I, being young, might come across some difficulties in port re-chartering, but that I would always find some elderly ship masters who would be glad to give me a helping hand. I got to London in time to sign on the crew, and with the guidance of Captain Robinson, the overlooker, everything went well. Having some business still to finish, the *Hazel Holme* left dock with Captain Robinson in charge. I stood on the pier-head until she was out of sight. During that short period I was overcome with love for the beautiful little barque that was now, as it were, "all my own". To me she was not a mere construction of wood and iron, but something that had come into my life as a living force that meant all the world to me. What I had always striven for – the command of my own ship – had come to pass in what, looking back, seemed a very few years and, as she faded away into the distance on that fine June morning, I turned away with a happy heart and some little moisture about my eyes. Having finished the business, I joined and left Gravesend at 4.00 a.m., June 12th, 1878, anchored in the Downs the same night and left on June 14th. Made very poor progress to begin with, got the trades on the 28th in 37 deg. N. Lat., 16 deg. W. Long. Sighted Madeira on the 30th,

Crossed the Equator July 20th in 21 deg. W. Long. The first little trouble arose on the 27th when we found one of our water tanks, which we had filled in the doldrums to the north of the Line, was nearly empty. As our second tank only held 400 gallons we certainly had not enough to last us out. As to further progress we sighted Trinidad Island on the 30th July, Tristan de Cunha, August 13th, and Amsterdam Island 10th September.

In good company

Our water supply being insufficient to last us to the Islands we decided to put into a port in West Australia, and on September 23rd anchored in Champion Bay and replenished, but it was a slow process as the water had to be carried of to the ship in hogsheads. We left Geraldton on September 25th, sighted and passed Sandalwood Island on our way to the Ombay passage on October 9th. Then we began to whistle for wind, for with contrary currents of 1, 2 and, at times, 3 knots we made little progress, a little bit ahead and a big bit astern and then the reverse, so it went on for ten days when two more vessels joined us, one no less a ship than the *Sir Lancelot*, but much cut down in masting and barque-rigged. We kept in company for the next sixteen days, sometimes ahead or astern of each other, but never far away. On the 5th of November we got a fresh breeze which lasted till we both cleared the straits together, but she soon left us and showed us the way with the fresh breeze. Two or three times we had a yarn with each other and found we were both bound for Yokohama.

The last time I had seen the *Sir Lancelot* was in July, 1869, when she made the record passage of 89 days. Somewhere about abreast of Hong we were standing to Northward on the starboard tack when we saw the *Sir Lancelot* coming down with a fair wind on his starboard quarter with every imaginable sail set and drawing. We passed across her stern close enough for the two captains, who were old acquaintances, to hail each other.

We reached Yokohama a few days after the *Sir Lancelot* and had a very pleasant and profitable time with Captain Brokenshar, of that ship, The *Lothair*, Captain Bolton, was there also. Having part cargo for Kobe, we proceeded there and afterwards loaded a cargo of rice for Melbourne and sailed on the 15th February, 1879. On the 23rd had a furious gale, which caused our cargo to shift and give us considerable anxiety for some time. We had not a stitch of canvas set, indeed I think it would have gone to ribbons if we had.

Deep sea surveying

On March 22nd, making our way southward between New Caledonia and the Fiji Islands, with a very light air and smooth water, on looking over the side we got a rude surprise, being able to see the bottom, where on the chart it showed odd soundings there should be 1,000 fathoms. Thinking, by the look of the bottom, we were less than five fathoms, we got another shock when on sounding we found 18, 19 and 20 fathoms, We took about a dozen casts and found no bottom at 90 fathoms, this quite suddenly from 20 fathoms. We collected the coral from the lead and with this our report, the Admiralty located the bank and surveyed it.

We arrived at Sandridge on 13th April without any further incident, and a few days later moored for discharge at the Town Pier. The *Myrtle Holme* was discharging at the Railway Pier, and as Captain Ritchie had his wife with him, I was invited, and gladly accepted, to take up my quarters on board, and a right royal time I had during my stay.

A little bargaining

Our next destination was Port Pirie, we duly arrived and loaded, we then set sail for Hong Kong where we arrived on the 7th August after a passage – East about – of 61 days. When we got among the islands near Hong Kong a pilot made signals about 10.00 p.m., so we backed our main yards when he came aboard, and the bargaining began by his asking had I been to Hong Kong before? "No" Had I a compradore? "No" "Well, you take my compradore, I takee you in for 30 dollars." "You no takee my compradore 40 dollars." But these figures were absurd. I offered him five dollars and his compradore or ten dollars or ten dollars without without compradore. He refused both, so I told the mate to brace up the mainyards and the pilot got into his boat, but before the ship got away he clambered aboard again and said quite contentedly "Can do, captain." A very capable he was and well-deserved the five dollars he got for himself.

After discharging we took in sand ballast and seven tons of cash – Chinese currency – with only one Chinese to look after all this money. We sailed 26th August 1879, for Quinhon, in Cochin China, arriving there 11th September. We were fixed to load a cargo of salt – principally – some Chinese general merchandise and to carry back to Hong Kong deck passengers. We were a month at Quinhon The port was under French jurisdiction, but apparently there were no regulations, and a good port seemed in a fair way of being spoiled by every ship dumping her ballast overboard just where she was lying. As this was the end of the season for trade purposes there was observed a great (what one might call) Harvest Thanksgiving. In the Hong we were loading for, they were making bamboo pyramids, about four feet high, and folding silver and gold paper into shapes likes pounds of tea, but nothing inside. I got quite adept at making these airy nothings, but they were to represent silver and gold. Then rice was boiled and stuck onto the bamboo pyramids; this gave the idea of mountains of rice, but they, like the silver and gold paper bags, were all hollow. Then real pigs and chickens were roasted and fish cooked etc.

The ceremony commences

A platform was erected outside the end of the Temple on pillars about 8 feet high and 20 feet long and 10 feet wide. All the good things were piled on the platform with a large lath and plaster Joss at the extreme end. Inside the Temple were seven priests, three on each side and one at the end of the table, each had a book in front of him and they were intoning at a rate of knots, while every few moments the one at the end, who had a bowl of uncooked rice in front of him, would pick up some rice in his hand, sprinkle it along the table, over books and all. But this did not disturb the others one bit, still intoning without a break. Outside the Temple all the inhabitants seemed to be gathering, the poorer class fighting for places in front of the platform where all the good things were on view.

Then four men appeared on the platform and some kind of ceremony was gone through which I took to be offering all these good things to the Joss, and on his refusing them the men set upon him with sticks, smashed him to pieces and bundled his remains of the end of the platform into a fire underneath, and all the baskets full of gold and silver paper bags on top of him, so they were all consumed together. All eatables were thrown on top of the rabble underneath, when for a moment or two it was pandemonium. The first man to appear from the tumult was a strong muscular native with a good-sized roast pig over his left shoulder, two men ran behind grasping a leg and a third man trying to secure his share by getting hold of its tail.

Profit made on spot

I was so interested in watching this helter-skelter race with the pig for a prize that when I turned round everything was gone, and there remained only the maimed and lame starvlings who were picking up the loose bits of rice with their finger and thumb from among the trodden dirt – a most pitiful sight to watch.

Immediately our cash was delivered to the Hong (or house of our charterers) many young women were set to work to re-string it from 1,000 cash per dollar to strings of 750 per dollar, which was making some profit. In use in the town and market were zinc cash, value four to a copper cash, and when one went to market one had to have a man with his shoulder stick and basket at each end to carry the money, and a measuring (half bamboo) stick marked to measure out the cash. There was some weight in 10 dollars worth of zinc cash. The charterers had to provide all stores and water for the deck passengers as per charter party. As most of them had one or two children the longboat, the longboat which was very large, was housed in for the youngsters, but there was no accommodation for the rest, who had to do the best they could. How these children were related to the men who were fathering them I could only surmise. A man and a woman came on board one day and offered me a boy about 12 and a girl of 14 for five dollars the pair – they said they were to poor to keep them – but I refused the offer.

Any children for sale

We finished loading in the outer anchorage and got all our passengers on board –

50 Chinese men and 48 children, the latter ranging from 6 to 11 apparently. We left on October 11th and on the 16th we had the tail of a typhoon to contend with, but nothing serious happened, it being the bare end of the tail. We arrived at Hong Kong on October 20th glad to see our passengers safely landed. As soon as the authorities knew of our children they came off, and after interrogating their owners took charge of the lot and carried them ashore for further investigations.

I heard afterwards that the owners were able to satisfy the authorities that the children were for household servants and not for sale. We had visits on board from Chinese, who wanted to buy any that the crew might possibly have, but, of course there, there were none.

After some waiting we chartered and proceeded to Tai-wanfoo (Formosa) where we loaded a full cargo of sugar, and after a long uneventful passage arrived in London (St Katherine's Dock) via Queenstown, F, O., on 8th August 1880, after a voyage of two years and two months.

A gentleman's agreement

After discharging our cargo of sugar we went on the berth for Freemantle and sailed from the London Dock on November 11th, 1880, and, taking in gunpowder at the powder buoys, proceeded and anchored in the Downs on the 12th, but owing to heavy westerly gales we were unable to sail until the 17th. Despite this bad start we hoped our luck would improve, but there was nothing doing, and we simply drifted to the Equator and made an average run of 87 miles per day, our best day being 204 and our worst 9. Nothing of outstanding interest occurred during the rest of the passage. We reached Freemantle safely on March 8th, and anchored in the Roads, where we discharged our cargo with our own crew, finishing on April 5th.

Our next engagement was a cargo of sandal wood for Shanghai. Two firms at Perth agreed, simply on a note of hand, to load the ship and dispatch her as quickly as possible, each firm loading its own chosen end of the ship. There was no charter party, the contract was based on good faith, which prevailed throughout, all went well, otherwise I should have been in the soup. Two stevedores packed the wood and got wages of 7s. a day. I wonder what they'd get to-day? Began loading April 8th, finished May 14th. It was a long job stowing the wood, which was in pieces from 18 inches to 8 or 10 feet long and 4 to 10 inches thick, every piece as crooked as a dog's hind leg, carefully cut and each piece stamped on both ends with the private mark of the shipper.

Chartered for life

During the time of the loading I had to make another kind of charter party; for after a correspondence of over three years, it was mutually agreed that the ideal young lady I had met in Rockhampton, should come to me to be married, as I could not get to her, and so it happened, as the stories used to say, "They lived happily ever afterwards," My agent Mr. W. D. Moore, a wonderfully fine man met the steamer on her arrival early one morning and took the young lady under his fatherly care, which was exceedingly kind seeing we were practically strangers in a strange land. We left Freemantle on May 17th, passed Java Head on the 30th, got through Banka Straits on June 5th, arrived at Shanghai on July 5th, and on the 30th left for London with a full cargo of tea, took the Eastern passage on September 14th.

A long weary journey through the Indian Ocean brought us to the Cape on October 23rd, and our thoughts to the conclusion that stun' sails would have been worth much on this voyage of light winds. Nothing of special interest happened during the rest of the passage. Running up the Channel with a heavy gale from S.W., were thankful to get into the Downs before the weight of it broke, and with both anchors down rode out the heaviest gale that I ever experienced, when at anchor the barometer fell to 28. 40. We discharged our cargo in Hay' Dock, London bridge on the Surrey side.

Something like a sea

Our next voyage was to Launceston. We left London, March 16th 1882, and after taking gunpowder at Gravesend, towed as far as the Downs. On the 26th when just west of the Lizards, we had a heavy gale which shifted to N.W. and blew harder. A heavy sea coming over the bows took the forecastle scuttle clean off by the deck and, of course, flooding the forecastle the watch below thought their last hour had come. The same sea smashed in the side of the galley, breaking in one side of the stove. We had to do our cooking for a day or two on the small cabin stove. The crew thought we should put into Falmouth to get a new stove, as the carpenter said he could not repair it, not having tools to drill the side if the stove. So we took charge of his tool chest, found something that did the work, and with a little ingenuity repaired the stove and kept on our passage, which was completed without further trouble.

We made Cape Otway on June 26th, and got a pilot at the entrance to the Tamar river and, with a fresh wind, sailed up the river 40 miles to the bar about half a mile below Launceston, where we anchored to discharge our powder. It was a very pleasant experience this sail up, for we were braced sharp on both tacks to round the many bends, and the weather leaches on the upper sails almost touched the trees over-hanging many of the high banks. Our stay in this beautiful little town is a particularly pleasant recollection. We were made welcome by the Y.M.C.A. inviting all hands to a tea in their institute, and soon all made good friends, and the time passed very pleasantly for everybody.

No homeward cargo offering on completion of discharge we ballasted and proceeded to Talcahuano seeking. We made an ordinary passage across the Pacific and after waiting some 14 days for instructions at Talcahuano we sailed on the third of October having been fixed to load nitrate at Iquique and Mejillones. Eight days later we anchored in Iquique and began loading the first part of our cargo, which was bound for Germany. We left on October the third, and on the 11th anchored in Iquique, where we loaded part cargo. During our stay here the usual hearty custom of celebrating the final loading of a vessel's cargo was duly observed. Three cheers were given for all the good ships, with an occasional groan for one which was unpopular. On sailing there was always a double crew to get the homeward-bounder under way, as several captains with boats' crews went on board to say good-bye.

A sudden send-off

A very unusual incident arose out of this latter custom which I will relate. Another ship, belonging to the same employ as *Hazel Holme,* had finished loading and was lying at single anchor, her sails loosened and, seemingly, all ready for sea. Five captains went on board to see her away and found her captain having his dinner. Captain Stoddart, of the *Remonstrant,* a big man with a loud hearty voice and manner, looked down the skylight, and seeing this, asked why he was wasting the nice breeze and why he could not eat at sea. So the old man came up on deck in quite a flurry, and could hardly speak. Stoddart took charge of the deck and before one could say the proverbial "Jack Robinson" she was under way with every stitch set. We then said good-bye and left, but his special friend went out a bit further.

Later in the evening this friend came on board my ship and said that the captain had not finished his business on shore and had no papers with him. Would I get them in the morning and carry them out to sea as he would stand off and on during the night and wait for them. As I had a boat rigged for sailing I was ashore pretty early, got the necessary papers and started out to sea, with nothing in sight it looked somewhat lonely, There was a nice breeze and we got along very well and soon saw a ship coming end on, so we made for her, but it was not the one we sought. Later we saw her coming on the starboard tack. About noon we got alongside and gave the captain his papers. He insisted on our going up for something to eat. In shaking her up to take the way off her she got aback, and at my request she was put on the port tack, so while we were eating our dinner she was leaving Iquique behind. When we came up on deck all that was visible of the port was the Zig-zag railway up the mountain side. We left him about 1.00 p.m. and had a pleasant sail, but towards sundown the wind began to die away and when a couple of miles off it fell dead calm. We had a heavy boat with only two boys to row. However, we dumped all the ballast and got on board safely sometime after dark.

Escort of sea lions

At 9.00 a.m. on November 10th, we left Iquique and anchored in Mejillones 5.30 p.m. Our cargo was all in a warehouse near the beach where it had lain for a year or two and was perfectly dry. It was the last cargo to be shipped from this port, as Caleta Buena was just opened as the port of shipment. We finished loading on the 20th of November, and had to go to Pisagua, 17 miles north, to clear. The vessel had a light 12 foot punt to pull, with two pairs of sculls, so started at 3.00 a.m. with two boys to make the trip. As usual at that time it was dead calm, so we started lively enough, yet when we lost sight of the ship's light and had nothing but darkness around us, the outlook was (to say the least of it) appalling. The sea lions were continually coming to the surface, and at times they came closer than was at all comfortable, and we felt like uttering the prayer of a Provencal fisherman, "Lord be good to me; Thy sea is so wide, and my boat is so small." However, we got there safely by 8.00 a.m. and were made very welcome on board one of Phillip Nelson's ships for the day.

Myrtle Holme.
With full spread of Canvas.

A dip to happy memories

Left in our boat 7.30 p.m., and had a calm passage, arriving on board at 1.30 a.m., November 23rd. Sailed for Cuxhaven for orders on the afternoon of the same day. Had nothing but light S.E. winds for 21 days, and it was December 25th before we reached the Horn. We did better to the Equator, which we crossed in 28 days, and thence to the Lizards in 22 days, arriving at Cuxhaven on February 19th 1883. We got orders for Hamburg, where we discharged our cargo which turned out dry enough to earn me the maximum gratuity.

After discharging this Cargo I left the *Hazel Holme* to join the *Myrtle Holme*. As a passenger on the steamer bound for London I gazed at the sweet little barque that had been my home for nearly six years and my heart was heavy within me as I watched the officer (left in charge of her) dipping the Ensign as we passed, and I thought lovingly of all our happy associations together and how in fair weather and in foul she had always been faithful and true.

Capt J. W. Millican
32 High Street
Maryport

"She moved like a queen on water, with the grace that was hers of yore,
With the sun on her shining canvas – what had she to do with war,?
With a world that is full of trouble and seas that are stained with crime,
She came like a dream remembered, dreamt once in a happier time."

C.F.S.

Winter scene The Old Ship Inn, South Quay, Maryport 1902.

Second Mate

You are probably Extra Master,
You have possibly passed in Steam,
And have at forty odd years of age –
Fulfilled each half-deck dream.
But a day has passed – one youthful day,
Has there been one day since to lick it?
That you went down to the Customs House –
For your Second Mate's Ticket.

You were then inclined to laugh at steam,
You had served four years in sail,
And rather than pass for a steamboat man –
You were ready enough to fail.
Six months you may have risked – perhaps,
But anyway you could stick it,
It enhanced the value in your eyes –
Of that Second Mate's Ticket.

Remember the traps examiners set?
How they treated you like a docker,
If they got you stuck with "How d'ye tell
Fore from mainsail in the locker."
You didn't know much – just thought you did,
But examiners played good cricket,
You admitted as much, that day you got
Your Second Mate's Ticket.

Remember walking down Castle Street,
To report you had passed at school?
And knowing perhaps you had answered
Several questions like a fool.
Remember that first night watch on the poop?
With the world at your feet – (did you kick it?)
Good days were they – five pounds a month –
And a Second Mate's Ticket.

C.J.F.

Hougomont's Adventures
Ship Survives Many Vicissitudes

T HE casualty which overtook the four-mast barque *Hougomont* on the 27th of February, 1903, when she stranded on the front doorstep of the little village of Allonby, not yet forgotten in West Cumberland. This fine vessel, 2,240 tons net register, built in 1897, was a unit of Messrs. John Hardie's fleet of big sailers, many of which bore names reminiscent of Napoleonic battlefields.

The *Hougomont* left San Francisco on 9th October, 1902, bound for Liverpool with a crew of thirty under the command of Captain C. Lowe, who was accompanied by his wife. The cargo consisted of 1,000 tons of wheat and 1,000 tons of barley in bags, together with 1,900 tons of tinned fruits and salmon in cases.

After an uneventful passage of 123 days *Hougomont* arrived off Point Lynas but was unable to obtain either tug nor pilot. The weather being southerly and dirty at the time she was driven to leeward. On the morning of the 25th of February, 1903, Maryport people were treated to a magnificent sight as a lofty four-master

The Hougomont *under sail.*

126

came sailing up the Solway Firth with nearly every stitch of canvas set. The crowd watched her reduce sail and saw her smartly rounded to anchor in Maryport roads there to await a tug-boat.

Speculation was rife as to her identity as no such vessel was expected in Cumbrian ports. It was the *Hougamount.* The owners sent the *Brilliant Star* to tow her to her destination and they set off at 4.00 p.m. on the 26; but destiny had prepared adventure for the *Hougomont,* as we shall see.

The weather broke that night. A sou'-west gale of hurricane violence, which was expected throughout the British Isles, sprang up and scattered desolation on land and sea. During the night tug and tow parted company. The *Brilliant Star* managed to reach Maryport Harbour in a battered condition and reported the loss of her charge.

Meantime *Hougomont* drove up the Solway at the mercy of wind and tide. Captain Lowe, who had commanded big ships for over thirty years, stated that in all his years experience he had never spent such a night afloat. Rockets were sent up and distress signals displayed but the weather conditions prevented their being seen. Finally, the vessel stranded at six in the morning in Allonby Bay, but she was not observed until day broke, when her towering mizzen and masts showed up above the haze which enveloped her.

Soon after she struck, her fore topgallant mast carried away bringing down the top hamper, which, in its train, brought down the main top gallant and royal masts, leaving a tangled and swaying mass to add to the terrors of the situation. Daylight revealed the forms of the crew clinging to the after-rigging, where they had to remain until the lifeboat from Maryport could reach the stranded vessel.

A tense situation

The wind hauled to nor'-west, and continued to rage with unabated fury which, combined combined with the rising tide, drove the vessel higher and higher up the strand on each successive roller until she came to rest near the Grapes Inn. Wind and sea were now broadside on and presented an indescribably grand but awesome spectacle as the great waves swept continuously over the decks of the stricken ship and spent themselves in multicoloured spray.

Havoc was wrought about the decks, and everything movable washed overboard. The cabin and crew's quarters were gutted, while the hatches were burst open and thousands of cases of tinned fruits and salmon were strewn along the beach. To the watchers on shore who were powerless to render assistance, it looked as though the ship must go to pieces and drown every soul on board.

Owing to conflicting orders reaching the lifeboat station at Maryport, it was high tide – about 11.00 a.m. – before the lifeboat reached the vessel and rescued the crew from their perilous and nerve-racking position, many of them being quite exhausted. On reaching the shore and rescued, every one of whom was soaked to the skin and chilled to the marrow, were shown great hospitality by the villagers, who supplied them with clothing, boots and food, all of which were doubly welcome after this terrifying experience. The following day, was gloriously fine, and the crew paid off, left for Maryport and entrained for their various homes.

The four masted barque Hougomont *high and dry in Allonby Bay 27th February, 1903. Eventually she was refloated by the late Sir Frederick Young K.B.E. The greatest salvage expert of his time.*

He spoke too soon

People travelled from near and far to see the way the elements had played with the big ship which presented a most unusual sight. Many of them did not go away empty-handed for they retrieved not only tins but cases of fruit and salmon. It is recorded that one worthy came with his horse and cart and secured a good supply of the delicacies of the Pacific slopes and waters. One night his premises were raided and stocks depleted considerably. The depredation was promptly reported to the police, who informed the Receiver of Wreck. One can readily imagine the chargin of the salver on being relieved of the whole of his "catch." Nevertheless, then and for long afterwards, there was no scarcity of those tasty viands in the vicinity of Allonby.

Captain (now, Sir) Frederick Young, of the Liverpool Salvage Association, appeared early on the scene and as a result of his labours *Hougomont* was refloated on the 15th March; but it took two ten-inch pumps going full bore to keep the ship afloat. She then anchored in Maryport roads, this time with a view to divers stopping the leaks, but bad weather came on before the task was completed. The following day Captain Young decided there was only one course left open to him if the Solway was not yet to claim his prize, and that was to put into Maryport.

Action was prompt. With the tugs *Cruiser* and *Wrestler* assisting, the harbour was successfully negotiated at high water. The excessive draft of the water-logged ship left only a few inches under her keel. As she wallowed along before a whole gale from West-North-West it is safe to assume that Captain Nelson, the harbourmaster, and Captain Dawson, his deputy, both had a bad five minutes until the big ship was clear of the channel and in a position of safety, which was achieved only by the skill and daring of those in charge of the respective undertakings working harmoniously together. In these circumstances *Hougomont* figured largely in the re-insurance at Lloyd's.

Deck scene aboard Hougomont as she lay in Allonby Bay, Captain Young,
as he was then, is seen on the left of the picture.

"The ship that came back"

After discharging a large part of her cargo at Maryport *Hougomout* was repaired temporarily and sailed on the 31st March, in tow of the salvage steamer *Ranger*, for Liverpool, where she completed discharge and then proceeded to Greenock to refit. This done, in a few months she set out for Victoria, B.C., in all the glory of her former rig and made an average passage of 139 days.

Five years later *Hougomont* was again very much in evidence at Lloyd's. After discharging a cargo at Coquimbo she was ordered to Tocopilla to load, and sailed accordingly on the 9th July, 1908. She never reached there that voyage – and thereby hangs a tale. The passage meant simply a drift of 500 miles up the coast. Unfortunately the wind fell away when the barque was off her port and the current whisked her northward as far as the latitude of Callao. After striving vainly for a month to get back Captain J. Macmillan – who is not to be confused with the D. S. Macmillan who commanded the big sailers *Corunna*, *Nivelle* and *Vimeira* of the same firm and was afterwards torpedoed and lost in their steamer *Caldergrove* – gave it up and bore away for Australia.

Meantime no little anxiety was felt for the safety of the ship and crew, which was reflected at Lloyd's where up to 80 guineas per cent, were paid on her for re-insurance. Making a fairly good passage across the Pacific *Hougomont* arrived off Sydney Heads where she signalled. With the reading of her numbers came the solution of what had up till then been another of the mysteries of old ocean. Great was the commotion in the shipping world, and great the joy among the relatives of the crew, when the report was flashed to this side. She was ordered to Newcastle to load for the West Coast, and while lying there was known as "the ship that came back."

Stout ship wins through

Yet another little adventure of the *Hougomont* may be of interest, On the 22nd of December, 1914, she left the Thames for New York with a cargo of chalk. During a dense fog on 6th February, 1915, she stranded on Fire Island, just outside New York, as portrayed in the photo.

Fortunately she was refloated a few days later little the worse for her experience. Having discharged her chalk cargo she loaded general for Melbourne and tripped out in 104 days.

Two years ago *Hougomont* was sold to Finland and is still sailing under her original name. At the beginning of last year she arrived at London from Lobos Isles via Panama Canal and so dodged the rigours of Cape Horn for once.

The foregoing remarks serve to show that the fortunes of the barque *Hougomont* varied no less than did those of the old Chateau on the field of Waterloo, after which she was named.

Capt G. A Cockell
132 High Street Maryport

Footnote: Captain George Albert Cockell became Harbourmaster at Maryport after a long association with the sea. He was originally from Sydney N.S.W. Australia, he served on both sailing ships and steam, it was on the latter that he met his wife who was the daughter of Captain James Ritchie of Maryport. George had joined the Holme Line of

Maryport and at the time was third officer on the Isel Holme of which Captain Ritchie was Master. They made their home in Maryport and after the Holme Line ceased trading as a fleet George joined a Glasgow shipping firm then aquiring his Captains ticket. During the war he served under the Admiralty, it was in 1922 he took over the roll as Harbourmaster after his predecessor retired. Captain Cockell was elected on the Maryport U.D.C. in 1925, he was also on the committee of the British Leigion, he was also involved in many of the towns activities and affairs, he was also Commandant of the Special Constabulary.

Sadly Captain George Cockell met his death by way of a strange accident. It was in September 1928 that he was cycling down Shipping Brow and as he approached the harbour bridge just passing the Queens Head Inn, which is now the Maritime Museum, a horse and trap suddenly appeared out of the turning from Well Lane, George swerved to miss colliding with the horse and was thrown off his cycle when he hit one of the chained mooring stobs that ran along the edge of the harbour wall, he sustained some nasty head injuries but was able to make his own way home to clean himself up. His wife immediately called Dr. R. Clark, who resided and practised in Fleming Square, the doctor attended to his injuries and told him to rest which he did for a couple of days after which he felt a little better, but this unfortunately did not last, he again retired to bed and sadly he died two days later due to his injuries. This was a sad loss to his family and to the town of Maryport, he was a fine and well respected member of the community.

J.D.W.

Cumbrian Coincidences

IN August, 1872. my father left Swansea in command of the barque *Cereal*, owned jointly by the late Mr. Wilfrid Hine, and my father (the late Captain James Ritchie). Both Maryport men. The vessel had a cargo of coal for Santos and all went well until she crossed the Line, when, one day, the strange antics of the ship's cat attracted attention. As a hatch was left open in the daytime for ventilation the cat was in the habit of going down the hold, but, this day, on coming up raced about the deck scraping her paws.

Soon afterwards a faint curl of smoke was seen and it was found that the ship was on fire. Matters looked hopeless, but everything possible was done to save the ship, boats were made ready and towed astern in preparation for leaving the vessel quickly if necessity demanded. However, the crew were spared the horrors of a long boat trip, for a vessel hove in sight. To the surprise of all – for many of the crew belonged to Maryport – the vessel proved to be the *John Ritson*, of Maryport, commanded by Captain George Curwen, a Maryport man.

By this time the fumes were very bad, so the *Cereal's* crew transferred to the *John Ritson* before nightfall. The two masters decided to take both ship's crews to the burning ship next morning and endeavour to save her. However, just as they were preparing to set forth the *Cereal's* hatches blew off and the vessel was quickly enveloped in flames. This was on the 28th September, 1872, in Lat. 4.30 S., and Long. 27. 45 W.

A fine launch. The Carl. 2,107 tons, built by Ritsons.
Lost off Cornwall in 1917.

The *John Ritson* was outward bound, so my father (and mother, who was with him at the time), his officers and part of the crew were transferred to the first homeward-bound vessel sighted, and she bore the Cumbrian name of *Portinscale*. Surely a chain of "Cumbrian coincidences."

(Mrs.) J. Cockell

The pretty barque Sverre, *shown leaving Maryport in 1926.*

The Netherby *leaving Maryport carrying a cargo of steel rails, 21st June 1906.*
She was lost with all hands.

A Missing British Ship

NOTHING has been heard of the Maryport barque *Netherby* since July 13th last, when she was spoken in lat. 19 N. Long. 25., on her voyage from Maryport to Talcahuano and it is feared that she has been lost in the vicinity of Cape Horn with the whole of her crew.

She left Maryport on June 21st last, and at the time she was due off the southern cape an enormous quantity of ice was reported, many ships having narrow escapes from disaster. The ship *Flottbek* collided with the ice, and it was with difficulty that she kept afloat until she arrived at a Brazilian port for repairs. The *Netherby*, which was at one time owned in Liverpool, signed on her crew at Maryport on June 15th last year, and the following is the official list of the crew which sailed from Maryport

Captain – Charles Gibbons (49), 5, Eastwood Road, South Woodford, Essex.
Chief Officer – John Wm. Caine (24), Post St Mary.
Second Officer – George Myles (21), 19, East Hill, Queenstown.
Boatswain – T. Gifford (30), Portland Place Downpatrick.
Carpenter – Alfred Ellerison (29), Elliot's Yard, Nelson Street, Maryport.
Steward – R. A. Thompson (23), 85, Upper Meadow Street, Belfast.
Cook – Fritz Langner (28), Seaton Street, Swansea.

Apprentices – Herbert Stanley Smith (21), Stepaside, Pembroke;
Cecil Ernest Lett (19), Bishop Wilton; Francisco Gonecalves (18), Madeira;
Thomas Alwyn Skelton (18), Maryport; Samuel Maxwell Dixon (18), Maryport;
and Edward Davison (19), Conndon.

Sails and A.B., C. Neilsen (54), 4, Frederick Street Liverpool.
A. B.s – James Mathews (24), Irish Street, Killyleagh;
Edward Wilcox (56), 72 Toxteth Street, Liverpool;
John Fox (29), 48, Lower Ditches, Southampton;
Wm, Wilson (28), 311, Ferries Street, Greenock;
Charles Linton (43), 4, Frederick Street Liverpool;
D. Macdonald (42), 2, Watt's Place, Greenock;
Thomas D. Hughes (32), The Lawn, Denbigh;
Jas. Seranagh Savanagh (48), 4, Frederick Street, Liverpool; and
Joseph Monks (19), 251, Bedford Road, Liverpool.

The *Netherby* was an iron barque of 1,448 tons gross, and 1,400 tons net register, built in 1886 by Messrs Ritson and Co., of Maryport, owned by her builders, and registered at Liverpool.

Lost on Uncharted Reef

Hard Times Foster Heroism

AFTER spending many years thrashing across the Atlantic in Captain John Suiter's Maryport fleet of wooden ships, among them the *Callixene, Clyde* and *Mersey*, which traded to Quebec in the season and to American lumber ports at other times, I decided to try a voyage in an iron vessel by way of a change.

At this time the *Henry James*, a trim little barque of 945 tons register. Built on the Clyde in 1882, Captain Ralph Lattimore in command, was loading a cargo of railway material for the Queensland Government in the Senhouse dock, which had been opened only three years before. I joined her on the 13th July, 1887, set forth on a voyage to Bowen, Port Denison, towing as far as St Bee's Head; but ere reaching that point a dozen stowaways were discovered and sent back by the tug when she let go. Very soon afterwards we found there had been a baker's dozen of the gentry as evidenced by a lad named Drummond, 16 years of age, who left his hiding place and threw himself on the Captain's mercy. We were favoured with a fair wind down channel and had an uneventful passage, if the bad weather incidental to running the Easting down be expected.

One dog too many in Bowen

Arrived at our destination on 7th November and not been long in port when Drummond, our stowaway, was fortunate enough to meet a lady who took pity on him and gave him a job in her stables. As he was a likeable lad I have no doubt he made good in Australia. While at Bowen on of our A.B.s, John Kennedy, fell overboard and was drowned, and his loss cast quite a gloom over his shipmates.

Another incident which occurred at Bowen concerned the Captain, who owned and carried with him a big fine dog which unwittingly caused his master to be fined to the tune of £10 and costs for an offence under the "Animals Act" for allowing it to land from the vessel. A local journalist, apparently amused by the incident, wrote the following ditty in his paper; "Captain Lattimore is the owner of a big dog. Now this dog is a very intelligent animal, and like all intelligent beings, he had heard of Bowen by repute as being a good place and a pretty one; what more reasonable, then, than that he should come ashore and see for himself whether all he had heard about us was correct? Accordingly he did come. He followed his genial master up the town, saw what there was to be seen, looked down upon the Bowen doggies with that supreme contempt which only a new chum can show for anything colonial, then barked, wagged his tail and went on board again.

Bolt from the blue

"But matters did not end here. The doggies who had to put up with the sneers and slights of the *Henry James* doggie took great offence and they reasoned among themselves and said, 'He has not paid his footing here, why then should he triumph over us? Truly his laughter shall be turned into mourning,' So reasoning they turned up the Act, which distinctly said that any dog coming from a far countree must pay his footing in a sum not less than £10 and not exceeding £50. Then the local doggie shut up the Act and acted upon it and they made the poor *Henry James* doggie pay £10 and other expenses. and he does not laugh now but will bite any J.P. within a radius of three miles of the Post Office."

After a long lie we completed discharge, ballasted and sailed for Newcastle, N.S.W., where we were chartered to load a cargo of coal for San Francisco. Arrived in due course and, as was customary in those days, soon had prospective passengers trying to secure births in our packet, although she was not a passenger ship by any means. Eventually the captain fixed up passages for a Mr. Taylor, his wife, and their two children, and Mrs. Taylor's mother, also two male passengers.

Having shipped our black diamonds we sailed on 15th March on what was destined to be an eventful passage. After a trying time in getting to the eastward owing to contrary winds we eventually met with fine weather and had a pleasant run through the Islands of Polynesia. We had crossed the Equator, passed Christmas and Fanning Islands, which lay to the east of our course and, standing on past Palmyra, which we expected to pass during the evening, we were congratulating ourselves during the dog watch that we were now clear of the dangers of the Pacific and had a clear run before us to 'Frisco, However, that same midnight – 10th April, 1888 – while making five or six knots under all sail, the barque ran up on a coral reef; our peace and security were rudely disturbed. Owing to the heavy ocean swell which beat upon the reef, the ship was creaking and grinding ominously.

Back to Palmyra

Soon we discovered that we had been seriously damaged, whilst seas began to break on board flooding the decks. Orders were given to abandon ship and, despite the darkness, this was done in an orderly manner. The lifeboats were provisioned, oil was poured on the waters to make it "smooth" and so aid us in passing the boats astern, for which purpose coils of rope had been got up from the fore peak. The boats were lowered but, notwithstanding the use of oil, one was smashed against the ship's side and lost. The other was all but swamped. The small boat was then got overside.

During quiet periods our seven passengers were lowered into boats from the poop, now the only dry place on the ship. The crew followed. The captain, true to the best traditions of the sea, was the last man to leave the wreck, and in doing so fell into the surf, being rescued with great difficulty more dead than alive.

The boats stood by the abandoned ship until dawn, when sail was set for Palmyra Island, situated in Latitude 5 deg. 51 min. N., Longtitude 162 deg. 23 min. W., about 35 miles from the position of the doomed vessel. This island, surrounded by coral reefs, we reached safely the same afternoon, but were in a sorry plight as our provisions, for most part, had been spoiled before getting away from the wreck and we had only what clothes we stood in, plus one pair of blankets. Nevertheless we counted ourselves fortunate in having *terra firma* under our feet once more.

Safe but miserable

We soon discovered that we weren't the first castaways to land on Palymyra as we found the remains – albeit scanty – of several huts and a quantity of cut wood and piled wood which were soon turned to good account. Sustenance was our first concern. There was an abundance of coconuts, as well as birds and their eggs and a species of land crabs, to say nothing of eels; but of water, that most urgent necessity of man, there was not a trace on the island.

However, we were able to catch sufficient rain from the torrential downpours which fell at infrequent intervals to quench our thirst between times. A hut was built at once to shelter the women and children, whilst the men made shacks for themselves.

But, even then, we had little peace or comfort as the island was overrun with leeches which attacked us after every shower of rain. These unpleasant creatures are very small, scarcely one inch in length and no thicker than a stout thread of wire, but are able to penetrate the meshes of the finest stocking, so we, with little or no covering on our legs, were an easy prey at all times.

Captain Lattimore set regular watches from the first and started a beacon fire. This was fed constantly until, one night, it was extinguished by the incessant tropical rain. As our last match had long since been used, the captain the next day, when the sun had gained strength, made use of the lens of his telescope, which had been saved, and so re-kindled the fire after the manner beloved of small boys with a burning glass. This fire was kept alight until we were rescued.

Slow starvation

The lack of water was most inconvenient, but by dint of much prospecting a copious supply was eventually found on an adjoining islet about two miles distant. Fetching it involved considerable difficulty owing to our physical condition as the unaccustomed diet had caused much sickness amongst us. This was aggravated by the want of clothing and the burning rays of the tropical sun, then nearly overhead.

A few days after landing, a boat party was sent to the wreck in the hope of salving something, but it returned the following day and reported the wreck submerged. Surprise was frequently expressed at the entire lack of flotsam on the island and reefs in our vicinity, as it is an accepted idea that such spots are usually strewn with them. Time passed, the days and weeks were mounting up, and we began to think we were in for a long spell on our island retreat. The chief mate, Mr. D. Mcdonald, was most anxious to set off for Samoa to seek help before the few provisions saved from the wreck, which had been jealously guarded against this contingency, were completely consumed or spoiled.

Heroic attempt succeeds

As Samoa lat 1, 300 miles distant, the captain was not at all keen on risking the lives of his chief mate and the volunteers who wished to join him, of whom there were many. Eventually he yielded to their entreaties and the boat finally set off with a solitary breaker filled with water, a few ship's biscuits, a little tinned mutton, a bottle of whisky and two or three hundred coconuts. The mate, bosun and two men, who compromised the boat's crew, set off on their long trail inspired by the God-speeds of those left behind.

They successfully accomplished their remarkable voyage in the space of 19 days, thus averaging nearly three knots on the trip, but it was achieved at the cost of much privation owing to scanty water and food supplies – the coconuts proved a delusion and a snare as they soon turned sour under the burning sun.

Their object attained they were satisfied, though they had to be lifted and carried from their boat. They were in kindly hands, and had the satisfaction of knowing that by their endeavours their erstwhile shipmates would soon be succoured also. Such a feat deserves to rank as an epic in the annals of the Mercantile Marine to which the plucky fellows added fresh lustre.

Small boat voyages – apart from the stunts of adventure – are mostly compelled by direct necessity, usually the sequel to an abandoned vessel, but here we have a volunteer crew risking all in the interest of others, as did Shackleton and his five gallant companions in their memorable small boat voyage from Elephant Island to South Georgia thirty years later. They, too, were merchant service men.

In kindly hands

The Oceanic Steamship Company's *Mariposa*, en-route from Sydney to 'Frisco, called in at Samoa, and her captain, on learning of the plight of the *Henry James* survivors, stated that he would call at Palmyra on his way north and rescue them if still there. He was as good as his word.

On the forty-second day of our sojourn on the island we were overjoyed to sight smoke on the horizon, and to note the steamer steering steadily towards us. Our captain sent the remaining boat to meet the approaching steamer, which turned out to be the *Mariposa*. She lay at a safe distance and sent her boat to meet ours. There was "joy in Israel" when it was learned that Mr. Mcdonald had got safely through. Soon the evacuation of Palmyra was accomplished, and we all clambered up the side of the hospitable American ship, amongst the passengers of which speculation had been rife as to our fate. We found solicitude on all sides. Our sores and wounds were tended, food and clothing provided, whilst the two women and children were once more able to enjoy the amenities of civilisation. The passengers of the *Mariposa*, not content with fitting us all out with clothing – needless to say, some of us looked very quaint in the rigs we donned – collected no less than £120 for our benefit.

Soon we reached Honolulu, where bade adieu to our new-found friends also to our *Henry James* passengers who had shared our vicissitudes with great fortitude and camaraderie and were now looking forward to reaching San Francisco.

Exonerated from blame

At the Navel Court – held on board H.M.S. *Carthage,* if I remember rightly – our captain and officers were exonerated from all responsibility for the loss of the *Henry James,* it being found that she had struck an uncharted reef.

This adventure decided me to finish up with sailing ships, so I worked my way home and, on reaching Maryport, joined Messrs. Hine. Bros Holme Line steamers, where I spent a dozen years, until 1900, I secured a post on shore which I still hold.

The crew of the *Henry James* dispersed at Honolulu, and of all my shipmates I know of only two who are now living, viz., Captain J. F. Crone, Maryport, who was second mate, and Mr. S. Young, of the neighbouring town of Workington, who was an ordinary seaman at the time we became castaways on the Pacific islands.

J. R. Wilson

> *"Wouldst, thou," the helmsman answered,*
> *"Learn the secrets of the seas?*
> *Only those who brave its dangers*
> *Comprehend its Mysteries."*
> *Longfellow*

The Brig Congress *– Built in 1818 (299 tons) discharging cargo of timber in the port where she was built. Lost in the Gulf of St. Lawrence in 1882.*

The fully rigged ship the Acamas *built at Maryport in 1897. Owned by the builder Thomas Ritson. Commanded by Capt. W. A. Nelson, the Master of Cape Horn, 1839-1929.*

– The Log of Davy Jones –

I'm nodding and a-blinking as I sit here at my ease,
And memory takes me back again to the days I sailed the seas;
And in the flickering firelight the ghosts flit to and fro;
Ghosts of those good old sailing ships I knew so long ago.

I can feel the old *Glenorchy* from the Cape come booming home.
Rolling down to Saint Helena, her bows a-cream with foam;
With the *Drummuir* running neck and neck, the *Palgrave* far away,
And the *Inchcape Rock*, that later left her bones in Algoa Bay.

From Garden reach to Esplanade they lay in serried ranks,
Those old Calcutta traders, the "Falls" and "Brocklebanks."
The "Bens" and "Glens" the "Fernie" ships and others as well known,
With Jimmy Nourse's coolie ships, the *Sheila, Erne* and *Rhone*.

The *Oakbank* and the *Otterspool,* both burned in far Peru,
The *Frankistan* and *Fannie Kerr,* the *Frank N. Thayer,* too;
Sir Lancelot, the beautiful, famed clipper in her day,
Loaded deep with salt from Muscat, when she foundered in the Bay.

Taitsing was wrecked on Zanzibar, *Eden Holme* on Hebe reef,
The *Flying Spur* on Martin Vas had also come to grief;
The *Flying Venus* on Penrhyn, *Loch Sloy* on Kangaroo,
Loch Vennacher had left her bones upon this island, too.

The *Nylghau* and the *Alex Mcneil* passed out on Pratas Reef,
Colonial Empire made eight bells on the rocks of Cape Recife;
The *Bangalore* went missing, likewise the *Oamaru,*
Lord Brassey and the *Manchester,* the good ship *Dalas,* too.

The good *Drumcraig* went missing, as did the old *Tamar,*
Peter Iredale and *Galena* on Columbia River Bar;
Midway Island took the *Carrolton,* Layson the barque *Ceylon,*
Ice took the ship *Geo. Peabody* and the bonnie *Rising Dawn.*

Glenberive on the Manacles, *Radient* on Crocodile;
The *Langrigg Hall* on Tuskar, *King Lear* on Lunday's Isle.
Seeadler, the pirate, wrecked on South Sea Isles afar,
Remembered by old sailor men as the "Pass of Balmaha."

Malden Island took the *Salamis,* Iquique the *Wynnstay,*
Persian Empire and the *Leverbank* both sank in Biscay Bay;
Glenericht, by collision, south of the River Plate,
On lonely Inaccessible the *Shakespeare* met her fate.

The *Allanshaw* and *Mabel Clark* on Tristan's rocky shore,
Glenhuntly and the *Beacon Light* nearby had paid their score;
County of Roxburgh and the *Savernake* on Paumotos made their bed,
Edward O'brian and *Dunreggan* piled up on Diamond head.

The *Primrose Hill* on Holyhead went down with all her crew,
The *Thracian,* on her maiden trip, took all hands with her too;
The *Ardencraig,* on Scilly, *Torridon,* sunk by the Hun,
Cape Wrath and *Cadzow Forest* took their pilots and were gone.

Kings Island took *Loch Levan,* likewise the *Kalahine,*
Lizzie Iredale went missing, with the *Heathbank* and *Loch Fyne;*
Powys Castle, Cosmopolis, Clenaird and the *Indore*
All made eight bells and closed their watch on Staten Island's shore.

Now the fire is getting lower and the ghosts have ceased to play,
And I think I heard a cock crow: It's near the break of day;
I'll make four bells and go below, and rest my weary bones,
But I bow my head to the men and ships that have gone to Davy Jones.

George Seeley

(Note: The last eight years of his sea service Mr. Seeley was in command of the vessel the *Glenorchy*).

Where are they now these ships and men?
Who's likes will ne'r be seen again,
For'er to sail the deep blue sea
On the white capped waves of eternity.

J.D.W.

Towing out to sea, the tug
Norfolk Hero. *Built 1848.*

The Great Eastern
Her Design and Launching

NUMEROUS accounts have been written about Brunel's wonderful masterpiece, but all of them are of her life and times and launching. Reading through an old book printed at the beginning of 1857, I came across an article on Maritime Conveyance which gives particulars of the *Great Eastern* as she lay on the stocks before launching. When she was being built, the largest steamer was the *Duke of Wellington*, – 240 feet long, and the largest merchant steamer was the Cunarder *Persia*, 390 feet in length and 54 feet beam.

The building of the *Great Eastern* was suggested by certain disadvantages which were inherent in all the previous steamers. Coal question was the greatest difficulty, the waste of time, through having to go out of the course to take in coal fuel, neutralised the advantages of a higher speed than the sailing ship; in fact, the clippers Australia bound often made as quick a passage out as the steamers.

A Wonderful Conception

In 1852, the Eastern Steam Navigation Company was formed, and the problem was discussed as to whether a steamer could be built large enough to carry fuel

The Great Eastern.

for the voyage out to and home from Australia; and, if so, could it be navigated safely and quickly. Mr. Isambard K. Brunel was called in to give a solution to this problem, and after mature deliberation the Company, upon Mr. Brunel's advice, determined to build a steamer nearly 700 feet in length. This ship was to carry 12,000 to 14,000 tons of coal, 5 tons of measured goods, and 4,000 passengers besides crew.

Mr. Scott Russell was selected to be the builder, and a piece of ground, adjacent to his works at Milwall, was leased by the Company as the place of building. This yard was prepared by piling to a great depth, and was provided with all the appliances for building an iron ship, and Mr. Jacomb was appointed as assistant engineer in its construction.

The length between perpendiculars was 680 feet, on the upper deck 692 feet; breadth of the hull was 83 feet, and including paddle boxes and fenders 118 feet. The height of the hull was 60 feet, weight of iron in the hull 7,000 tons, and the weight of the whole ship loaded was to be not less than 25,000 tons. At that load she would draw 30 feet of water. More than two million rivets were used in fastening the ribs and over 10,000 plates together. In the interior of the ship there were 10 or 12 watertight bulkheads, extending up to the upper deck, with no openings below the lower deck.

Three Strings

Accommodation was to be arranged for 800 first class passengers, 2,000 second class, and 1,200 third class passengers and soldiers. The crew were 400 in number, and were accommodated forward, while the upper deck was to be flush fore and aft, thus giving a promenade of about an eighth of a mile in length. As the old narrative has it; "The means of propulsion are vast in power, and unprecedented in combination since they include the paddle, screw, and sail." The wheels were 56 feet in diameter, with floats about 13 feet long. The engines for these were made by Scott Russell, and stood nearly 50 feet high. The cylinders of these engines had a diameter of 74 inches and a 14 foot stroke.

The screw was 24 feet in diameter with four blades, with a shaft 160 feet long and of 60 tons weight. It was driven by engines made by Messrs. Watt of Soho, with four cylinders of 84 inches diameter and with a four-foot stroke. There were four boilers for the paddles and six for the screw. Her six masts carried 6,500 square yards of canvas, and she had auxiliary steam on deck to hoist sails, anchors, etc. There were 10 anchors and 800 fathoms of cable, whilst gas was to be made on board to light the various parts of the ship. For life-saving purposes there were boats enough to take all passengers and crew, including two screw steamers of 90 feet in length, hung on the davits abaft the paddle boxes.

The great length of the vessel necessitated a new plan for launching, and accordingly two timber platforms were built from the ship's position to the low water mark. They were of immense strength, and measured 80 feet in width, having a slope of 1 in 12 towards the water. Two cradles of timber were built temporarily under the hull, and at low water mark she was to be launched. This ends the account of her building on stocks.

As is well known, Brunel was rather timid over the launch, and checked her when she had only travelled about three feet down the ways broadside. She maintained this position for several months, and was then launched by hydraulic jacks. Her launch alone cost her owners £120,000, and incidentally ruined them.

Her after history is well known. She was sold for £160,000, but her new owners found her unsuitable for the North Atlantic trade. She left Southampton for New York in June, 1860, making the run in 11 days. During that and the next year she made several more trips. In 1865 and '66 she laid the Atlantic cable, and from 1869 she laid some of the most important cables in the Atlantic, Mediterranean and Red Sea.

In 1884 she was sold for £26,200, and in 1886 was owned by the London Traders, Ltd. She was sold in 1888 for £58,000, and was broken up in Liverpool in November, 1888.

So ended the dream of I. K. Brunel and Scott Russell, which might have come true had it not been for that fatal check when she was being launched.

E.A.W.

This monument is erected in memory of William Harrison, Commander of the Great Eastern, who was drowned in Southampton Water January 21st 1860. Born at Maryport 1812. An accomplished navigator, he crossed the Atlantic upwards of 200 times. Erected by public subscription.

Things in General at Maryport

APRIL 9th, 1938

Maryport Link with Shipping Centenary

ON a large headstone in Maryport cemetery an inscription reads "In memory of William Harrison, Commander of the *Great Eastern*, who was drowned in Southampton Water, January 21st, 1860. Born at Maryport, October 1812, He was an accomplished navigator who crossed the Atlantic upwards of 200 times." The last fact has little literal meaning to the present generation, who already have the facility of an air service across the South Atlantic, and are soon to have one linking North America and Europe. However, its importance measured by the standards of this former Maryport Captain's generation can be best explained by stating that he was in a similar position to the Commander of the modern *Queen Mary*, selected for his skill and experience as a navigator and his exceptional knowledge of the North Transatlantic crossing, as Commander of the first big Transatlantic liner. His position as such is recalled this week, because Monday was the centenary date of the first Transatlantic crossing made by a ship under continuous steam power.

On April 4th, 1838, the paddle steamer *Sirus*, of 703 tons with engines of 302 h.p., left Cork Harbour and reached Sandy Hook on the afternoon of April 22nd. On the following morning, St. George's Day, she proceeded up New York Harbour, where a tumultuous welcome awaited her. The success of the *Sirus* was followed very soon afterwards by a regular steam liner service provided by the *Great Western*. Of 1,340 tons, with engines of 750 h.p., the *Great Western* was the creation of Isambard Kingdom Brunel, the great engineer and builder of the Great Western Railway. As Bristol was to be his railway terminus, he conceived the idea of extending the service to New York by steamship. Brunel formed the company, the ship was built, and continued to ply across the Atlantic for nine years, being commercially successful for a number of years. The *Great Western* led in less than twenty years the *Great Eastern*, launched at Millwall in 1858. She was a paddle liner of 22,800 tons, then by far the biggest ship afloat. Captain William Harrison of Maryport was selected as her commander. That she was in size before her time and did not pay commercially, being used later for cable laying in the Atlantic and Mediterranean, does not alter the honour of his selection. Nor does it alter Maryport's link with a chapter of British Mercantile Marine progress that laid the foundation of a world lead in steam ships that has been maintained for a century, although it is becoming increasingly difficult to do so in present times owing to the great vast tonnage sunk during The Great War, coupled with the increasing competition of foreign – owned vessels aided by Government subsidies.

Roman artifacts on display in the Portico of Netherhall.

Macleod Macphail

Light up your pipes for a salty lay that sings of the days of sail,
A song of the roaring windbag days when I sailed Wi' Macleod Macphail,
A hard-case Scot of an olden day, with a thin stiff upper lip,
Who'd chance if something carried away to get the speed on his ship.
When the wind was right and the gear was tight and the log showed twelve-point-three.
Then his jaw was set and his eyes were bright with the pride of his years at sea.
For Mac was a sailor from Sailorville, with all the spunk of his clan,
Bending his ship to his stubborn will with the strength of a Hielandman.

Mac was a man with a grown-up mind and the heart and soul of a boy;
Though his ways were harsh, still his heart was kind and his ship was his grown-up toy.
He'd pull her to bits and build her up, like a lad with a plastic set;
And he did not worry for bite nor sup while his soul with spray was wet.
Truck to keelson and stem to stern, a sailorman true and brave,
Who battled and cared not what he'd earn this side of a watery grave,
Setting the stunsails when winds were light and cracking on in a gale,
Seeing ahead with uncanny sight – that was Macleod Macphail!

I met Macphail when the war was on. Though the years had wandered by.
Twas the same old Mac that I gazed upon, with the same old glint in his eye.
His hair was grey; and his wrinkled face, tanned with the tempest's shocks,
Brought to me visions of lee-fore-brace and the cursing of countless blocks.
Face to face after twenty years, in a Mediterranean port,
Both of us landed in quaint Algiers in naval jobs of a sort;
Mac marooned on a "sweeping" craft, and I on a naval tug;
As he shook my hand he grimly laughed in tune with his shoulders' shrug !

"This is no game," he said with a frown, "or a sailorman to play.
The blinking Navy has got us down and – mark me she'll have her way.
Flying a blanked lootenant's bands on a d-d hot water can,
With never a sailor amongst your crew, but soldiers every man!
Fakements to blow up submarines, smoke-screens to blur their way –
If it's sailor's work in these d-d machines it's sorry I'm here to-day!
But it's too late now to take a pull. It seems like a loathsome dream.
Gi'e me white sails wi' their bellies full and the wind abaft the beam!

"Do ye mind the time in the Wings O'Dawn, when we ran our easting down
With hardly a stitch o' canvas on till we came to Melbourne town?
Straining her guts till the pumps grew tired of keeping the water low –
But her speed was all that a man could ask, and God! that was good to know!
I'm dodging now on a trawling scow, out here for my country's sake –
Two stripes and a curl's my part of the show, and I – I am just a just a fake!
A cog in a wheel and a paltry one; and I fear that my wits will fail,
If this thrice-damned war is not quickly done, and I get me back to sail."

But Mac was settled like many more, in a scrap with a submarine –
Fritzie and he three miles off shore both slithered to Fiddler's Green!
For the whole "duration" he couldn't stay; and died at his country's call –
He took his discharge in a seaman's way and went down, stripes and all!
I can see his quaint old shoulders shrug. I can hear the laugh he laughed
(I marooned on a naval tug, and he on a sweeping craft);
And my thoughts go back to the good old days when the pulse of the sea was Sail,
While my heart keeps singing its meed of praise for the ghost of
Macleod Macphail!

Albatross, *The Sydney Bulletin*
September 1925

White Star Line

After Many Days

THE MISSING BARQUE *MIDAS*
(MESSAGE FOUND IN A BOTTLE)

A DISPATCH dated Portland, August 10th, says: What has every appearance of a genuine message from the lost barque Midas was found floating in the breakers off Stot's Place, about four miles north of the Colombia River Tuesday. The slip of paper was found in a bottle, and as far as it could be interpreted by handwriting experts the message reads as follows:

"Brit barque Midas, ballast shifted, all in small boats, first mates boat capsized, will all drown –"

Captain Thomas Messenger.

The *Midas* sailed from Nagasaki for Portland in January, 1898, with a crew of twenty-five men under charter to C. W. Tracy to load wheat. Soon after leaving the Japan coast a heavy storm swept over that region, and two other ships which afterwards reached Portland narrowly escaped foundering. On receipt of the message the signature was compared with that of Captain Messenger on his clearance papers at the Custom House. The resemblance is so striking as to leave small doubt as to its being made by the captain of the *Midas*.

Captain Thomas Messenger had served as mate on the well known Whitehaven built ship the *Dunboyne* built in 1888, he was one of the first mates to serve on her, and carried on doing so for some four years until he took his first command as Captain of the Maryport built vessel *Ladas*. She was a three masted barque, of some 1,200 tons net, and built by Ritsons in 1894.

Captain Messenger was one of the last of the old sailing ship captains, a man raised in a hard school, but also in an era that was very special, apparently he commanded his ship with the authority that was expected of a man in his position, he was a tough old sea dog, he never demanded respect, but respect was shown and given to him by his crew, to which he presented himself not as a hard task master, but more of a fatherly figure, who expected his wishes to be obeyed.

Any reader wishing to know more about this fine seafaring captain, about his life and his voyages up until his tragic end, can be found in the pages of a book published in 1998. which is a must, especially for the nautically minded the title being:

Dear Daughter
The Messenger Letters.
Voyages Of A Sailing Ship Captain.
(1890-1898)
ISBN 0 9534609 0 8.

The above is a genuine manuscript, compiled from letters sent by Captain Messenger to his only daughter while on his voyages at sea, which gives a great insight into the man himself, and life at sea in that period, when seafaring was a tough job, but a magnet to those with the spirit of adventure. Men like Captain Messenger are moulded by their surroundings and act accordingly, my grandfather being a seafaring man of that period, I recall him being of similar temperment, incidentally, he knew Captain Messenger quite well, and was twenty two years old when Captain Messenger took command of the *Ladas*. My grandfather at that time was with the Holme Line, running steel rails out to Canada for the Canadian Pacific Railroad, and making return voyages with cargoes of timber and wheat, and also to Australia with similar cargoes, some of these voyages were of long duration, some up to two years.

During periods of family conversation as a teenager shortly after my grandfather had passed away. I recall the names of Captain Millican, Captain Brown, Captain Ritch, my grandfather had sailed on numerous voyages under the command of these well known seafarers in his early years, many stories of voyages, the busy docks and port, characters of the town. now only memories of an era that has passed.

Captain Messengers daughter Mary Adelaide lived in her later years with a friend of long standing at 39 Curzon Street, I myself lived only a few doors away at number 53, I can remember the elderly lady quite well, as I was in my teens at the time, my grandmother used to often chat with her and Mrs Cameron, who resided at number 49. Miss Messenger rented a flat in the quite large property from the early 1950s until 1963. She passed away on August 10th 1963, aged 81 years. There is a double sided headstone to the Messenger family in the Crosscanonby Parish Churchyard, which includes an inscription to Captain Messenger.

The book the *Messenger Letters* is Edited and Introduced by Mr. Graham Hindle. who's great aunt was the lady with whom Miss Messenger lived, and was her close friend. Graham himself at that time lived at the same address.

J.D.W.

The Midas.
One of the last big sailing ships to be built at Maryport.

From *The Cumberland Evening Star,* September 1st, 1952

In 1894 there occurred two very epic events. A horse called Ladas won the Derby and a ship called *Ladas* was launched at Maryport. Both were champions.

As a two year old, Ladas had won the four races for which he was entered, he also beat Matchless in the two thousand guineas. Ladas was considered a certainty for the Derby.

That this famous horse did win at the prohibitive odds of 9/2 on is all the more glorious, for Ladas had to stand with his near hind-leg in a bath of hot bran until a few days prior to the race.

When Ladas, owned by Lord Rosebery, won the Derby it was a momentous occasion, for the owner was then the Prime Minister. It is therefore very understandable that when J. & T. Ritson, Ship Builders, Maryport, had a ship ready for launching that year, the name *Ladas* should come easily, for the ship too had grace, beauty and, it was hoped, a good turn of speed.

The building yards of Messrs. Ritson were famous for their broadside launches. *Ladas* was a three-masted barque of some 1,200 tons net, and her first voyage with Captain. Thomas. Messenger of Crosby in command, was the conveyance of a load of steel rails from Senhouse Dock to Chile. This maiden trip which took place around the end of August 1894, was also accorded a great ovation. The dock gates and pier were crowded with people, swelled above the normal by a large number of trippers from Carlisle and neighbouring towns.

It must also have been an especially great day for a young Maryport man called Hodgson. who joined *Ladas* on her maiden voyage as an A.B. Captain Hodgson as he is now known in Maryport, served for three years in the *Ladas*, leaving her on May 7th, 1897, to sit for his higher certificate.

He had some wonderful tales to tell of his days 'in sail'. There are instances fraught with great danger, but ever uppermost in Captain Hodgson is a strong affection for the *Ladas* – a great ship manned by good men. The *Ladas*, like the horse after which it was named was indeed a very speedy vessel, and Capt. Messenger a holy terror for carrying sail. The *Ladas* was in Buenos Aires docks in 1915, then under the Norwegian flag.

The Midas *in sail.*

From Editor, the *Evening Star*

A reader tells me that the Master of the barque *Ladas* was Captain Messenger, and that her crew had reason to be grateful for his true seamanship when she encountered some rough weather on a voyage to Australia in the early months of 1895, about a year after her launching.

The account of the voyage given in Captain Messenger's report is reminiscent of the recent troubles of the Theron taking our antarctic expedition to the South Pole. They left Coral in Chile on February 7th and ran into ice on March 1st. The report goes on 'we hauled the ship up to the South East and stood on until 10 a.m. Then found the ice to be one continuous field, with mountains at apparently the extreme ends of it. We steered in various directions for at least ten miles, but at 7 p.m. found we were sailing into another bay, as ice was all around.

After running about 60 miles in a circuitous course to get clear of the ice, the vessel only succeeded in running into another bay. Up to 47 degrees South and 42 degrees East the vessel was sailing through the ice and frequently came into collision with small bergs that did some slight damage'.

An anxious and trying time was spent by those on board, all of whom attributed the safe arrival of the ship to Captain Messenger's seamanship.

The AF Chapman *launched as the Dunboyne in Whitehaven in 1885. She survives today as a tourist attraction in the harbour at Stockholm. She was used for some years as a training ship for the Swedish navy and is the only surviving Whitehaven built vessel that is still intact today.*

A Famous Son of Maryport
LIEUTENANT EDWARD SMITH – V.C., D.C.M.

EDWARD Smith, or Ned, as he was affectionately known in his home town, but to his military associates he was better known as Ben, was born at number one North Quay, on the harbourside at Maryport in 1899, Ned was one of a family of eight children. As a youth attended the old National School in Maryport. When finishing his schooling which was at the age of 14 he took a job at the Oughterside Colliery, and whilst working there he joined the Army reserve this was in 1915, he was then only 16 years of age. Ned then enlisted, and was shipped to France, and in December 1916. he joined the 1st-5th Battalion, The Lancashire Fusiliers. Ned took to service life, and he gained promotion quite quickly. In the month of August 1918 he was made Sergeant.

The following details were given in the *London Gazette* supplement of October 18th, 1918. – Sergeant Edward Smith, D.C.M., Lancashire Fusiliers, while in command of a platoon, personally took a machine gun post with rifle and bayonet, killing at least six of the enemy, regardless of the hand grenades they flung at him. Later he led his men to the assistance of another platoon he saw in difficulties, he took command, and captured the objective. During the counter attack the next day he led forward a section and restored a portion of the line. His personal bravery, skill and initiative were outstanding, and his conduct throughout an inspiring example to all. Ned was awarded for his bravery and outstanding skill and courage with his country's greatest honour. The Victoria Cross.

When Ned arrived home to Maryport it was to a tumultuous welcome, he was a hero, not only in the town, but the whole of

Edward Smith, V.C,. D.C.M.

Cumberland, and a great reception was laid on in his honour.

After the war Ned returned to his home town where he resumed with his previous occupation at the colliery. This was not to last very long, missing military life and his former colleagues, he returned to rejoin his former regiment, where he served in Dublin, becoming Drum Major. In 1924 he was again promoted, this time to the rank of warrant officer, as Colour Sergeant Major where he served in Malaya for three years. He then became Regimental Sergeant Major, serving with his battalion in the Far East. Ned finally bid farewell to the services in 1937, receiving an inscribed tankard presented by the officers of his regiment in appreciation of his gallantry and long and illustrious career.

Edward Smith was back in uniform again at the outbreak of war in 1939 again with his old regiment. He was Lieutenant Quartermaster. Ned was tragically killed in France serving his country with pride as always. He died on Friday 12, January 1940 age 41 years. He is buried at BEUVRY COMMUNAL CEMETERY EXTENSION Pas de Calais, France.

IN MEMORY OF

LIEUTENANT EDWARD SMITH VC,DCM

107894, 2ND BN., LANCASHIRE FUSILIERS
WHO DIED AGE 41
ON FRIDAY 12 JANUARY 1940.
LIEUTENANT SMITH, NATIVE OF MARYPORT, CUMBERLAND.

REMEMBERED WITH HONOUR
BEUVRY COMMUNAL CEMETRY EXTENSION

COMMEMORATED IN PERPETUITY BY
THE COMMONWEALTH WAR GRAVES COMMISSION

Commemoration Photo.

The following poem was sent to Ned by one of his wartime comrades on his heroic return to Maryport.

Sergeant Ben Smith V.C., D.C.M.

Sergeant Ben Smith of Maryport,
V.C. and D.C.M.
Brave and gallant soldier
I give you greetings Ben,

You're a credit to old Cumberland
And the town of Maryport,
Also to your regiment
Who through the war have bravely fought.

The soldier's "Star of Hope," the Cross,
Right gallantly you won,
A boy in years, in deeds a man,
You proved unto the Hun.

No less than six before you fell,
Upon that eventful day.
No wonder with such gallant lads
Old England had the sway.

Heaven's blessing on thy mother
Who reared such a gallant boy,
Honour to thy native county
How their hearts are filled with joy.

Cumberland lads will proudly greet thee,
Old Maryport will be en-fête,
For the colliers swear that you Ben
Are a chap thats hard to beat.

Sergeant Ben Smith of Maryport
All honour to thy name,
You're a credit to old Cumberland
And the town from whence you came.

Also to your Regiment
The Lancashire Fusiliers,
Hat's off my lads to sergeant Smith
Let old Maryport ring with cheers.

Written by Mr. James Campbell,
The – K.O.R.L., One of the old Contemptibles.

Ned's neice, Mrs. Margaret Barlow.
Pictured outside her cottage on Shipping Brow.
Margaret passed away in 2004. Photo 2003.

The far cottage to the left is the Harbourside home where Ned Smith was born and raised.
1 North Quay Maryport. Photo 2003.

Footnote: Ned Smith was a sergeant of only nineteen years of age when he was awarded the D.C.M. One month later he was awarded the Victoria Cross for Gallantry, Bravery, and leadership in the face of the enemy. Personally taking six lives of the enemy. Ned was also a keen sportsman, He was battalion boxing champion while stationed in the Far East. The Lancashire Fusiliers disbanded in 1973, and were amalgamated with the Royal Regiment of London, which is based in the Tower of London.

A Cumbrian Legend – Douglas Clark

International Rugby League Footballer, Cumberland and Westmorland and all-in World Champion Wrestler Born May 1891 – Died February 1951 – Aged 59 Years
(THE PEOPLES CHAMPION)

THE year would be about 1949, I was a young boy, of ten or eleven years of age at the time. It was the year before my grandfather passed away, we were living at 53 Curzon Street, the property being quite substantial, my parents and brother lived there together with my grandparents. This particular day I remember quite vividly, my parents at the time were away in Kent visiting my younger brother who was a patient in the Royal Eye Hospital in Bromley. My grandmother asked me to run an errand for her to Skelton's confectioners, whose premises were in Wood Street. When I returned home my grandparents were in the front room chatting with two visitors, they were both men and both large men, one of them in particular, it was summertime, the shorter but the much more powerfully built man of the two was wearing a pale blue short sleeved shirt, he was very suntanned and heavily muscled, he was the first to speak when I entered the room "hello young man he said in a softly spoken voice, he then smiled and said I take it your name is John,? to which I answered yes, he then patted me on the head and replied, and a nice name to have son". Even at that young age I was impressed by the man, even though I had never met or set eyes on him before, I had the feeling that there was something very special about this person, My grandfather introduced me to Mr. Douglas Clark, and then to the other taller man who was very similar in looks, this was his younger brother Mr. Ainslie Clark. I had been introduced as a young boy to a man who was already a legend, not just locally, but all over the Globe, and wherever people gathered to talk rugby and wrestling. I was to learn much more about this very special man as the years unfolded ahead.

Douglas Clark on that particular day was on holiday visiting family and friends, my grandfather knew John Clark, Douglas's father quite well. John Clark was a coal merchant who used to deliver coal to our family home in the past years, and likewise, grandfather delivered fish and fruit to the Clarks home in Ellenborough, and it was through this that he got to know the Clark family very well and they became quite friendly, a cup of tea at either home on delivery days and a chat. Ainslie the younger brother of Douglas was a chief Inspector on the Cumberland Bus Services, and would often stop for a chat when passing. I remember Ainslie quite well during my teenage years, a very smart upright military looking man, and one thing I remember in particular about him was, how light on his feet he was for a big man and when walking moved very catlike. On this day in mention, the two brothers had been passing and had called in to say hello, as a young lad at the time I had no idea who this man was or where he came from, all I felt was that there was something special about the man, he held my attention, for some reason feeling drawn to him. I also remember my grandfathers words to me after the two men left. "You have been very privileged today son, that man you have just met is a war hero, and also the greatest sportsman and the strongest man this county has ever produced, when you go to school tomorrow tell your friends who you have met".

Douglas Clark
World Wrestling Champion.

Douglas Clark was born in May 1891, In the Civil Parish of Ellenborough Maryport, he was the fourth born of eight children, four boys, and four girls, his father John Clark was a coal merchant, his mother was Elizabeth Clark, of the children, Sarah was the eldest, Archibold was second born, then came Margaret, Douglas, Mary, William, Ruth, and Ainslie the youngest.

Douglas and his brother Archibold had worked for their father John, helping to deliver coal around Maryport and district, it was said that at a young age Douglas was a very powerful young man, and that it was not unusual to see him carry a one cwt sack of coal under either arm, he revelled in hard work, as he was a health and fitness fanatic, hauling coal helped to build up the wonderful physique that he was to attain and the strength that was to give him the title of the strongest man on the planet!

Douglas Clark was not a man who was all brawn and without a brain. Duggy, as he was fondly named was a thinker. He thought out the moves on the field of rugby, of which he was a top class player, and was dubbed in his time as the finest loose forward the game had ever produced, and likewise in the field of wrestling, of which he would became World Champion, both in the Cumberland and Westmoreland style, and all-in wrestling.

In his later life, as a recreational hobby Douglas took up the game of golf, he also painted in watercolours, he was very fond of the great outdoors and wildlife, a family man who was kind generous and fair. In all respects a true sporting gentleman.

The year after I met Douglas my grandfather died, this was in 1950. Sadly one year later in 1951 after a short illness this supreme sportsman and war hero died, he was only 59 years of age. Blown up on two occasions in 1917 in France, he suffered multiple shrapnel wounds while searching for and helping wounded comrades. Confined to a wheelchair and discharged from his unit, it would seem that he was finished as a service man and also as a sportsman, a few months later he was back in action with his company. After the war Douglas was awarded the Military Medal for valour during engagement with the enemy.

He had lived most of his life in Huddersfield, where he was treated like a son, they took this great man to their hearts to which he gave loyalty in return. But in the end he would return to his roots, and be interred in Maryport cemetery, where he rests with his wife Jennie. Douglas always loved his home town, and it does seem rather sad that he had to make his name elsewhere, he was idolised by local sportsmen and highly admired by the people of the town district and county, but seemingly the powers that be who were in office at the time were somewhat blind to talent and achievements of this very special man. People of much less achievement have gained higher popularity and acclaim, put upon pedestals and had streets named after them. This is by no means due to the working people of the town, the people of Maryport have always been loyal to their town and should be given more say towards its future and prosperity. Hopefully in the future this may happen, for the town is now taking on a new and brighter look which has been long awaited, long may it continue.

Hopefully should a new sports centre be built, it will be named after the greatest sportsman that the county has ever produced. I would think without doubt if he were alive and in his sporting prime today, Douglas Clark would be chosen as the sportsman of the year, which would have been a just and due reward.

J.D.W.

Fartown Affairs – Douglas Clark
By Rouge December 29th, 1932

Was it of Fox that the story goes? When this statesman died, his friends were desirous of a distinctive epitaph, and asked the best brains of the time to supply one. Of all sent in, the prize was awarded to the man who wrote "Charles James Fox." Now in every writing of any former Fartowner I feel very much in sympathy with the man who solved the question of Fox's epitaph, and feel the best thing I could have done was to write the above heading, and leave it at that. "Doug" is so well known throughout the land that I am faced with the difficult task of painting the lilly. But an inexorable Sports Editor is totally lacking in sympathy, so I must make the best I can of it. A further difficulty will be that once started on this varied subject I should know when to stop, so to simplify matters I shall practically confine myself to Clark's football career. All of us recognise his greatness in the wrestling world, but to many of the younger generation Clark the footballer is just one of the great ones of a past generation.

A Physical Marvel

As was the case a couple of weeks ago, Cumberland again comes into the case, for it was at Ellenborough in that county that Douglas Clark was born. With parents who held strong views on fresh air and simple life, physical fitness became almost a religion with Douglas in his boyhood days, and this accounts for what to many appears to be the most wonderful thing about Clark – that in middle-age, after going through experiences which would have killed many and would have made others invalids for life, he is still capable of dealing with the world"s strongest men. He soon made his mark in football, which appealed to him more strongly than any other sport. He played with his school, but on leaving at the age of fourteen he found it no easy matter to keep in touch with his beloved game. He assisted his father in a coal business, and often on Saturdays his work was not finished in time for him to get off to the matches. Did he give in? not he, He followed the example of the "meenister,"who was divided by the calls of golf and his vocation. He used his pocket money and induced some of his pals to finish for him. When fifteen years old he joined Brookland, Rovers and before he was sixteen won his first medal as one of the team which carried off the championship of the intermediate competition for youths under eighteen. When sixteen he played in the under twenty-one Section, and his team was successful in every match that season. In this season and the one following, when he was admitted to the ranks of the seniors, Clark added six more medals to his fast growing collection, and in the following season the late Mr. Joe Clifford persuaded him to throw in his lot with Huddersfield. When he first came Douglas was played in the reserve team, out of deference to his father's wishes, but it was soon apparent that this sturdy young Cumbrian was equal to the strain, and on September 23, 1909, he played his first game with the senior team. The match was against Hull Kingston Rovers, not the most drawing room type of players in those days, but Douglas came through with honour, and from that day was a regular member of the team which grew up to greatness along with Clark's reputation.

A Wonderful Career

Thus started, Clark never looked back, and when he retired from the game some twenty years later he had gained practically every honour attainable. He played his last game with Huddersfield in the 1927-28 season, but his last big match was with his native county against O'Gorman's team of Australians in 1929. A truly fitting termination to twenty years of eventful and varied football!

Clark came to Huddersfield just when the club was beginning that wonderful climb from a long period of obscurity to the most dazzling heights ever reached by a town team. The Oxford University teams in the early 'eighties, and the Fettesian-Lorettonians for about a decade were wonder sides, but I doubt if even they stood out more conspicuously from their contemporary clubs than did Huddersfield above their contemporaries from 1911 until the war.

Then during the war Clark, together with several other members of the Huddersfield team, played under Rugby Union rules with Grove Park, and did his share in the astonishing feats of that team. Only last month I was discussing Rugby League football with a R.U. enthusiast. Clarks name came up, and my friend asked if I meant the Clark who played with Grove Park before going out to France. When I said yes, he told me that a friend of his who saw a lot of the Grove Park matches, considered Clark the finest forward he ever saw. That is a big thing to say, but few will deny that Douglas was one of the great men of the game.

Clark was one of the "Four-Cup" team, which was a member of the teams which carried off the Challenge Cup three times, and also the R.L. Championship, and numerous Yorkshire Cups. He repeatedly represented his County, his Country, and the British R.L. against Australia, including the celebrated "Rorke's Drift" conflict, in which he became a serious casualty, but even that could dim his admiration for the marvellous display of his captain, Harold Wagstaff.

I should doubt, however, if he ever felt greater satisfaction at the result of a match than when in his later years (1926 was the date) he led Huddersfield to victory against Wakefield in the final of the Yorkshire Cup at Headingley. In this match Huddersfield were considered to have a very thin chance, but clark so inspired his men by his example and his infectious enthusiasm that "Jonty Parkin" and his team were thoroughly subdued. This after seventeen years of continuous football, bears testimony to the wonderful vitality of the man.

When Douglas joined Huddersfield they had never won a trophy of any description, or made any appearances in any finals, but things were about to make a change, he was an inspiration to his team. Douglas was a man of all seasons, the perfect specimen, he would let nothing beat him, the greater the challenge or the odds. He was gassed on two occasions, and blown up during the War and was awarded the Military Medal. While in the forces he was wrestling champion of the British Army "all in style," he was also "World Champion" in the Cumberland and Westmorland style, he won the Grasmere Cup in 1922 also in 1924 collecting many trophies and medals along the way. The stories of his immense strength have almost become folklore, there was the story of Douglas breaking the neck of a stubborn Bull in a field in Patterdale while walking his dog, apparently he was unaware of the animals presence until he was about to leave the field through a gate, when his dog by barking warned him of the bulls imminent presence, as Douglas turned he was face to face with the animal, and his back was apparently only a few feet from the gate, and the animal almost upon him, he instinctively gripped the horns of the animal hopefully to twist its head to one side and wrestle it to the ground and make his escape from the field before the bull regained itself into the standing position, but unfortunately this did not occur, the bull held its head upright not giving in to be grounded, Douglas had to use his powerful shoulders and arms to extent to down the animal, which resulted in its neck being broken. Douglas when asked on occasion never denied the happening of this story, as he was an animal lover and was upset at the outcome of the incident and avoided questioning. But the happening was well talked about in and around the local Pubs and Hotels of Patterdale at the time. I myself do believe the story, as my grandfather told me that Douglas had broken the neck of a bull, he would have known if the story was true or false, for he was a friend of the man in question.

The Man Himself

The first impression one receives from contact with Clark is his wonderful physique. A huge frame wonderfully muscled up, houses a constitution as sound as a bell, Add to this the suprising speed for a man of his build, and you have the foundation upon which a wonderful reputation has been built. On better acquaintance with him one realises that of even greater value to him have been his enthusiasm for all that is best in sport, his quick thinking, and his genuine desire to convert a political cry into a football slogan, "Each for all and all for each." His team spirit was common to all his comrades in the old days. Enthusiastic and unsparing of himself as he was a deadly tackler and a strong runner, It could be said of Clark that he was never guilty of misusing his great strength. Not once but many times have I seen him jump over a defender rather than risk causing serious injury, sometimes at the expense of loss of ground.

It must not be thought that he was lacking in dash or that he did not realise the value of his strength. Ask Bolewski and Johnston who used to play for Leigh, or the great Billy Batten, or Chas Seeling, his greatest rival as a loose-forward for many years. Scrupulously fair, ultra-conscientious as regards training, full of such a love of the game that he could not help giving his best, no better model could be found for a young aspirant for football honours than Douglas Clark.

On his first team debut at Hull Kingston Rovers on September 25th, 1909 it ended in a 3-14 defeat. Douglas was to play 485 games for Huddersfield, twenty years later he and his team had become ledgendry in the annals of the game. The team led by the the great Harold Wagstaff ("Prince of Centres") were now known as "The Team of All the Talents." Douglas Clark was one of the most talented men in the team also one of the proudest, he was dubbed one of the finest loose-forwards the game has ever seen.

Huddersfields finest season ever was in 1914-15 lifting all four cups, the team was so majestic the matches were practically walkovers. Douglas's test career had the span of eleven years from (1911-1920) and his last game as an International was at Workington on February 7, 1925. He toured Australasia as a Lion in 1914 and 1920, and scored the winning try in his last test appearance against New Zeland beating them 11-10 at Wellington on August 14, 1920.

Already mentioned was the memorable test at Rorkes Drift against Australia on July 4, 1914, Britain won the ashes 14-6 this took place in Sydney. Douglas was a casualty in this game breaking a thumb and dislocating a shoulder, he had to forcibly led off the field in tears wanting to carry on playing despite being injured. The Australian public took to their hearts this wonderful British Lion team for their courage and determination and will to win. But this was not the last time they would see Douglas Clark, He would return to their shores playing a different role, that of a World Champion wrestler, he would introduce some holds in the All-in-Style never been seen before, they would be introduced to Cumberland and Westmorland style wrestling, and begin to wonder what this man was made of.

Douglas played his last game of rugby for his own County of Cumberland against Yorkshire on his home ground Fartown, he was only a few months short of his 39th birthday. He was a great servant to his own County, he was capped 31 times and made captain in 1923, he even came out of retirement to represent his County for three fixtures in 1929 and 1930. In all Douglas played competitive rugby for twenty years a feat within itself.

A favourite place for training even when living as far away as Huddersfield, was the Salt Pans on the coast road between Maryport and Allonby, Douglas trained here as a young man when he played his school rugby and for Brookland Rovers. As mentioned previously his family were great believers in good clean living, plenty of fresh air, outdoor activities, where would one find a better place than the Solway Coast. I remember once watching the great Gus Risman training on the sands at Flimby near Maryport.

After the tide had receded he would wear heavy work boots or clogs, then try to run as fast as he could in the heavy wet sand, this was to build up the calf and thigh muscles in the legs, this gave him extra pace when on the field of play, this was in the 1950s, Gus was captain of Workington Town, a popular and well respected sportsman. Years before this is how Douglas had trained at the Salt Pans, as well as wearing the heavy boots or clogs, he would also have strapped to his shoulders a military type rucksack or knapsack as they were called, this piece of equipment was filled with dry sand which would add another twenty eight pounds to his own bodyweight, a lot of training was done there on the sands. Douglas brought other wrestlers and rugby players to the area to train, he had a small chalet of his own at the Salt Pans, the training sessions became popular to the local people, they came to watch this multi-talented sporting legend train, he was a local lad idolised by many. This gave Douglas the idea to develop a centre in the area, a physical training camp as you might say, which would attract athletes and sporting types from near and far, this was in the 1930s times were very hard, it would offer employment that was badly needed, it would attract business and business people to the area. A few small huts or chalets had been erected where these sportsmen stayed while on training sessions Douglas's being one of them. The proposal was rejected by the Cockermouth Rural District Council, the chalet's and huts had to go, as they did not confirm with local planning and health regulations, even though at the time the area was littered with broken down buses, a couple of burnt out caravans which had stood there for a few years, the area was generally untidy with litter etc. Douglas had the backing of the other chalet owners, also the local Press, newspapers etc, but this did nothing to alter the decision of the Council, the huts were to be removed, with the huts so went the sportsmen and the dream of Douglas Clark, he was by all accounts very disappointed, likewise many local people, who could see what the proposal if it had

materialised would have offered them. But as always seems to be the case, Maryport's loss was now Huddersfields gain.

He was and still is today held in high esteem where the knights of the round table gather to talk rugby and wrestling in Yorkshire, Douglas always remained loyal to his home town and County, even though his proposals were rejected, he always remembered his roots, the town where he was born, he made regular visits to see family and friends, and still made the round trip of nearly 300 miles to train at his favourite location when able, watched by his fans and the young hopefuls of the time.

J.D.W.

Douglas Clark
Cumberland Rugby Career

	Opponents	Venue	Score	
October 25th, 1910	Yorkshire	11-28	Dewsbury	Try
November 24th, 1910	Lancashire	8-13	Workington	
October 9th, 1911	Lancashire	28-7	Warrington	
December 9th, 1911	Yorkshire	16-13	Millom	Try
September 28th, 1912	Lancashire	11-0	Workington	
December 5th, 1912	Yorkshire	5-19	Hull KR	
September 29th, 1913	Lancashire	3-24	Broughton	
October 11th, 1913	Yorkshire	8-3	Workington	Try
November 8th, 1919	Lancashire	5-3	Millom	
November 6th, 1920	Yorkshire	6-27	Maryport	

Huddersfield Rugby Football Team Season 1911-1912.
Left to right. Back row. *H. Bennet Asst. Trainer, H. Sherwood, W. Brook, C. Byme, B. Gronow, D. Clark, Sir Charles Sykes, R. Lockwood.*
Middle Row. *A. Bennet Trainer, W. Trevarthen, T. Grey, E. Wrigley, H. Wagstaff, F. Kitchen.*
Front Row. *A. Rosenfeld, Wildman, J. Bartholomew.*

Huddersfields team of all talents winning three cups in the season.
Douglas Clark pictured third from the right, second row.

	Opponents	Venue	Score	
November 14th, 1921	Yorkshire	12-30	Halifax	
January 7th, 1922	Australians	12-25	Workington	Try
January 21st, 1922	Lancashire	7-18	Maryport	
October 28th, 1922	Yorkshire	4-9	Maryport	
November 15th, 1922	Lancashire	9-46	Swinton	
September 29th, 1923	Lancashire	5-24	Whitehaven	
October 17th, 1923	Yorkshire	12-51	Hunslet	
October 18th, 1924	Yorkshire	20-0	Whitehaven	Try
October 29th, 1924	Lancashire	0-8	Warrington	
September 26th, 1925	Lancashire	5-6	Whitehaven	
October 29th, 1925	Yorkshire	31-13	Huddersfield	
January 8th, 1927	New Zelanders	3-18	Workington	
March 23rd, 1927	Lancashire	5-12	Salford	
September 24th, 1927	Lancashire	27-2	Whitehaven	
October 15th, 1927	Glamorgan	18-12	Pontypridd	
November 30th, 1927	Yorkshire	11-5	Wakefield	
October 20th, 1928	Glamorgan	15-5	Whitehaven	
November 17th, 1928	Lancashire	5-10	Swinton	
December 9th, 1929	Australians	8-5	Workington	
December 21st, 1929	Glamorgan	6-14	Cardiff	
January 22nd, 1930	Yorkshire	3-9	Huddersfield	

Great Britain Career

	Opponents	Score	Venue	
December 16th, 1911	Australia	11-11	Edinburgh	
January 1st, 1912	Australia	8-33	Villa Park, Birm.	Try
June 27th, 1914	Australia	23-5	Sydney	Try
June 29th,1914	Australia	7-12	Sydney	
July 4th, 1914	Australia	14-6	Sydney	
June 26th, 1920	Australia	4-8	Brisbane	
July 3rd, 1920	Australia	8-21	Sydney	
July 10th, 1920	Australia	23-13	Sydney	
July 31st, 1920	New Zealand	31-7	Auckland	
August 7th, 1920	New Zealand	19-3	Christchurch	
August 14th, 1920	New Zealand	11-10	Wellington	Try

11 Tests Played – (Three Tries)

The Wrestling Champion

For many years Douglas Clark was the champion Cumberland and Westmorland wrestler, carrying off the title at the Grasmere Games, where for many years he was an outstanding figure, in 1924 he won the heavy-weight title for the fifth time, and so became the possessor of the Rawnlsey Cup, which was to go to the heavy-weight who was the first for three years in succession, or who had five victories in the class. His old rivals, "Big Bill" Knowles, J. T. Brewer, and Dick Greatorex were competing, and since he and Knowles had each four successes to their credit and Brewer had won in the previous two years everything pointed to a great struggle, which turned out to be the last for the cup. Clark had to meet Knowles in the final, a fitting pairing, and as they came out on to the grass the band played "Silver Threads Among the Gold," a tribute to two of Grasmeres oldest and most famous wrestlers, Clark threw Knowles twice in succession, and so won the cup.

Douglas's attention had already been turned towards all-in style wrestling, where he was just as successful. In the early 1930s he beat Athol Oakey, of London, on points for the British title, and later was to spend much time trying to get Oakey into the ring for another bout.

He won the T. Herbert Kaye belt for the World Championship when he beat the Belgian, Gerstmanns in an open air show at Fartown following a draw at Headingley.

Some of his best known fights were those against Bernadi Esseratti, whom he beat at Wakefield: Henri Irslinger, with whom he drew one fall each: and Ben Sherman, who failed to throw the Huddersfield man three times within the hour as he claimed he would, in fact, he didn't throw him at all!

In 1934 Douglas fought the pride of Devon, the giant Carver Doone, Doone stood 6 feet 8 inches tall and weighed in at 23 stones, Clark was not a tall man he, was 5 feet 9 inches and weighed in at 16 stones, but every inch of that 16 stones was solid muscle, the forecast to the fight was a walkover in favour the giant Doone.

The result was very different to the forecast. It was a brutal fight, it ended with Douglas battering Doone to the floor in only 13 minutes. After the contest Doone had commented on the strength and skill of his opponent.

The Following articles are from newspapers of the time.
That relate to the career of Douglas Clark.

— 1931 – CLARK RETAINS HIS TITLE
A SHORT BOUT
TWO FALLS IN 73 SECONDS

Opponent Injured

All-in "Wrestling came to Huddersfield on Saturday, when at Fartown, Douglas Clark, the famous former International Rugby League forward, and the heavyweight champion of England at this style, met "Johanfesson" described as the middle-weight champion of the world, and light heavyweight champion of the world.

The bout was for the heavyweight championship of England. Clark won, and the spectators were elated at his success, as they showed by their cheering as he left the ring,but their satisfaction on this ground was tinged with some disappointment with the bout itself, which only lasted seventy-three seconds, and ended with "Johanfesson" being carried out of the ring suffering from a broken shoulder. "Johanfesson" appeared in the ring first, and he was quickly followed by Clark, who received a fine ovation from the spectators. The usual preliminaries over, the men advanced to the centre of the ring and quickly got to close quarters. Clark got his opponent in a hold and threw him over his shoulder to the ground, pounced upon him and pinned both his shoulders to secure the first fall in 25 seconds.

"Johanfesson" lay prone on the ground, and it was obvious that he was hurt, he was assisted to his corner where he received attention, and then Mr. J. T. Withers, the Fartown club's trainer, who was in Clarks corner, went across to examine the Chesterfield man's shoulder. It was found that his collar-bone had been knocked up, but "Johanfesson" decided to continue.

When the next round started it was plain that the injury was troubling him, and only 48 seconds sufficed for Clark to secure the second throw, and the match. It was then announced that "Johanfessons" shoulder was broken, and he had to be carried from the ring to the dressing-room.

ALL-IN-WRESTLING – OCTOBER 1931
CLARK'S FUTURE

It was a distinctly good piece of work on the part of Douglas Clark to draw with Irslinger, better, perhaps, than those who lack complete knowledge of the full circumstances realise. Apart from other considerations, the American has had a much wider experience in this form of wrestling than the Huddersfield man – he has won more than 500 contests in America, Australia, South Africa, and other countries – and there are few holds and so forth that he has not encountered in his many contests. Clark taught him a new one, just as Irslinger introduced a fresh lock to Clark.

Clark's future in the sport will depend on the turn of events in the next few weeks. He believes he can beat Irslinger, and is particularly anxious to gain the verdict over that redoubtable exponent.

Another chance has been promised him, and there seems good reason for anticipating that the Cumbrian would have his ambition fulfilled. Irslinger is his immediate object, and after him there few challengers to be going on with, with the Australian tour in the offing.

A SPORTSMAN'S WAY

All-in wrestling is by no means everybody's taste in sport. There is a side to it (or can be) that many do not and can not like, but Clark approaches the game with the cleanest of hands and according to the best Traditions of sportsmanship. It is a pleasure to hear him speak of his attitude towards the sport. He freely admits the possibility of tricks of more than doubdtful character, and with the characteristic sportsman-ship and no athlete had a better name for playing the game fairly than Clark – he declares his determined intention to meet any questionable tactics by fair methods. His view is that shady tricks are not merely undesireable, but are totally unnecessary, and to use his own phrase "there is a back door to such-nonsense."

There is some talk of making another attempt to popularise all-in wrestling in this country, and some of the greatest wrestlers in the World are expected over here. The rules to be adopted for this new campaign are to be those in operation in America, which permit "butting, gouging, limb breaking, and other unpleaseantries." Bad as all this sounds, Clark is not in the least perturbed, and he told me that subject to his manager's consent he will wrestle any one of them for the love of wrestling or for reasonable side-stakes, and they can try their butting, etc., but he will wrestle purely as a catch-as-catch-can man should wrestle. That is a spirit to be admired, and what we all expect from Clark.

I see Atholl Oakley is being described as the heavyweight champion of Great Britain. This is distinctly unfair to Clark, who beat Oakley in the last championship, and is the present champion. It will be interesting to see what happens when next these two meet. Clark has challenged Oakley, and is willing to meet him at any time and at any place.

(1930) CLARK WINS FINE CONTEST
SKILFUL WRESTLING AGAINST THE MASKED MAN

A full house at the Parochial Hall, Fitzwilliam Street, last evening enjoyed what was probably the best Programme of the series up to date, writes "Looker-on." The principal bout, that between Douglas Clark and the "Masked wrestler,"was a splendid affair, and revealed more of the champions resources than any of his previous contests at this hall.

The disguised opponent was a wrestler of great strength and much technical skill, with a marked preference for mat work, at which he was happier than standing on his feet.

He was an opponent worthy of Clark, even though he was definitely his inferior in the art, and we might add, the artifices, of wrestling. Clark gave what amounted to a first-class exhibition of all-in style.

Cleverly varied and in the main neatly executed. One uses the phrase "in the main" advisedly, for the masked man was sufficiently a good wrestler-when he wasn't the fighter to prevent Clark from finishing at times what he had attempted. The Huddersfield man was by no means as relentless as we know he can be, and one often felt that had he pushed home the advantage on a few occasions he would by sheer strength, have forced the other into submission. Invariably he had the measure of his man, and to watch him scheme for position was often as attractive as the actual execution of a throw or hold. This is not to suggest that Clark was never troubled, "the Masked Wrestler" had a disconcerting trick or two, and close to the fourth round he had Clark well held in head scissors, a hold which taxed the Champion's ingenuity to the utmost. Before that, however – after three minutes forty seconds in the second round – Clark had gained the first fall, from body scissors which forced a submission fall. It was in the sixth round of a most entertaining contest that Clark obtained the second and deciding fall. He flung the other man to the mat with the hipe which Clark can apply in such a thrilling manner, but he did not go for the pin. A moment or two later, however, he repeated the throw and gained the fall.

ALL-IN STYLE OF WRESTLING A GROWING SPORT.
AN INTERVIEW WITH DOUGLAS CLARK (1931)

"All-In" wrestling, which is so popular in many parts of the country at the present time, is a sport about which Huddersfield folk, mainly through lack of opportunity, know very little, but if the plans of Mr. George De Relyskow, who is the manager for Douglas Clark, the famous Huddersfield wrestler, fructify, the town should be able to see some of the foremost practitioners of this style of wrestling in the future.

During a recent conversation I had with Clark and his manager, Mr. De Relwyskow said: "I am proposing to match Douglas against the best men we can get, and bring them to Huddersfield, because I want to show the people here how thrilling and skilful this style of wrestling is." In a talk on the sport, Clark told me that any lock, hold, throw, or bar – wether from ju-jitsu, catch-as-catch-can, or Cumberland and Westmorland style – is allowed in all- in wrestling, and that a throw is secured by throwing an opponent to the ground and pinning his shoulders to the floor. Rounds are of ten minutes' duration, and the wrestlers strive to get the better of six of these, victories are gained on points, knock-outs, or the retirement of one of the contestants, who, if he finds himself in a hold from which he cannot escape, may tap on the floor three times with his foot.

GOOD REFEREEING ESSENTIAL

Speaking of fouls, Clark said that sometimes difficulties arose because holds and locks which were allowed in one of the styles wrestling were not permissible in another, but if they were practised in any of the three main styles they were also allowed in "all-in" by virtue of this fact sport lends itself to some sharp practice, and Clark here stressed the importance of good refereeing, and said that with a good official and two men in the ring who loved the sport and wrestled cleanly, a bout could be very exiting and exceptionally interesting. As in football or any other form of sport, for that matter, the opportunity was there for underhand tricks, but they did not pay, neither did playing to the gallery with holds and actions that were by no means so effective as they appeared to the uninitiated. He is full of enthusiasm for this form of wrestling, and is very confident as to its future. He talked of its growing popularity in this country, particularly in centres like London, Manchester, and Newcastle, and added that it was rapidly gaining ground in America, where in many places boxing contests, which formerly had been the principal events at tournaments, were taking second place and were included in the programme as preliminaries to the wrestling bouts. Boxers who had been paid well in the past were now getting acknowledgements for being there. Wrestling was drawing large crowds of spectators, and attendances of between forty and sixty thousand were by no means uncommon.

THE LEADING EXPONENTS

When I asked him how he thought "all-in" compared with Cumberland and Westmorland wrestling, his native style, at which he is the World Champion and the winner of several prominent tournaments, he gave me one reason why he hoped to be more effective in the former. In the Cumberland and Westmorland style a wrestler has to keep his hold, if it is broken he loses. In "all-in" the hold can be broken and renewed time and time again.

Clark gave me the names of the most prominent "all-in" wrestlers of the world today, they are Jim Londos, a Greek, who lays claim to the world's championship; Boganski, the Russian champion; Moderich (Italian), Esseraltz (Italian), Athol Oakey (ex-British champion, who Clark beat recently in London), Irslinger (Austrian, now naturalised American), Bull Dog Gannon (Welsh), and Billy Riley of Wigan, the English middle-weight champion.

"NO MERCY"

Mr. De Relwysko told me that anyone who had seen Ju-Jitsu, catch-as-catch-can, or Cumberland and Westmorland wrestling, and thought he had seen "all-in" was quite wrong. Whilst it enabled him to use rugged strength to the full, it also gave him an opportunity to show gentlemanly actions. "As a matter of fact," he added, when I have introduced wrestlers from the ring I have always used these words, "these men will ask for no mercy, and I do not expect that either of them will offer any mercy. The best man must win."

He has a high opinion of Clark's capabilities, and said to me "I think in Clark we have the best man in Britain and possibly a contender for greater honours."

Mr. De Relwyskow is a former champion wrestler and won the British title four times. He won for England the Worlds Wrestling Championship at the Olympic Games, held at the White City in 1908, and in 1924 was the trainer of the British Olympic Games Team in Paris.

CLARK'S BOUT A WEEK HENCE

(1935) The world championship all-in wrestling contest between Douglas Clark and Constant Le Marin has been fixed for next Friday at Greenfield Greyhound

Stadium, Dudley Hill. It will be in the open air, and will have a really first-class supporting programme, including a re-appearance in the north of the popular Huddersfield wrestler, Harry Brook. Clark tells me (writes "Looker-On") that he has almost completed strenuous training – and when Clark says strenuous, he means it. He keeps in wonderful condition, and is never really out of training. He has been taking on as many as five opponents, non-stop for an hour and a half, and on Thursday, after a hard spell, he finished with a swim in Cupwith reservoir, beyond Nont Sarah's, at 11-30! He is now off to Cumberland for a day or two to brush up on his Cumberland stuff, with the assistance of Bill Knowles and other leading exponents.

THEIR RECORDS

The records of the two contestants are "billed" as follows:- Clark: Winner of Kaye World Championship Belt, winner of Grasmere World Championship (Cumberland and Westmorland style), three times winner of Championship cup at Lane's Club, London; recently defeated Bulldog Bill Garnon (Wales) For British Championship at Belle Vue Manchester; defeated Laurant Gerstman for World Championship at Huddersfield; and defeated Jim Burnett (Vancouver) for belt; and is undefeated.

Clark is unquestionably the leading British wrestler, and is one of the best we have had for many a year. Will he meet his match in Le Marin, who is one of the leading International exponents? Here is Marin's "bill matter": Weight 17 stone, height 6 foot 1 inch, winner of nineteen international tournaments including those at the Paris Folies Bergere (thirty-eight participants), Casino de Paris (forty competitors), Cirque de-Paris (sixty competitors), and Madrid. Won the gold belt at a World championship tournament (seventy participants) at the Casino de Buenos Aires; has defeated Zbysko Gerstman and the famous Hans Schwarz in Graeco-Roman style. A great record.

DOUGLAS CLARK AUSTRALIA BOUND

December 20th, 1935. World Championship Bouts Arranged.

Douglas Clark is to leave on January 18th for his third trip to Australia and New Zealand, this time to fulfil a series of wrestling engagements. Twice previously he has gone out on Rugby League football tours, in 1914 and 1920.

Clark is going out on the invitation of the Inter-State Wrestling Syndicate, and his provisional programme includes two World championship contests, one with Lurich, the Russian champion, at Sydney, and another with the Australian, Billy Meeske, at Brisbane, and about twenty other contests.

Arrangements will be made, so far as possible, for Clarks more important bouts to coincide with the itinerary of the Rugby League touring team, which in course, will give a great fillip to the tournaments.

In which the Huddersfield wrestler will be engaged. In addition to Sydney and Brisbane, Clark will appear at Adelaide, Perth, and Melbourne, and after the Australian tour he will go to New Zealand.

If possible Mrs. Clark will join her husband about the time the touring team reaches Australia.

Both in Australia and New Zealand there is something of a wrestling boom at the present time, and there are several prominent wrestlers from America in those countries, as well as the Indian "Crack" Gulua. Clark should have a most profitable tour, for he became a most popular figure "down under" during his footballing days, and will certainly be remembered by the hosts of Rugby league followers.

HOMEWARD BOUND
Friday, September 18th, 1936

Douglas Clark and Mrs. Clark were due to leave Australia on the Orford yesterday, and expect to arrive in London on October 22nd. Last Saturday, Clark tells me in a letter received this morning (writes "Looker-On"), he was to meet Billy Meeske at Adelaide for the British Championship, but the result of course is not to hand. At the time of writing Clark had the very good record of sixteen victories and three draws from twenty-one matches. To sustain only two defeats on a tour of this sort, and at Clarks age, is a great Tribute to the Huddersfield man's wrestling ability very fine physical condition.

Eight Meetings With Lurich

Lurich is the "big shot" of Australia, and Clark has met him five times, Clark won on five occasions, drew once, and lost twice. One of these contests was billed as being for the Empire Championship, Clark's honourary manager and adviser, "Harry" Miller, who is secretary of the New South Wales Rugby League, would not agree to it being a British Championship Contest, because Lurich, who is a Russian, refused to show naturalisation papers, and also because the referee was Lurich's brother-in-law, In spite of protests at the appointment. It later transpired that Lurich was not naturalised. The contests with Lurich were a great draw, and double prices were paid by full houses. Another apponent was a clever Indian, Harbourd Shinge, at Sydney, the best man on his feet that Clark has met. Clark won one of the contests, and drew the other. Both meetings were described at the time as the best wrestling ever seen in Sydney.

"The Gentleman Wrestler"

I have before me a very long newspaper report of Clarks bout with Hori Tiki, a Maori, who played for the New Zealand Rugby League. By way of introduction the writer stated; it was something out of the ordinary for wrestling fans to see a wrestling match minus caveman tactics, Clark is really one of the finest built wrestlers ever seen in this State. Clark stripped at 16 stone 2 lbs, and the Maori two pounds heavier. Clark can be termed a true gentleman wrestler, but at the same time cannot be taken other as a man who is at the top of the tree in the wrestling world. The ring manners of both were nicely commented upon by the large audience." The wrestlers obtained one fall each.

Old And New Friends

"We have made some wonderful friends" writes Clark. My old Rugby friends have given Mrs. Clark and me the best time of our lives. We were delighted to watch England win the Ashes so convincingly, and to see how Australia took, in true sporting spirit, a defeat which must have awfully disappointing after their first brilliant Test win. I was guest of a former Kirkburton man, Mr. Sykes, engineer and plant installer, who is president of the Returned Soldiers Club, which cost over £36,000. Another old Huddersfield man, Mr. Bower, is now carrying on an undertaking business here in Adelaide. I spent a happy week-end with Pat B. Walsh, one of our old players. He is very well. His wife is a Huddersfield-Cumberland lady, and they have two charming daughters. Pat sends his regards to everyone.

THE END OF AN ERA

Douglas Cark passed away on February 1st, 1951. This was after a short illness of only two weeks, this came as a complete shock to his family, the sporting world in general, and to the legion of fans and followers of Rugby and Wrestling alike. Young men in particular from his home town of Maryport who idolised this great athlete, and all that he stood for. People of his adopted home Huddersfield, where he was also idolised and treated like a son.

There has not much been brought to light in recent years on the subject of this local hero, or what he achieved in his very full life, so I made it my duty while compiling this book to let the reader know who this man was, and all that he stood for. Putting pen to paper, I have only given an insight into his life as a sportsman and a gentleman, hopefully this will enlighten the reader on the life and times of this very special man. While writing this chapter of the book I feel so honoured to have met this man as a small boy all those years ago in Maryport

J.D.W.

HUDDERSFIELD, FEBRUARY 3RD 1951
Local News
DOUGLAS CLARK – A GENEROUS OPPONENT
AND A GENUINE SPORTSMAN

Douglas Clark, whose sudden death was a shock to all of us who attended the game at Fartown, was a great man, great not only in the sense that Nature had endowed him him with uncommon physical strength, but also in spirit and character.

He was easily the strongest man any of us ever knew. The stories of his feats of strength have already passed into legends both here in Huddersfield and in his native Cumberland. It was in Cumberland where his fame as a wrestler keeps his name as alive as that of John Peel, that I heard the most remarkable of any of the stories about him.

It is that once going through a field with a dog, he was surprised by a bull.

Duggy.

Douglas, being cornered, took the animal by the horns, intending to throw the beast by twisting its neck, but the bull hadn't the sense to follow its horns, the result was that Douglas broke the animals neck. I heard the story in a Patterdale Inn. No-one in the company doubted it, nor do I find it difficult to believe.

On the football field he was strong enough to carry two or three men with him, and thousands of Fartown followers will have memories of him going over the line festooned by opponents hanging on to him. He was hard to get low, and there were few in the game who could do anything with him by going high.

I said last week that Huddersfield once had "policemen" in the side. Douglas was one of them. Once a Lancashire side playing at Fartown, began some rough stuff, the climax came when their full-back swept a Huddersfield player off his feet by as flagrant an effort of trip by kick as I have seen. The referee did nothing. The Huddersfield players had a hurried little meeting, and soon afterwards sent the ball straight to the full-back, who was then shepherded into the waiting arms of Douglas Clark. The powerful arms closed about him in a bear's hug, the man shrieked; Douglas opened his arms for the offender to drop at his feet. All that Douglas had done was to give him a squeeze. The man carried off, insisted that his ribs were crushed. They weren't, for Douglas knew his strength. After that the game was much quieter.

I recall, too an incident of a very different kind. The game was at Dewesbury. Clark whipped down the blind side. The only man in his way was the wing, a boy of eighteen, playing in his first game you could see the boy quail, but he dived low and brought Douglas down with a neatly-timed tackle. Douglas regained his feet first, and the boy remained on the ground as though struck with fear of retribution for having brought down the great Douglas Clark.

With a smile on his face, Douglas patted the boy on the back and said something complementry, so that for the rest of the game the lad played with an extra inch of chest expansion That was characteristic of Douglas, for he was a generous opponent, and a genuine sportsman. It cost him nothing to give an encouraging word to a lad on the other side – indeed. Being so interested in the game for its own sake, it was natural for him to do so. He never took undue advantage of his great strength, and only as a "policeman" would he use it to punish an opponent he was too clean a man, in thought and action.

To descend to unworthy tactics.

It is easy, remembering his great physical prowess, to think of him merely as a man of brawn, but that would be unfair. He was an intelligent man. When not on the field of play he had other interests, apart from keeping fit, he was a family man, he was a non smoker and a teetotaller – with a complete sense of self-dedication to the game. He took an interest in watercolour painting, he even played chess, and took up the game of golf. His daily life was dominated by an incorruptible sense of decency, "He nothing common did or mean."

DOUGLAS CLARK INTERRED AT HIS NATIVE MARYPORT
FEBRUARY 6th 1951

Between heavy showers of snow and sleet Douglas Clark, sporting hero of several generations of Cumberland youth, was interred at his native Maryport this morning after a service in St. Mary's Parish Church.

A bus strike which affected all West Cumberland, prevented many attending, but there were large gatherings inside and outside the church and at the cemetery. Every section of Rugby Leauge Football were represented – the Commissioners, the Cumberland League, the schools; the three Maryport clubs Clark's own Brookland Rovers, Maryport and Glasson rangers, and Workington Town, together with Maryport golf club, of which he was a member.

The Huddersfield club representation was led by Mr. J. Wood Beever (Football Committee Chairman) and Mr. A. Archbell (Secretary). Wrestlers and Rugby League footballers acted as bearers. The six were; William Hodgson (captain of Brookland Rovers Under 17 team, in which Clark first played and won his first football medal). Faragher Southward (ex-Salford and Cumberland). Jonty Irvine (ex-Halifax). Joe Watters (an old Playing colleague). Jack Fisher (secretary of the Cumberland Westmorland Wrestling Association).

ORGANIST FRIEND

The Rev. D. G. Blake, Vicar of Maryport, took the service, and the organist was Mr. A. Hirst, a Yorkshireman, trained at the Huddersfield College of Music. For forty years he had been a friend of Douglas Clark, and for the hymn "Oh Rest in the Lord" he specially selected the West Riding tune "Wyke" by Leslie Howard.

Rugby League footballers present ranged in age from Jack Kimney, Wigan's star winger of fifty years ago, and Billy Dixon, Oldham. And contemporary of Clark with Cumberland, to Lowther Hayston, Clark's nephew, recently with Workington Town. Mr. W. H. Hall, close friend and former referee, made a long journey from Lancashire to be present.

Douglas Clark has four brothers and four sisters, and there was a big family representation, including R. B. Fearns, brother-in-law, ex-Cumberland County full-back, and John Clark, nephew, ex-Cumberland County amateur centre.

J.D.W.

Footnote: To the readers who are familiar with the name of Douglas Clark, and to those who now know a little more about him, don't you, like I myself, think it's time a memorial of some description was erected in his memory? Be it in the form of an inscribed monument, or sports centre named after him. We are all familiar with the song – dy'a ken John Peel, well how's about dy'a ken Douglas Clark! This was a real man. I say this with no disrespect at all to Mr. Peel, he most probably would have agreed with me.

Merseyside

Queen of the North, where merchants trade;
And sailing craft of every grade
Come in from shores of distant lands,
From frozen seas to burning strands.
Thy docks swing back their ponderous gates,
And ships unload the precious freights
Amid the clang of trucks and wheels.
Cotton and wool for busy mills;
Grain, fruit and oils, and goodly wines,
Produce and ores from foreign mines.
The world's leviathans at rest,
Swing to the tides upon thy brest,
Till soon, outbound, their human freight
Will wave farewells, and crowd the deck.
The siren booms, the hawser clears,
'Mid fluttering handkerchiefs and tears.
By day, is heard the rumbling jar
Of city traffic, hooting car;
The sound of hammers, windward borne;
And ferry craft flit to and fro,
Like time and tide's unceasing flow.
While screaming gulls, in hungry mood,
Dip, circling round in search of food.
By night, the lights along thy banks,
Decked out like giant fairy lamps,
And masthead, port and starboard lights,
That shine for helmsmen in the night;
While through the fairway to the Bar,
Each signal twinkles like a star.
Queen of the North, there's non like thee
For haven, coming home from sea.

C. Wilson Fearon

Maryport lads "Three of a kind".
Left to right. *Tom Dawson – Crown Inn Yard, Charlie Smith – 1 North Quay.*
R. Docheray – 47 Crosby Street. 1939.

Plaque – 28 High Street, Maryport   *Joseph Lord Lister*

A Winters Day, Netherhall Road, Maryport 1904.

The "Mossrose" of Maryport. A lonely vessel in a silent dock 1935.
Eighty percent of the town were unemployed at this time. An era which has left its mark to this day.

Whitehaven

Port with a History

WHITEHAVEN, seaport and market town, is seated on the Irish Sea near a small creek which forms the harbour, bounded and overlooked on the other sides by green hills, which rise abruptly from the outskirts of the town. In the sixteenth century it was so inconsiderable a place as to be unnoticed by Camden, but owes its rise as a seaport to the exertions of the family of the Earl of Lonsdale, who have been Lords of the Manor for about two centuries.

In ancient records it is called Quitofthaven, Whitofthaven and Whyttofhaven, and is supposed by some to derive its name from the whiteness of the rocks near the harbour when compared with the dark red sandstone about St. Bee's Head. Others take the name from the circumstance of the first fisherman who frequented the bay being of the name of White, and that he built a small cottage here in the old town, over the door which was carved the date 1592. The latter derivation cannot be correct as in the registry of the Priory of St. Bee's the place is named at a much older period as Witofhaven and Quitofhaven, sufficient to prove the fallacy of the latter etymology.

Town's Early Days

During the reign of Queen Elizabeth (A.D. 1556), as appears from a Survey of the Shipping and Trade of the County of Cumberland, taken by virtue of a commission under the Great Seal, Whitehaven was a small fishing village containing six houses. The only vessel belonging to the place was a pickard, of eight or nine tons, employed in fishing, and in 1852 the Earl of Lincoln, Lord High Admiral, having commanded a general muster of ships and mariners within the County, there were only twelve small ships under 80 tons and 198 mariners and fishermen in the County. In the return of ships at the time of the attempted Spanish invasion the *Bee*, of Whitehaven, 10 tons, appears as the largest belonging to the County.

Land, which had formerly belonged to the Priory of St. Bee's, was bought by Sir Christopher Lowther (second son of Sir John Lowther, of Lowther), who settled at Whitehaven during the life of his father. His mansion was at the west end of the town, at the foot of the rock. Sir John, dying in 1644, was succeeded by his son, Sir John Lowther, who built a new mansion house (on the site of the Castle), described by Mr. T. Denton, in 1688, as a stately new pile of buildings called the Flatt.

Beginning of the Harbour

At this period, as appears from an old print, "The South-east Prospect of Whitehaven in the year 1642," Whitehaven consisted of about forty houses; the little old chapel mentioned by Nicholson and Burn, was an humble edifice with a bell, turret and a cross at the east end. A few pack-horses, probably just arrived from Kendal over Hardknot and Wrynose, are seen approaching the town along a road strewed with large stones and partly overgrown with grass.

About the year 1666, Sir John Lowther, of Whitehaven, obtained from Charles II a grant of all the "derelict land at this place," which yet remained in the Crown; and in 1678 all the lands between high and low water marks, for two miles northward, on payment of a yearly rent to the Crown. The latter contained about 150 acres, being in breadth 200 yards.

Sir John, thus having laid the foundation of the future importance of Whitehaven, commenced his great work and lived to see a small obscure village, which in 1633 had consisted only of nine thatched cottages, grow up into a thriving and populous town, which in 1693 contained 2,222 inhabitants. A pier was erected by Sir John Lowther before 1687; Mr. T. Denton describes the harbour as rendered so commodious by it has to be capable of containing a fleet of 100 sail.

Paul Jones' Raid

From this period Whitehaven rose to commercial importance in a steady yet rapid manner, in 1685 there were 46 vessels belonging to the port, exclusive of boats, of from 12 to 94 tons, equal to 1,871 tons. The largest of these, the *Resolution*, of 94 tons was commanded by Richard Kelsick, in which he crossed the Western Ocean more than once to the province of Virginia, there he took a cargo of tobbaco and discharged the same at Whitehaven.

One of the most important historical facts connected with the annals of Whitehaven is the daring attempt of Paul Jones, the noted pirate, to fire the shipping lying in the harbour. On Thursday, the 23rd April, 1778, he landed with about thirty armed men from the American privateer *Ranger*, mounting eighteen six-pounders and six swivel guns, which had been equipped at Nantes expressly for this attempt.

Jones was a native of Galloway, he had served his apprenticeship as a seaman on board a vessel belonging to Whitehaven, and his acquaintance with the port enabled him to undertake its destruction. He and his men set fire to three ships, expecting the flames would spread through the one hundred then in the harbour; but, in consequence in the defection of one of the men (David Freeman) who alarmed the inhabitants, this was prevented by their timely defence. Before any force could be collected Jones and his crew re-embarked in two boats and all of the guns in the nearest battery were found spiked. Three of them were, however, soon cleared and several shots were fired, a few of them were observed to fall between the two boats but not to take effect. The boats were afterwards seen to reach the ship, which about nine o'clock stood audaciously towards the harbour, with the flowing tide, and with the appearance of preparing to bombard it, but on a discharge from one of the fort guns she sheered off, and as it afterwards proved the crew landed on the opposite shore of Galloway, where they plundered the house of the Earl of Selkirk.

After this daring attempt great exertions were made to put the harbour into a proper state of defence, a subscription for this purpose amounting, in the space of four days, to £857 5s. 3d. Grim visaged war having smoothed his wrinkled front the batteries had so long been neglected that they required the chief part of that sum to render them efficient for defence; and an additional grant was received from Woolwich.

Measures for Defence

At the latter end of the last century the batteries were thus described; The whole number of cannon is now 98, amongst which are 12 42-pounders and 18 of 36 at one of the forts of the military guard is kept, and it is always the depot of the regiment. It is situated at the entrance to the new quay and commands the whole of the harbour and approach to it from the northward.

At about 200 yards distant, nearer St. Bee's Head, is the Half Moon Battery, so situated as to command the whole bay. On the opposite side of the harbour is the open battery on a place called Jack-A-Dandy, in which are mounted four of the heaviest pieces and some smaller guns, the Fort is on the height directly above the Half Moon Battery, commanding not only the whole bay but the coast towards Harrington and Workington.

Acts of Parliament for improving the town and harbour of Whitehaven were passed in 1708 and 1711, other acts for making the former more effectual, and for repairing roads leading to the town, passed in 1740, 1816 and 1818.

Growth of the Harbour

The harbour may be described rather as spacious than easy of access; it has seven stone piers, some of which are on a magnificent scale, and on these piers are three lighthouses; the two principal ones have been recently built and are highly advantageous to the port. A tonnage duty had been established by two Acts of Parliament passed in the 7th and 11th years of Queen Anne for the purpose of improving the harbour, to which many additional works have been added during the last fifty years. The New Quay was lengthened in 1767; the north wall was begun in 1770 and finished in 1784. The new work, formerly called the Bulwark, has been entirely rebuilt on a larger plan; the Old Quay was lengthened in 1792, and various other improvements were affected about the year 1809, so that several hundred large vessels may now lie with safety in the harbour. The new West Pier was commenced in 1824 and finished in 1839; it is a noble construction of great strength, and was under superintendence of Sir John Rennie at a cost of upwards of £100,000. The magnificent round head on which the lighthouse is built cost £30,000. The new North Pier is also a noble structure, but is not yet completed.

In the year 1772 there were 197 vessels belonging to the port; in 1790, 216 vessels; in 1810, 188 vessels, tonnage 29,312; in 1882, 181 vessels, tonnage 26,220; in 1828, 197 vessels, tonnage 30,960; in 1840, 217 vessels, tonnage 36,800.

A lifeboat was stationed at Whitehaven in 1803, and the Custom House was erected in 1811. A very considerable part of the shipping was then engaged in the coal trade with Ireland. Several large vessels, however were employed in the importation of West India, American and Baltic produce. Large quantities of lime were shipped to Scotland; and iron ore, from the Parishes of Arlecdon and Cleator, for the furnaces in Wales. Shipbuilding was also carried on here to a considerable extent and on a system that acquired for the artificers a high reputation. Ships of 500 tons were then frequently built, and some of considerably greater burthen. The principal shipbuilders were Daniel Brocklebank (afterwards Thos. and J. Brocklebank), W. Bower (63 ships), J. Scott (38 ships), W. Wilson (50 ships), R. Hardy (15 ships), W. Palmer (2 ships), A. Green (1 ship), W. Younghusband (2 ships), L. Kennedy & Co. (66 ships), T.

The Brig Swallow *(114 tons).*
Built by Messrs. Thos. & Jno. Brocklebank, in 1806.

Cowen (18 ships), R. Eilbeck (2 ships), W. Coulthard (3 ships), H. Stockdale (23 ships), Jas. Shepherd (34 ships), H. Williamson (14 ships), W. Huddart (3 ships), Shepherd & Leech (8 ships).

Among the many claims of this old port as a pioneer may be mentioned that of municipal gas lighting. In the year of 1754 a Mr. Spedding, an agent of Sir James Lowther, after experimenting with gases at the coalface at Howgill Colliery, offered to supply the trustees of the harbour with whatever gas they wanted to light the town if they would be at the expense of conducting it through the streets. The gas was accordingly conducted by pipes from the pits to the open air where the flame was constantly seen burning. It can also be claimed to have been one of the first towns to be illuminated absolutely by electricity; as far back as 1888 or 1889 there was not a public gas lamp left in the town.

In 1870 a company was formed and styled the Whitehaven Shipbuilding Company, who built and launched their first ship, the *Patterdale*, in 1871, and incidentally the last wooden ship of any note was launched on the same day, the *Beckermet*. A wet dock at this time was also talked about, and the same was started in 1875, which practically put an end to wooden shipbuilding, as the dock was built on the site of the last of the early shipyards.

The Iron Shipbuilding Yard was situated on what is now the flour mills of Messrs. John Pattinson & Sons, and was responsible for the erection of many of the finest sailing ships of their day, both in model, workmanship and sailing qualities. They also built some very fine steamers, and their activities were carried on until 1889, at which time the decay of the sailing ship had set in and the yard could no longer be carried on as a paying proposition, so that another great industry had to be forfeited.

Not only was the building of ships forfeited but kindred trades, such as ship carpentry, boat builders, blacksmiths, ships painters, riggers, block makers, sparmakers, roperies, ship chandlers and sailmakers, all had to be sacrificed owing to the decline in the shipbuilding trade.

Business transferred to Liverpool

Other industries carried on in the town at that time were sailcloth making, cable making, coarse linen, iron goods and pottery ware, which industry gave employment to approximately 150 hands. The decline of the port was not due to the failure of shipbuilding alone but to the progress of competitors, such as Liverpool, whose natural position enabled it to become the clearing house for the whole of the industrial South-West Lancashire. Even the shipowners of Whitehaven themselves found it necessary to remove their businesses to other ports. Among the foremost of these may be mentioned firms such as Wm. Lowden & Co., afterwards Lowden & Edgar, now styled as Lowden, Connell & Co.

There was also Fisher & Sproats, who owned the "Meres," George Nelson & Sons, who were responsible for some very nice ships, including the *Amethyst*,

Irton, Bootle and the Silverhow, as well as a fleet of coasting steamers.

In the year 1860 we find William Kennaugh at West Strand engaged in the business as Sailmaker and Ships' Outfitter, whilst W. S. Kennaugh and Company commenced shipowning in 1883, and carried on for many years from premises situated on Queens Dock, Whitehaven, until their removal to Liverpool.

This firm is well known in the coasting trade, in which business they have principally engaged, entering into it at a time when coasting steamers were superseding the small sailing craft, and to-day is one of the oldest established coasting business in the country.

Still under Whitehaven Registry

Their first vessel was built by Messrs. R. Williamson & Son at Workington in 1883, and named *Scale Force*, and which was also the first steamer built at Workington. Since that time Messrs. Williamson have built most of the fleet, and there has always been a close connection between the two firms.

The present fleet consists of the following steamers, ranging from 700 to 1,400 tons: *Skelwith Force, Eden Force, Stock Force, Rydal Force,* and *Greta Force*. These little steamers with their cream-coloured funnels and engines placed aft, still retaining Whitehaven as their port of registry, are very well known, particularly on Merseyside.

It is interesting also to note that in the years 1892 and 1894 Messrs. Archibald Macmillan & Son built at Dumbarton for the firm, two fine steel barques, *Friars Crag* and *Eagle Crag*, 1,338 and 1,346 tons nett register, respectively.

A.L.H. Sea Breezes

June 1928

From Sail to Steam

Record of Service from 1750

THE commencement of the firm dates back to the year about 1749, when Thomas Connell, master mariner, born in Kirkcudbright, and the son of a burgher of Dumfries, settled in Whitehaven, then a port of rising importance and a great maritime town. He there married a Miss Caldbeck in 1752, and after being in command for many years, became owner of the *Mary* and *Nelly* in 1786.

His son and grandson were masters of various vessels, and Captain Thomas Connell, his great grand-son, built the *Iron Crag* and *Ladstock*, two iron sailing ships at Whitehaven.

The Lowden family, originally came from Glencaple, the port of Dumfries, settled in Whitehaven about the year 1840, and Samuel, the brother of Mrs. Connell, commenced what became probably the principal private school in West Cumberland. His friends joined him in purchasing the brigs *Globe* and *Dryad* from the Brocklebank firm. He then built the brigantine *Eskett*, sailed by his father, and later the *Huasquina*, commanded by his brother.

The first iron sailing ship was built in conjunction with his brother-in-law, Captain Connell, and was named the *Limari*. On the death of Samuel Lowden, who had combined shipowning and the position of school-master with signal success, the management of the vessels was taken over by his brother, Captain William Lowden, who was at the time master of the *Huasquina*. He built at Whitehaven the *Greta, Angerona, Candida, Hala* and *Benicia*, in partnership with Mr. John Edgar.

Captain Lowden joined his nephew, Sir Robert Lowden Connell, K.B.E., J.P., a son of Captain Thomas Connell, in the year 1890, and formed the firm of W. Lowden & Co., afterwards Lowden, Connell & Co. The fleet then consisted entirely of sailing ships, the *Greta, Angerona, Candida, Hala, Mitredale, Eskdale, Iron Crag* and *Ladstock*. The last sailing ship built by the firm was the four masted 4,000 ton, *Mashona*. She was built at Londonderry after the Whitehaven yard was closed.

Transfer to Steamers

In 1898 the firm that built their first steamer, the *Athena*, and owing to their close association with the Chilean nitrate trade, formed the British and Chilean Steamship Co., Ltd.

Among the steamers owned by the company have been the *Baroda, Caprera,*

Delmira, Escalona, Ferrona, Helvetia, Wabana, Empire and *Manx Isles.* The company lost most of its tonnage during the Great War.

The *Manx Isles* is now owned by the United Molasses Co., Ltd., of which Sir Robert Connell is a director. This company, as part of its operations, owns a dozen vessels, most of them over 10,000 tons burden motor-driven and of the most modern construction.

It will be observed that the Connell family has been actively engaged in either sailing or managing ships, or both, since the year 1750, and the partners in the firm are now Sir Robert Connell and his brother Mr. Alfred Connell.

The Peter Iredale, *a fine and well-known Ritson built ship. Together with the* Auchencairn *they were recognised to be two of the firms favourite vessels, the* Peter Iredale *had a gross tonnage of (2,075) (1,994 Net RT). She was 287¹/₂ feet in length with 39 foot beam, her hull was of steel and iron.*

Britain's Oldest Shipping Company

Sailors, Shipbuilders and Shipowners

WHITEHAVEN has the distinction as claiming as one of her sons Captain Daniel Brocklebank, the founder of what is certainly the oldest shipping line in Great Britain, if not the oldest in the world. Born in 1742, Captain Brocklebank went to America, and in 1770 established a shipbuilding yard in New York, where he constructed five vessels. When the War of Independence broke out he decided to return to England, coming over in 1775 in command of the fifth ship, the *Castor*, a brig of 220 tons, armed with 20 guns, and just completed. Four years later the *Castor*, then registered at Whitehaven under the command of Captain Brocklebank, was given "Letters of Marque" by George III; She was fitted with 26 guns and a crew of 45 men.

Having obtained a suitable site for shipbuilding at Whitehaven, in 1778, the *Perseverance*, of 155 tons, was launched, being the first vessel he constructed in this country. Each year finer and larger vessels were completed at the Brocklebank Yard, and as the ships were very strongly built, of the best materials, and excellent workmanship, and of the highest class, their fame soon became world-wide.

Captain Daniel Brocklebank died in 1801, greatly respected by all who knew him, and he was buried at Trinity Church. Whitehaven, having just retired from the firm which had been carried on in the name of Daniel Brocklebank. His sons, Thomas and John, continued the business, altering the title to Thos. and Jno. Brocklebank. As shipbuilders, shipowners and merchants they continued to prosper, and during the early part of the last century were trading with Russia, Newfoundland, Canada, United States of America, the West Indies, and also South America, both East and West Coasts.

On the abolition of the East Indian Company's trade monopoly in 1813, one of the Brocklebanks ships, if not the first, was one of the earliest to enter the Port of Calcutta, and their connection with that port has remained unbroken to this present day.

In 1815 Brocklebanks launched the *Princess Charlotte*, of 515 tons, for the Calcutta trade from the Mersey, in which year Mr. Thomas Brocklebank went to Liverpool, while his brother, Mr, John Brocklebank, remained in control at Whitehaven. A sister ship to the *Princess Charlotte*, namely, the second *Perseverance*, of 513 tons, was put in commission in 1819 – the first-named was armed with 20 guns, and the latter had 18 guns, and they were amongst the largest merchant ships of that day.

During 1829 Brocklebanks extended their operations to the Far East, despatch-

The two piers at Whitehaven, with a typical sailing coaster leaving for sea.

ing the *Superior* (240 tons) from Liverpool to Batavia and Singapore, while in 1853 a service was inaugurated to Bombay. The vessels were very popular with shippers owing to the excellent condition in which they carried and landed their cargoes – the ships also conveyed a lot of produce on Brocklebank's own account, as they were extensive merchants.

Mr. Thomas Brocklebank, who was considered one of the greatest shipbuilders of his day, died in 1845, his brother John having predeceased him by fourteen years. With the completion of the *Mahanada*, of 1,002 tons, and the lease having expired, the shipyard at Whitehaven closed in 1865, but during the years 1788-1865 Brocklebanks had built there no less than 152 wooden ships, including the well-known *Crown, Hindoo, Patriot King, Tigris, Patriot Queen, Princess Royal, Thos. Brocklebank, Rajmahal* (of 1,302 tons, in 1858, which was the largest ship they constructed), *Burdwan, Bowfell,* and many others. They also built the paddle steamer *Countess of Lonsdale,* 150 tons, in 1827, and the *Earl of Lonsdale,* of same tonnage, in 1834, for the Whitehaven Steam Navigation Company.

In 1865, Brocklebanks transferred their business to Liverpool, which is now the home port of a fleet today that to-day consists of 28 large, modern, fast freight steamers of a total of 208,449 tons gross.

The title of the Company is Thomas and John Brocklebank, Ltd., the Chairman being Sir Aubrey Brocklebank, Bart., while his son, Mr. Thomas A. L. Brocklebank, is one of the Directors – the fifth and sixth generations of the family! The has been in existence 157 years – surely something for the town of Whitehaven to be proud of.

A Doctor – Shipowner

Two of his Earlier Vessels

WILLIAM Burnyeat, founder of an old Whitehaven firm, was born in 1819, and died in 1894. He was a descendant of Phillip Burnyeat, who acquired the Beckfoot estate in 1696. On leaving school he went to sea, then studied and passed for a doctor, but then later became greatly interested in shipping, being at one time the largest 64th shareholder in ships in the world. He owned and managed, amongst many others, the well-known brigs *Sarah Burnyeat* and *Emily Burnyeat*. In 1881 he started the firm of Burnyeat & Dalzell, ship store merchants (now Burnyeat, Dalzell and Nicholson, Ltd.), and the firm of Burnyeat, Dalzell & Co., Whitehaven, which commenced business in 1875, as iron ore proprietors, railway wagon proprietors and shipowners, managing the steamers *Armathwaite*, *Solway King*, *Solway Queen*, and the *Solway Prince*.

Mr. Burnyeat's eldest son, bearing the same name, became very well-known in Cumberland, holding many directorships covering banking, Mr. Wm. senr., was also a director of the Whitehaven Shipbuilding Yard, and later turned his attention to coal mining in South Wales.

Two of Mr. Burnyeat's vessels, *Sarah Burnyeat* and *Emily Burnyeat*, had fairly long careers, The *Sarah Burnyeat* was launched in 1861, having been built by Gowan at Berwick. She was a barque of 317 tons register, and for a long time was engaged in the West Indies trades. This vessel is still serving a useful purpose, being a lighter in Sydney, Australia.

The *Emily Burnyeat* was a brigantine of only 127 tons register. When she was first launched from Gowan's yard at Berwick in 1862, she was not schooner-rigged and employed wholly in the coasting trade. She had not a long run on the coast, being altered into a brigantine, carrying a royal, and put into the foreign trade, mostly in the Mediterranean, African and Canary Islands trades. She was eventually put back into the coasting trade, and her spars cut down considerably. Her last owners were Arklow men, who put her into a schooner-rig, and she was engaged in the home trade until the war, and at the finish she was either sunk by gunfire or torpedoed by the Germans about 1915 or 1916.

This vessel had a very thrilling time coming home from abroad to the Mersey. She was running before a heavy south-west gale, when a very heavy sea broke aboard and everyone aboard was disabled excepting the master and a boy of about 14. The disabled crew were got below and remained there until she arrived in the Mersey, some four or five days later.

The captain could do nothing but run before it under the small sail, to which the vessel had luckily been reduced before the accident to the crew happened, but somehow he got into the Mersey, although the weather had been getting worse. There was no chance of heaving-to for pilot or getting one aboard, so he ran her aground in the Sloyne and immediately afterwards collapsed. The Customs officials came aboard and a doctor was procured, who forbade all communication with the master for some days. When he did come to he was asked for his position on a certain day (the day of the accident). On refering to his log book (he had not had a sight that day) it gave his dead reckoning. The reason for the enquires was to find out how far he had been from the ill-fated *London*, which had foundered. The logbook of the *Emily Burnyeat* on the day of the accident showed her position to have been within a few miles of where the *London* had gone down.

1904-5 Maryport Residents on a trip out of town.
John and Ada Birkett & Daughter, Martha. (Pictured far left second row, seated).

The Brig *Kitty*
A Staunch Old Craft

PROBABLY the most interesting vessel belonging to Whitehaven was the *Kitty*. There were two or three other old ships, but *Kitty* was the first favourite. She was built at Whitehaven in 1765 by Mr. William Palmer, on the site of the old Patent Slip, the builder died about the close of the year 1778. She was constructed to the order of Captain B. Fisher, her first master, who died suddenly on board his vessel on the 24th May, 1786, on passage from Dublin to Whitehaven. He was 70 years of age.

The *Kitty* was remarkable, amongst other things, for the very few captains she had since she was launched; and for the further fact that she stayed all her life in the same family.

In 1860 she underwent a thorough overhaul in the same yard in which she was originally built, and made, I understand, 12 feet longer, the addition being made to her aft, which caused her to have a very narrow stern, and proved a most noticeable feature. A remarkably successful money-making ship, she was said never to have met with a single casualty of any importance up to the time she was lost.

Llala, a fine Whitehaven vessel. 1,329 tons, built in 1882 for Captain Wm. Lowden and his partner, Mr John Edgar.

I was always interested in the old brig, as I joined her as an apprentice, to serve five years for the princely wage of £40 for that period. That was in 1865, and she was then 100 years old. She was a splendid sea going ship. Her registered tonnage was 137 tons; but after the addition made to her she carried about 250 tons.

I remember my first voyage. We left this port with a large fleet of vessels which had been lying wind-bound, and the old *Kitty* was the second ship to anchor on Cardiff mud, the first being the brigantine *Exel,* a vessel built some 60 or 70 years after *Kitty.* We had a mixed crew of eight. The master (Captain – M. Shealor) was a Dutchman; the mate, an Irishman; cook, a Manxman; three able-seamen, two Irish and one Dutch; an Irish apprentice belonging to Droheda, and myself (English).

The brig was lost when she was 118 years old. On November 28th, 1883, she loaded a cargo of 244 tons of flint and 11 tons of whiting at Dieppe, France, for Runcorn, and sailed with a crew of six hands. On December 3rd, owing to stress of weather, she was put into Falmouth, leaving the latter place on December 8th, and was supposed to have foundered during the heavy gale of December 12th. This was the end of poor old *Kitty.*

There were three other old vessels running in the coasting trade at the time, namely the brig *Endeavour,* built at Rockliffe near Carlisle, in 1762; the brig *Senhouse,* built at Chester, in 1873; and the brig *William and Mary,* built at Whitehaven, in 1768.

Joseph Wear

High Street, Maryport.

An Old View of Whitehaven

By "Onlooker"

(Reproduced in *Sea Breezes* by courtesy of *Cumberland News*)
February 8th, 1936

A S the port of Whitehaven has been greatly discussed in *Sea Breezes*, I desire to use some space to note some of the things concerning that town that I have gathered. First, let me thank Mr. E. L. Nanson, of Whitehaven, for his informative note in reference to the old print dated 1642 of Whitehaven. Mr. Nanson asks: "Do you think that the print referred to is one of an engraving which was taken from a pen and ink sketch with the title 'The South-East prospect of Whitehaven in the year 1642'? There are quite a number of such prints extant, and it is possible that an examination of the watermark of the paper upon which they are printed may give some clue to the date of the engravings. I may say that I own the original pen-and-ink sketch, having bought it at the sale in 1921 of the contents of Whitehaven Castle. There is one curious point about the drawing, viz., it does not, in fact, show the south-east of Whitehaven, neither is it taken from a south-east point of view".

Mr. Nanson, I imagine, is quite right in his view that the engraving referred to is not nearly as old as 1642. The view doubtless was taken in that year, but it is, as I said a fortnight ago, extremely unlikely that the engraving was as old as the original drawing. The topographical engravings of this county do not date near so far back. Buck's views, which are among the earliest, are dated 1739. After that time there came a perfect spate of engravings of all makes, sizes and qualities, and some of them as unlike the place they pretend to represent as night is unlike day.

In this connection take the series of engravings of the Bewcastle Cross. It is perfectly apparent that some of the artists have never seen the cross at all, and have given a guesswork picture. Mr. Nanson, who is as well qualified to speak on any Whitehaven topic as any man living, has shown how in his drawing and the engravings from it there is a gross perversion of the point of view. To the old topographer, such a thing was a trifle. One thing I am glad of, and that is that the original is in such safe hands as those of Mr. Nanson.

The Whitehaven-built steamer the *Countess of Lonsdale*

Returning now to the story of Whitehaven, I notice in the autumn of 1825 a really important event in the commercial history of the town, the event was the laying of the keel of the first steam vessel ever built in the town. The steam vessel was intended for the Whitehaven and Liverpool trade, and was further intended to be strong opposition to the well-established services then running from Port Carlisle to Liverpool – a service of which the Whitehaven folk were extremely jealous, the *Cumberland Pacquet* more than once accusing the Carlisle papers of undue favouritism in the matter. Then the Editor of the *Carlisle Patriot* was not a man to take a charge of that kind lying down. He gave as good as he got; and quite fairly, I think, showed he held the reins of impartial judgement between the two services.

The notice of the laying of the keel of the *Countess of Lonsdale* is referred to in the following brief paragraph from the *Patriot* of October 21st, 1825: "The keel of the new steam packet intended to ply between Whitehaven and Liverpool was last week laid down in the building yard of Messrs. Thomas & John Brocklebank. It is about 114 feet in length, and the vessel when completed will measure upwards of 130 feet upon deck." Twenty months later, in June, 1827, appears the notice of the launch. "*The Countess of Lonsdale* steam packet was launched at Whitehaven on Tuesday last. She is spoken of as a very fine vessel, and will be handsomely fitted. On Tuesday next the owners intend to treat their friends to an excursion in her to the coast of Scotland, by way of trying her power."

By the time *Countess of Lonsdale* took to the water, the Carlisle and Liverpool Steam Navigation had got a good start. They had two steamers on the Port Carlisle-Liverpool service, and were paying seven and a half per cent. dividend No wonder they did not very heartily welcome *The Countess* into the same trade as they themselves were so very successfully covering.

A so-called pleasure trip in the *Countess of Lonsdale*

I give the account of the first trip – the pleasure trip of the *Countess of Lonsdale* from a private letter written to a Carlisle gentleman. I cannot do better than give the exact words of the writer. The letter was written on June 21st, 1827. Here it is: "I congratulate you and my other kind friends at Carlisle that your engagements prevented you from taking part in the much talked of 'excursion of Pleasure' in our new steamer on Tuesday last. Ma conscience! as Bailie Nicol Jarvie would have said – it proved anything but pleasant, and happy were they who were disappointed of the trip. The *Countess of Lonsdale*, as arranged, left the harbour at 7.00 a.m. with some two hundred folks on board, of various grades, from the purest china to coarsest red earthenware.

"During the night a good deal of rain had fallen, and the morning looked extremely dull, but flying banners and lively music cast a feeling of cheerfulness over the livestock who crowded the decks of the packet, and off she went with three cheers from the numerous spectators on shore, quickly returned by those on board. We stood off for St. Bees Head, on our way to Scotland, and having neared it – not Scotland, but the head – the vessel was put about to exhibit to those few straggling individuals whose breakfasts (if they had any to eat) might not be ready, and who might perchance see us from the piers of Whitehaven, Parton, Harrington and Workington.

"From off the latter place we stood to the Scotch side; and now having got into the seaway and running ten knots the 'pleasures' began. Males as well as females – not in solitary blushing ones and twos, but in tens and twenties (how pleasant! that one might not laugh at another!) alike fell victims to ocean's power; and had you, who have visited so many cascades in various parts of the kingdom, had the felicity of being on board your eyes would have been regaled with innumerable specimens of these works of nature, you would have allowed, superior to anything you had before witnessed.

A Lady as Lord High Admiral

"The births (berths, I believe, is the proper word in the steam vocabulary, perhaps because there is less to sicken in an 'e' than an 'i'). The berths were soon filled with the bodies of the tender and delicate sex (their souls were in their stomachs and, therefore, I have said bodies) and there lay, wondering what ailed them, and their bodies in sad a state of jumblement as their heads. If the ladies were thus afflicted, the men with a few exceptions were not much better. One friend was soon rendered powerless, and submitted without much resistance, if not without murmuring. For a great part of the day he lay at full length upon the cabin floor, unable to move; and only capable, now and then of turning his head. His very hat seemed to be off colour, for its rim was turned the contrary way all round, and his face was precisely the colour of a piece of dirty white paper.

"Miss – was the heroine of the party, she walked the deck 'mid the storm and rain like any Admiral; I question if the Lord High Admiral himself could have done so well, and never for one moment gave way to the womanish qualms which overcame all around her. But, to proceed, we stood towards Scotland until we had reached two-thirds of the way across, when lo! by some orders not comprehensible, the vessel was put about, and bore away until within the sight of Whitehaven, where she was brought to anchor in Saltom Bay, where she lay from about one o'clock until near six, patiently waiting for the water to enter the harbour.

"It was near seven when we came in. The piers were clad with people. Can you pardon the spectators? Every face was dimpled with an arch smile. We landed at the Lime Tongue, and such was the marked civility of the crowd that formed for us a narrow avenue, extending the length of the pier, along which we had to walk one after another, like a colony of half-drowned rats emigrating from one ship to another.

Twelve hours' sail – Whitehaven to Saltom Bay and back

"The good nature of the lieges was amazing. They all viewed us with looks of pleasure, amounting to lively satisfaction, and some of the kindest congratulated us upon our pleasurable twelve hours' sail to Saltom Bay. Our excursion however, proved more than one fact of some importance. The packet sails extremely well, is very comfortable, and so firmly put together that one cannot feel the least shaking when the engines are in full operation. Don't you wish you had been with us to have shared in such pleasure? Mr. Nutter missed some charming views of both animate and inanimate nature. Would that he, at any rate, had been present to have immortalised by his pencil some portion of 'our excursion of pleasure."

I have given the lively writer's account of the first steamboat sailing from Whitehaven for more reasons than one. First, it was an historic occasion, the forerunner of a long line of steam-propelled ships that sailed from that harbour. Secondly, it resembled very much the first of *The Solway* (which I related six weeks ago), belonging to the Carlisle and Liverpool Steam Navigation Company – the same rain, the same discomfort, and general failure of arrangements that would have been pleasant but for the Clerk of the Weather. Thirdly, *The Countess of Lonsdale* was the first steamship to be built in this county; the Carlisle steamer having been built in Deptford.

I know full well how some of the West Country readers of this paper will treasure this sprightly account of the first trip of the *Countess of Lonsdale*. Personally, I hope Mr. Gelding or some readers will send it on to *Sea Breezes* for permanent preservation in its pages.

The remains of the Peter Iredale *on Clastsop Beach, the mouth of the Columbia River, USA. Photo 1926.*

Replica of Paul Jones Bust for Whitehaven Museum

WEST CUMB TIMES JUNE 10th 1939

T HE Whitehaven Museum has been fortunate in acquiring a plaster replica of Antoine Houdon's bust of John Paul Jones (1747-1792) whose famous attempt to fire the shipping in Whitehaven harbour on April 23rd, 1778, was one of the outstanding events in his career. The original was executed in 1785 at the request of the Lodge of the Nine Sisters, of which Jones was a member, and reproduces "the, keen, shrewd, strong features, the forceful concentration, the virility of purpose, and doggedness, without which he could never have succeeded." Jones had eight replicas made and sent to friends in America.

In his "History of the Rise and Progress of the Arts of Design in the United States," William Dunlap writes: "M. Houdon was born in Versailles in 1741. The celebrated sculptors of France Immediately preceding him were Coisevoix, Vancleve, Lepautre, Legros, the two Coustons, and Bouchardon. The works of these masters, placed under the eyes of the young man, had their influence in forming his taste, without even his being conscious of the aid he received from them. These masters were in fact were the only instructors of Houdon, until he had, by his untutored efforts gained admission into the academy; and he continued his studies without placing himself under the formal direction of any professor. By his diligence he progressively advanced to skill, until he gained the great prize for sculpture in 1760, at the age of nineteen." After spending ten years in Rome he returned to France where his style placed him far above his rivals. His fame reached America, and he was invited to the United States to execute a likeness of Washington in marble.

Bust of John Paul Jones (1747-1792). By Antoine Houdon.

Among the many other portraits from his chisel may be mentioned those of Voltaire, Franklin, Gluck, Rousseau, D'Alembert, Buffob, Gerbier, Sacchini, Barthelemi, and Mirabeau.

During the Revolution he was accused of devoting his talents to the cause of oppression, but the skill of his lawyer who defended him saved his life and Houdon terminated a long and honourable career on the 16th July 1828.

The plaster cast in the Whitehaven Museum has been made from one of the replicas sent to America by Jones, and now preserved in the Pennsylvania Academy of the Fine Arts.

Artist unknown

The Museum has on loan a portrait of Paul Jones which is described as "an authentic portrait painted as a youth visiting Whitehaven. – Artist unknown." It may be the work of Strickland Lowry (1737-1780?) a native of Whitehaven who had quite a considerable local reputation as an artist and whose son, Wilson Lowry (1762-1824) achieved more than ordinary fame as a lithographer in London, but one cannot be dogmatic on this point as the history of art in Whitehaven in the eighteenth century still remains to be written.

The story of Paul Jones has frequently appeared in print. The son of a Scottish peasant, he was born in the village of Arbigland, Kirkcudbright. He made his first voyage in 1759 as a boy of 11, and at the age of 22 had accumulated a thousand guineas.

In April 1773, he left the sea, and settled down as a planter in Virginia, where his brother, John Paul Jones had left him an estate. Trouble broke out between Britain and her American colonies, and Jones was among those consulted on the question of getting together an American fleet. He sailed for France in command of a small vessel called the *Ranger*, and fought his first battle under the Stars and Stripes in her when he beat Drake off Carrickfergus, Ireland, in April, 1779.

He determined to carry out a raid on the English coast, and decided on Whitehaven. At the head of a number of sailors he landed at night spiked the guns, and set fire to a ship in the harbour. Jones got clean away, while people of the North fumed at the "insult" and referred to him as a pirate.

Before leaving the Solway Firth he descended on the castle of the Earl of Selkirk with the object of capturing him. The Earl was not at home and all that was taken were some pieces of silverware by members of the crew. Jones afterwards purchased this himself and returned it to the Earl.

When the war with Britain ended Jones went back to France as prizemoney agent and became plenipotentiary agent to the Court of Denmark.

Next he accepted a commission as a rear-admiral in the Russian navy commanding a squadron of ships in the Black Sea and taking action against the Turkish fleet.

Jones finally settled down in Paris in 1790, and died there on the 18th July, two years later.

Footnote: Prior to his attack on Whitehaven, Jones, on another raid took prisoners of a Scottish schooner in the Mull of Galloway, also sinking a vessel from Dublin. It was shortly after these raids of so-called 'piracy' that he decided to raid Whitehaven.

It was due to these raids, his excellent seamanship, courage and bravery, that John Paul Jones became an American hero. But after settling in France after such a distinguished career he faded into obscurity and into poverty. He died in Paris in 1792, and was buried in the protestant cemetery just outside the city.

However it was in 1905 that his body was exhumed and fully identified as that of John Paul Jones.

His remains were then transported with full honours to the United States, where they now rest in the crypt of the chapel of the United States Navel Academy in Annapolis, Maryland, this took place with honour and ceremony on the 24th of April 1906. A full address was given at the ceremony, by the then President of the United States, Theodore Roosevelt. It was then that John Paul Jones became recognised as the founder of the American Navy.

J.D.W.

"We sailed wherever a ship could sail,
We founded many a mighty State,
Prey God our greatness may not fail,
Through craven fears of being great."

Kipling

The Cottage of John Paul Jones.
Situated in the grounds of the Arbigland Estate, near Kirkbean, 13 miles south-west of Dumfries.

The *Cutty Sark*

I saw her last in Falmouth Sound,
The clipper of the seas,
Anchored and held to her cable's length,
A greyhound in the breeze
Eager to slip the iron leash,
And longing to be free,
White wings aspread, and running wild,
Out on the rolling sea.

But silence reigned upon her deck,
Where oft tramped busy feet;
There stood no helmsman at the wheel,
With eyes and ears Alert;
No flag nor pennon flew aloft,
No galley-fire aglow;
Her spars all bare; and running gear
Swung idly to and fro.

Yet not long since, the ocean's pride,
In all her beauty shone,
Stately, with all her canvas set,
She glided like a swan;
Or beam alee, and shortened sail,
She raced ships of renown,
The roaring forties far behind,
To run her Easting down.

Her horny-handed, tarry sons,
Shall lay aloft no more;
Nor to the chanty, haul the brace
Cheerily as of yore.
One by one, her skipper and crew,
Shall follow the beckoning hand;
Aye, Aye! sings out, as the call is heard,
And they pass their watch beyond.

The grand old ships must now give place –
Forgotten, and laid aside –
For the throbbing-engined, smoke-stack craft
That bide not wind or tide,
But rush on like the speed-mad world,
In the seas from pole to pole,
Till in turn they shall have their day,
And change as the years they roll.

Chas. W. Fearon

*Aboard the vessel the **Alfred**, 7th December 1775. As 1st Leiutenant, John Paul Jones "hoisted the flag of America, it being the first time it was ever displayed." Jones then took part in organised warfare against his own country.*

Maryport and Pier 1907.

Chanties and Folk-Songs

A Landman's Views

HAVING always been keenly interested in folk songs and folk music, I look upon chanties as another branch of this very entertaining section of the world of music. Many old sailor songs and chanties have appeared in back numbers of *The Journal* of the Folk Song Society, amongst them "Sailing around Cape Horn." I had the pleasure of hearing an old seafaring friend sing this at a social gathering at Maryport some years ago and was struck by the similarity in style of the singing to that of the real (and alas fast-disappearing) old-world folk songs. Like most folk songs the chanties have a simplicity and tunefulness of melody that make them pleasing even without the artificial aid of harmony, sung unaccompanied they still appeal and, in addition, from the nature of the work helped have a rhythm that is most decided and attractive. Still, this does not mean that the chanties, as musical items, are better unaccompanied, as they were sung in the vast majority of cases on board ship.

Although I cannot claim to be other than an absolute landlubber, like many other inhabitants of this island I appreciate the value of sea and the extent of our dependence on it for our position amongst the nations of the world. Moreover, I appreciate, from factual contact from seafaring friends, the sterling qualities of those who "go down to the sea in ships." Having been fortunately located for some years at Maryport on the shores of the Solway, with opportunities of contact with seafaring folk, it was only natural that a mind already bent towards folk music should turn somewhat greedily to sea chanties. The ultimate outcome was a musical evening entitled "Sea Songs and Sea Pictures," which took place recently under the auspices of a local Baptist organisation, being the first occasion on which chanties were sung in public at Maryport. In my remarks on sea songs I differentiated between the landsman's, or parlour, type of sea song and the true sailor songs, forebitters and chanties.

Various examples of these were given. The soloists were Mrs. H. O. Marsden and Mr. J. J. Brown, two leading lights in the Local Amateur Operatic Society, whilst the choir led the audience in the singing of the chanties. There were many old seafaring men present, and from the effect they must have been enjoying the time of there lives. Interspersed between the items appropriate lantern views were shown depicting life at sea in the days of mast and sail, also views of local interest relating to the recent visit of the herring fleet. In giving the lecture, I acknowledged my indebtedness to Captain W. B. Whall's authoritative work on chanties, and to the many articles in back numbers of *Sea Breezes*, which describe the chanties and included also the music of many of them.

It might be interesting to give the writer's idea as to the order of popularity of these chanties. *John Brown's Body* has always been a favourite, with *Rio Grande* a good second; *Shenandoah* is well appreciated, though perhaps more suitable as a solo. Other favourites are *Sally Brown, Billy Boy, Blow, my Bully Boys, Blow,* and *Johnny, comes down to Hilo.* As an example of the forebitter type, the writer recommends *The Chinese Bumboat Man* and *The Merchant's Ship* in Mrs. Clifford Beckett's book on chanties and forebitters.

The writer hopes these observations may be of service to others who may wish to carry out a similar type of evening.

J. E. Christopher

The Barque Ladas *pictured here when she was under the ownership of Rasmus F. Olsen. She was commanded by several of Maryport's notable captains. One being the Master of Cape Horn, Captain William Andrew Nelson. She was wrecked on Christmas Eve, off Denmark in 1923.*

St. Mary's Parish Church

A Brief History

(Extracted from the late Mr. J. B. Bailey's
"History of the Churches in the Rural Deanery of Maryport.")

For the Bi-Centenary Souvenir Programme, 1763-1963

THE Church Register records that Maryport was built in 1760 by Humphrey Senhouse, Esquire as a Chapel of Ease to the Parish Church of Crosscanonby and was consecrated by Charles Lyttleton, Lord Bishop of Carlisle on August 4th, 1763.

It had one bell inscribed "Prosperity to Maryport, Wm. Evans Fecit, 1761" but was without a chancel until 1763 when this and a transept were added at a cost of £265.

In 1837 the Church was lengthened by about 38 feet. The total cost of this work was £920 and a mural tablet in the Church states that approximately half of the sum was met by "a munificent donation from the personal representatives of the late William Jenkins, Esq., of Shepton Mallet, a pious and liberal Presbyterian, who, whilst he differed from the forms, preserved the doctrine and the spirit of the Established Church and earnestly desired her welfare."

The present tower was built in 1847 and further alterations to the building were made in 1870 and in 1880, in which year the organ was moved from the west gallery to its present position. The many alterations and additions eventually resulted in the old Church becoming ill

St. Mary's Parish Church, Maryport.

adapted for the requirements of a modern place of worship. It had galleries on three sides and the – pews of all kinds and sizes – were privately owned and were even bought and sold at public auctions.

The pew owners were by various expedients induced to surrender their private rights and interests and the work of re-building the Church was then commenced. It was completed in 1892 and was dedicated by the Lord Bishop of Carlisle on 6th April of that year. The total cost of the building was about £5,000 exclusive of personal gifts of stained glass windows, bells and various furnishings to the value of £2,380.

With such a beautiful Church there now came a laudable wish to have it declared a Parish Church. As a preliminary step it was declared a Consolidated Chapelry in 1893. Its boundaries were the centre of the Maryport and Carlisle Railway beginning opposite Ellengrove and ending at the Solway Ironworks. All between this line and the sea was to be in charge of the Minister at Maryport, but it had to wait a further 25 years – until the death in 1918 of the Rev. W. I. Marsh, Vicar of Crosscanonby – before it became "a Parish or a Parochial Chapelry."

A Memorial Chapel in memory of those who fell in the First World War was dedicated by the bishop of Carlisle on February the 8th, 1921 and additions to commemorate those who fell in the Second World War were completed in 1949. The Vestry was extended in 1957 at a cost of £1,500.

In recent years there have been many beautiful additions to the furniture of the Church, including new Sanctuary and Chancel carpets, new standard candlesticks, and new almsdishes.

In 1960 the tombstones in the Churchyard were removed and positioned against the boundary walls and the ground was levelled and converted into a spacious lawn. The Urban District Council accepted their responsibility for its care and maintenance and they are to be congratulated on the excellent job they are doing.

Altogether, St. Mary's is now a beautiful Church in a beautiful setting.

The Vicar's Bi-centenary letter

My Dear Parishioners,

As you come into St. Mary's Church and stand by the Chuchwardens' pews you will notice above your head a stone, in the centre of the archway, with the date 1760 carved on it. Having seen that you may think we are three years late in keeping our Bi-Centenary. It is true that St. Mary's Church was built as a Chapel of Ease to the parish of Crosscanonby in 1760, but the building was not *consecrated until* 1763. This date was most important to us as Church people for it marks the day when our Church building was set apart for the service of God in this community of Maryport.

For 200 years this Church has served as a witness to God. it has stood steadfast amid all the changing fortunes of our land, amid all the changing fortunes of Maryport. In the year of its consecration England was at the height of its power and had just won great possessions in Canada through the defeat of the French. Her trading ships moved untroubled through the oceans, protected by her great navies. This was the time when Maryport first became a port, thanks to the initiative of its local Squire, Humphrey-Senhouse. The Church was still standing as a witness when the country was threatened by invasion, first by the French in 1805 and then by the Germans as recently as this last war. It has seen material prosperity in Maryport, and it has lived through the dreadful days of depression. All this time our Church has preached the same gospel of Jesus Christ, administered the same Sacraments of Baptism and Holy Communion: baptised, married and buried members of our community. People have come to this Church in times of sorrow, and in times of joy. Here many have received answers to prayer and grace to continue whatever the difficulties may be.

A Bi-Centenary is not merely a thanksgiving for 200 years, it is also a looking forward to the future. We of today have inherited a beautiful Church, a hallowed place made sacred by prayer, sacrament and worship. We have inherited the tradition of faithfulness from many generations. It is our duty to hand on this glorious tradition unimpaired to all those who are yet for to come.

I would like to end this letter with a quotation from the scriptures, which sums up so well our duty in our inheritance – "What doth the Lord require of thee, but to do justly, and to love mercy, and to walk humbly with thy God?" (Micah 6v.8).

Yours very sincerely,
R. Eckersley

Interior of St. Mary's Church.

Vicars of St. Mary's

1761	John Gilbanks		1902	F. A. Taylor
1794	Anthony Dixon		1907	J. A. Richards
1845	R. N. Featherstone		1923	G. H. Hawkins
1850	William Bewsher		1927	G. B. Code
1867	Alfred Oates		1933	E. G. Hymas
1880	W. P. Schaffter		1942	D. G. Blake
1886	Edward Sampson		1958	C. A. R. Eckersley

The Rev D. G. Blake was the Vicar of St. Marys Church when I attended there as a young boy, I got to know him quite well over the following years, being a member of the Church choir, also a member of the Church Scout troop of which he ran. He was a man who had his own beliefs, and stood by them. He was

highly criticised when he introduced his high Church background and beliefs to the Church by many of the local people, but despite initial misgivings Father Derek was finally accepted into the parish because of his dedication, qualities, and commitment to the parishioners. If I or any member of the family were sick or unwell, he never failed to call upon the household and pay his respects. Father Derek served his time as an architect after leaving school before being called into the priesthood, and it was he who designed the extension to the Vestry in 1957 which was built by William Eve of Netherton.

Rev. D. G. Blake as a young man.

After leaving Maryport he moved to St. Aiden's in Carlisle. From there at the age of 59 he moved to Holme St. Cuthbert near Silloth, and up until he was 76 he was responsible for Allonby. He retired at the age of 80 to a small cottage in Broughton, eventually in 1966, to Holmewood Residential Home in Cockermouth where he died in March 2004. I will always remember him as a fine man dedicated to his profession, and also a good friend to myself and the family, he was aged 94 years.

J.D.W.

The C. B. Pedersen
"The 4-masted Barque"

There sailed a barque on the seven seas
Under billowing clouds of white
And tall rose her masts in the whispering breeze
And her hull was made for flight.

She roamed the Oceans and seas so long
Till she knew by herself where to steer
And she rocked so easy and ran so strong
Where was there a ship so dear?

No gales were too strong for that ship to ride,
No Doldrums too weary for her,
Her crew of youngsters were quick to abide
Her command if a breeze should stir.

She knew the continents white and black,
She knew the harbours and roads,
And she knew so well where the tides ran slack,
As she travelled the narrows and broads.

No longer now will she roam the sea
Under billowing clouds of white,
No longer adorn a river will she,
Nor a roadstead in morning light.

One pitch dark night when homeward bound
Under press of canvas that beautiful barque
Was rammed by a steamer that sent her down
To her grave in the unknown dark.

I sigh for the ship that was my abode,
My home for ten years and four,
She speaks to me still in a sailor's code
Though gone to oblivion's shore.

Capt. Hjalmar Dhalstrom (Sweden)

Dennis Owen Law
School Teacher and Sportsman

DURING the course of one's lifetime we will visit a particular place or meet up with a particular person who will stand out, creating a picture and an everlasting impression in the mind. In this instance I refer to the latter, I recall this person very clearly, even though it is many years ago when I attended Solway House School in Maryport as a pupil. The gentleman I refer to was a

school teacher, who took the sport classes, taught maths, and also the P E classes as they are known these today, in those days they were known as P T – (physical training. As teachers go he stood head and shoulders above the rest, he was a special teacher who came from a special mould, a mould that unfortunately seems to have been discontinued for quite some time.

Dennis Owen Law was born on the 24th of October 1924 in Kirby Street, Maryport, the son of Margaret and Percy Law, Percy was a coalminer who worked in the local mines, they had one other child Mary, who was younger than Dennis.

As a young boy Dennis was keenly interested in sport, mainly athletics and rugby, he competed in most of the annual athletic events as they came along, and he became an excellent sprinter winning many events, this was to be an asset to him in his future years as a top class rugby

Dennis pictured as President of Cumbria Rugby Union.

player, his playing position on the field being that of fly half.

He started his education at the British School at Maryport. He then attended the Workington Grammar School from 1935 until 1941. Dennis had his mind set upon attending college and studying to become a teacher when he finished at the grammar school. He was a sharp and clever pupil who was well liked amongst classmates and teachers alike, possessing very good potential in his work and studies, and still finding plenty of time to indulge in his passion for the field of athletics and especially the game of rugby, in which he became a very fine player and attaining a great knowledge of the game in general.

The Second World War was to intervene with his proposed plans to attend the teachers college, it would have to be put on hold for the time being.

Dennis joined the Royal Navy in 1941 where he trained to be a telegraphist, he was then shipped out to the Far East to do his service. During his service he worked and was in communication with the Enigma Code Breakers at Bletchley Park in Buckinghamshire, and was one of those responsible for de-codeing of the Japanese morse-code.

While overseas he carried on with his passion for sport when the time allowed, competing in athletics, and playing rugby for the Royal Navy.

When the war ended in 1945 Dennis returned home and commenced with his plans to attend the teachers college which was at Bamber Bridge near Preston. During this period at college, as previously in the Royal Navy, he was very much into his sporting activities, competing in the college and local athletics, and was really in his element playing rugby for the well known Preston Grasshoppers.

When his studies and college training were completed, Dennis first taught under Mr. Issac Kennedy at the Dearham Junior School. While teaching at Dearham he was courting the then Miss Jean Storey of Camp Road, Maryport. They married on Boxing Day in 1949. Dennis and Jean lived in the house where she was brought up in Camp Road from 1949 until 1972. They then moved to Papcastle near Cockermouth.

Finishing teaching at Dearham he transferred to Solway House School at Maryport which was in two parts, the main building which was situated on the Sea Brows overlooking the Solway Firth. The other part of the school were two pre-fabricated single storey oblong buildings, that were known as the huts, these were situated on the site of the old British School which had been bombed and totally destroyed by enemy action in July 1940 in which seven people were killed.

Dennis taught at Solway House from 1950 until 1955, It was during this time that I became one of his pupils. He was a no nonsense school teacher, he was there to do a job, and to use an old expression, if a job is worth doing, it is worth doing well, that about sums up the man. He did have a good sense of humour, and could see the funny side of things when they presented themselves, he was a strict teacher who expected the full attention of his pupils during his working day, if any pupil was distracted or not giving their full attention, he or she would be hit by a very well directed piece of flying chalk, which usually made contact with the head, it was only on very rare occasions that he missed the target.

Dennis Law was a very fair man, if you had a problem you could express yourself to him and he would listen, he was a regular man, not a man of moods. If he ever did have any personal problems they were certainly not on show to his pupils. His lads looked up to him, especially those who were sports minded, but this made no difference to him, he had no favourites. If a pupil excelled at rugby or running etc, it made no difference to him. The pupil who was no physical marvel was praised for trying and doing their best, but if you were lazy, and tried to get one over on him you were wasting your time, he would be upon you in a flash.

A lesson taught

I recall on one occasion a young smaller pupil was being bullied on a regular basis by an older and much bigger pupil from a higher class, this was always at school break times, and also when school had finished for the day, for some reason the young pupil would not retaliate and just put up with his tormentor, one day out of the blue Dennis appeared on the scene, carrying two pairs of boxing gloves, he then promptly marched the bullied and the bully down to the old Church rooms in High Street, where the school woodwork and metalwork classes were held. In the building there was a spare empty room adjacent to these, where P T classes were held in the winter, or if bad weather had prevailed for the day.

The gloves were laced and the only words spoken were "get on with it and make it clean". The outcome was what Dennis had most likely predicted, it was short and sharp, and needless to say the tables had turned, the persecutor became the persecuted by a barrage of hefty punches around the face and head, and to finish the job one good punch under the ribs put him on his knees. The gloves off, Dennis then said to the jubilant winner "why didn't you do that to start with to save your agony"? He then said to the big fellow "how does it feel to be on the wrong end of the sword and be taken down a peg or two"? for future reference keep today in mind. On the way out of the hall Dennis grinned at the winner and said, "ever thought about taking up boxing lad"? I do believe Dennis had predicted what the outcome would be, or he would have approached the situation in a different manner.

Solway House Rugby Team 1952-53 .
Back row left Mr. Sharp, Headmaster, and Mr. Bell. Right Mr D. Law.

The art of self-defence

Returning to the art of self defence, one wet day we again find ourselves in the Church rooms in High Street, this time as a class. We were to be paired off as near to matching weights as possible, to indulge in the fine art of making a mess of each other. After the lower and middle weights had completed a three minute round apiece, we then arrived at the heavy end, be it fat, well built, or indifferent. One lad was left without an opponent, he was a good school friend of mine, by the name of Tom Bell, Tom was quite a sturdy powerful lad, who with his elder Bobby, who at that time worked for the local firm of P. Greggains Haulage Contractors, indulged in weight training etc. Dennis said "right Bell, you are near enough my weight," and commenced to put on the boxing gloves, I can remember Tom looking a bit bemused at this and staring at Dennis as though in slight shock. "Now then" said Dennis, I will Demonstrate on how to ride a punch "right Bell, I want you to throw a punch at my chin, "come on gloves up" Tom with feet apart and hands held high in typical boxing stance, but still looking as though in shock, prodded out his left glove tapping Dennis on the chest, "come on Bell, stop messing about, on the chin lad, on the chin, and as hard as you can. Tom gave a slight nod, and at the same time threw a fast hard punch straight from the shoulder, it was right on target, Dennis went staggering back four or five paces, almost going down. It was his turn to have the look of shock, he had fully intended to demonstrate on how to ride, or dodge a punch, but Tom's punch had landed before he could put his move into operation. Composing himself he said,

"Right Bell you've proved you can hit, and I have proved I wasn't quick enough" he then turned to the rest of the class and said "If any of you lot fancy your chances against Bell forget it" Tom looking much happier and grinning, said "I can hit harder than that Sir, I was holding back." "Really" replied Dennis, "Lets make sure you get a different opponent next time", and with a smile said, "well done, boxings over for today lads, in future we will concentrate on the finer arts of rugby."

The straight drive

The boxing ring was now a thing of the past as far as our class was concerned. It was now midsummer, and we find ourselves on a lovely summer day in the playground of Solway House, padded up for cricket, with Dennis talking about long legs, short legs, silly mid-ons and offs, slips and gully's etc. etc.

When we finally attained a basic knowledge on the fielding positions, we were then introduced to the cricket ball, and instructed on bowling, fast, medium fast, and spin bowling, that involved googly's and chinamen, the googly's and chinamen were the slow bowlers specialities Dennis explained, which could not be executed on a tarmac surface, using a ball with no seam, and made up of a mixture of cork and heavy rubber. When this ball was flung down at pace to the batsman, who was holding a bat for the first time in his life, by a bowler who thought he was at the fairground knocking over coconuts at a coconut shy and believing that he was a reincarnation of Harold Larwood, the bodyline specialist of the 1930s, it was no joke, the ball on occasion making no contact with the pitch at all, passing over the batsman's head with feet to spare, or if it did bounce halfway down the pitch it would rise about fifteen feet in the air, fly over the batsman's head and end up at the end of the playground. Dennis called things to a halt, to calm down the ferocity of the missile projector, and to inform the batsman who didn't really need a bat, that the war was over for the time being. After things had calmed somewhat, we now find Dennis with bat in hand making some classic cricket strokes, when the bowler was able to pitch a ball in a straight line somewhere in the region of the wicket, which if lucky was once an over, an over consisting of six balls.

Netherhall rugby union team. Dennis pictured front row right.

Dennis began to explain on how to play the majestic straight drive back over the bowlers head, and was waiting for what seemed an eternity for the right ball to arrive to execute this shot, in time it did finally arrive, which put an end to the cricket for the day, the ball pitching perfectly for the shot, with Dennis making perfect contact with the ball. The ball left the school playground completely, travelling long and high, the ball then started its descent crashing through the window of a house on the other side of Camp Road, coming to rest in the front room, which fortunately or unfortunately was that of Dennis's home. "Well lads said Dennis you have now seen how the straight drive is played, a shot to be proud of, even though I say it myself. but at a cost of which no doubt I will soon be informed."

Solway House School, Maryport.

Dennis Law taught at Solway House from 1950 until 1955. He then moved to the new school at Netherhall where he taught until he retired as Senior Master. I often saw him around the town after leaving school, he always showed great interest in how his old pupils were faring in the real world, it was a genuine interest that he portrayed that shone through the man. I recall on one occasion I met him on the Athletic ground at Maryport at a rugby match, I was on embarkation leave at the time during my national service, waiting to be shipped out to West Africa with my unit, The Kings Own Royal Border Regt. National call up was due to come to an end some 18 months later, and I recall Dennis saying it should never be stopped, it did a young man good, it gave him pride and also the opportunity to learn a trade. Or even to take up service life as a career, as in the late 1950s and early 1960s, the prospects of securing a regular job or gaining an apprenticeship were pretty low. We chatted right through the match, and at the end I could not bid him farewell without a reminder of boxing and cricket, to which we had a good laugh, with Dennis rubbing his jaw smiling and saying 'aye, that Tom Bell could pack a wallop for a lad at school.

Dennis played rugby for the County on many occasions, and was deeply involved with the game on and off the field, eventually in later years becoming The President of Cumbria Rugby Union. I recall also in those days, There would oft times be a gathering on a Saturday lunch time in the late 1950s and early 1960s, this would take place on the corner of Crosby Street and Senhouse Street, when the local supporters and the Knights of the world of rugby would congregate together and get lost into the mists of the sport with Dennis centre stage holding council.

In his later years he took up the peaceful game of bowls, still a verbal force in his beloved rugby, and a highly respected specialist of the game.

My memories of the man are very clear. He had a strong personality combined with honesty, together with a witty charm, he could put on a serious look and be quite funny at the same time. To his pupils he was leader of the pack, and his pack in those days held their leader in high esteem. He was the genuine article. Sadly after a longish illness Dennis died on the 30th March 2003 aged 79 years.

Leaving his wife Jean and their three children. The eldest Christopher, who lives in New Zealand. Stuart, who lives in Spain, and Julia their daughter who resides in England.

He was a fine teacher, sportsman and gentleman, who will be sadly missed by all who knew him.

J.D.W.

Solway House School mid-1952.
Back Row L/R. T. Johnston, J. McIvor, H. Bland, J. Wells, F. Whitehead, R. Stoddart, J. Nicholson, F. Harrison, C. Murray. Centre Row L/R. G. Wignall, T. Bell, I. Moore, D. French, E. Fletcher, M. Irving, S. Bethwaite, A. Hodgson, G. Hodgson, C. Wigham.. Front Row L/R. J. Brown, E. Wood, J. Elliott, M. Dixon, J. Mossop, M. Fearon, R. McManus, M. Armstrong. H. Wood.

Old British School. Bombed and destroyed in 1941. Seven people killed.

The Chief Steward

The captain of a liner is
A most important man,
He's been a haughty autocrat
since liners first began;
But tho' he rules upon the bridge
He's but an empty show –
The C.S. is the actual man
That makes the ship to go!

The Officers are splendid chaps
To work the ship and crew,
as keen as mustard to excel
In all they have to do,
But are they indispensable
On board a steamer ? No! –
The C.S. is the actual man
That makes the ship to go!

The engineers are clever folk,
and experts in their way
Their life is one of constant toil,
with very little play,
But tho' they work by day and night
And risk their lives below –
The C.S. is the actual man
That makes the ship to go!

He's pushful, but he's tactful, too,
He calmly goes ahead,
The kind of man who sidles in
Where angles fear to tread.
and I maintain, without a doubt,
Without irreverence,
The C.S. is the actual man
That bosses providence!

Greville E. Matheson

219

Dr. J. W. M. Crerar

J.P., MB., F.R.C.S. ED.

of Maryport

THE Crerar family were of Scottish origin. Dr. John W. M. Crerar was born in Maryport in 1869, and brought up in the town as a boy, eventually leaving to attend University to study Medicine. His father John senior was a medical practitioner who with his wife Catherine arrived and settled in Maryport in the early 1860s to take up practice in the town. He became very well known in his profession, was quite a striking figure, with a strong personality, a very caring practitioner who was well liked by his patients, building up a large and popular practice in and around the town.

The Crerar's brought up quite a large family. Christina their daughter was the eldest who became a school governess, followed by John who was two years her junior, who on his fathers death returned to Maryport after a Brilliant career in the field of medicine at university to continue his fathers practice. He had a younger brother Charles, who was also a student of medicine, who eventually took up practice in Silloth. Sir James Crerar another brother, received a knighthood for services rendered in India. The remaining and younger children in the family were the three girls Kate, Jessie, and Sarah Margaret, the two boys, Donald and Duncan. The Crerars were a brilliant family, and all attained high positions in their chosen professions.

When John junior took over his fathers practice after his death, it carried on in the same manner, he was a very popular young doctor at the top of his tree, and inherited quite a lot from his father, being outgoing, forthright, and also with a strong personality, a very caring doctor, who treated the wealthy and the poor alike, there was no upper or lower class where he himself, or his practice were concerned, as was with his father before him. He was our family doctor for many years, and was a great favourite of my grandmothers, she thought very highly of him, and would not call on any other practitioner for herself, or any other member of the family while he was available. I myself can remember being taken as a very young boy by my grandfather to his practice which was also his home, at number 11 High Street, a large house at the south end of the town. I was to be treated for an ear infection. The door bell was answered by a gentleman in a grey uniform – (military type) wearing knee length and highly polished boots, who then led us into the surgery. I was to be informed later that the above gentleman was a lifelong friend and companion of the doctor, who was also his valet and chauffeur for 55 years or so, his name was Mr. Claude Mann. I was later to see both doctor and chauffeur on occasion when they visited our home, Mr. Claude

Maryport's first car, a 1902 3.5hp Swift. Owned by Doctor John W. M. Crerar seen here at the wheel, his passenger, friend and chauffeur, Mr. Claude Mann. This photograph was taken at Birkby near Maryport.

Mann always immaculate in peaked cap and light grey uniform. The Doctor a very polite and charming man, who would spend all the time that was necessary with his patients, and on occasion time to chat to my grandparents, on the past history of the town or local current affairs and events of the time. Dr. Crerar practised until well into his seventies.

He was noted as being the first person to own a motorised vehicle in Maryport, the type being a 1902 Swift, of three and a half horsepower, which at top speed would travel at not much more than 20 mph.

Doctor Crerar was very involved in the town and its affairs, he took a deep interest in its history, and was looked upon as the towns historian. Over the years he attained a great knowledge on the town, of its founders, its Maritime history etc. He was very interested in the Christian family, and I recall him chatting to my mother and grandmother on one of his visits, regarding Fletcher Christian of the Mutiny on the Bounty fame, also the Fletchers of Moresby, and of Cockermouth. My grandmother being called Fletcher before her marrage, was born and raised in the village of Dearham near Maryport, He was sure that if her family history was looked into in depth, a family connection would be found that would link her to that of the family of the famous mutineer.

Doctor Crerar shown here on the doorstep of number 11 High Street, his home and practice for many years. (Photo 1938)

The Doctor was also very interested in the story of John Paul Jones who raided the town of Whitehaven, writing a short story on the subject, a subject which was gone into in great detail.

The life of Mr. James Brooker, the ornamental wood carver of ships figure-heads and sterns, this was another subject of great interest to the doctor. The shipbuilding history of the town, the builders and the launches of these fine ships.

Doctor Crerar was a man who's life was seemingly lived to the full, not a moment wasted. Fully in-volved and dedicated in his work to the people of the town in his profession, writing and collecting as much historical memorabilia, photographs etc, as time would allow regarding the history of the town and its people.

The collection of this mem-orabilia after the Doctors death was presented by his family to the County Archives in Carlisle, which is housed in Carlisle Castle. **Dr. John W. M. Crerar. J.P., MB., F.R.C.S. Ed.** A man who's work and loyalty to his town makes him an outstanding figure in its history.

The Birkett Family
of Maryport

Gatehouse of Fleet

I have seen few scenes naturally more beautiful and
ornamented than this, within the bounds of one landscape, the
eye beholds the river fleet discharging itself into the Firth; the
houses of Ardwell and Cally; the beautiful and populas village
of Gatehouse; and the ancient castle of Cardoness, with a large
extent of adjacent country, either cultivated and thickset with
farmhouses, with abundance of woodland interspersed, or –
towards extremities of the prospect – widely picturesque.

Robert Heron 1792

Gatehouse of Fleet.

GATEHOUSE of Fleet, this neat and beautifully situated village stands to the south-west of the parish on the banks of the River Fleet. The town only dates back to the mid-1700s. In 1795 Gatehouse had four cotton mills, a brewery, a soap factory, brickworks, brass foundry and tanneries, and a population which then was double of that of today. Within the two parishes of Girthon and Anwoth, the population was in the region of 2000, today the population just 1000. It was known in those days as Little Glasgow, or the Glasgow of the South, which is hard to imagine to the visitor of today. But traces of the past still linger in this beautiful and tranquil village.

The Mill On The Fleet, once a large mill is now a visitor centre, one of the factories owned by the Birtwhistle family who originated from Yorkshire. The laird, James Murray of Broughton and Cally (1727-1799), planned the town and encouraged the development of industry. The population and the town grew steadily between (1760-1790) to its present size, but there was much competition the cotton industry, mainly from those in Glasgow and in Lancashire, its importance in the industry declined as a manufacturing centre after 1850, and eventually the other industries faded away also, the brickworks and tanneries, the brewery and soap works, the ship building that once flourished there, and the repair yards. Port Macadam once the towns harbour, lies on the River Fleet, it used to take up to 150 ships, the quay is used today by small pleasure craft.

Gatehouse is centrally and ideally situated for visitors exploring Dumfries and Galloway, there is much to see. The village is surrounded by spectacular countryside, ideal for walkers and riding enthusiasts, it is alive with wildlife, a haven for birdwatchers. It has a fine nine hole golf course and tennis courts, the village has a post office and bank, there are numerous and independent shops which supply everyday needs, as well as gift and craft shops. The only drinking houses left in the village today are the Anwoth Hotel (formerly the Ship Inn), where the writer Dorothy L. Sayers, wrote her best selling novel (The Five Red Herrings). There is the Masonic Arms, and the Murray Arms Hotel, the latter once being a hostelry, where the poet Robert Burns is reputed to have written the poem (*Scots Wha Hae*) having composed it while journeying from the neighbouring village of Laurieston in a thunderstorm.

Gatehouse Of Fleet is a beautiful village, and well worth a visit to the traveller or holiday maker who is seeking peace and tranquillity, and to be made more than welcome by the local people. This I can vouch for, having spent a most enjoyable week while staying at the Murray Arms in the month of June 2004 while researching material for this manuscript.

Ambrose Birkett

Ambrose Birkett arrived in Gatehouse Of Fleet sometime between the years of 1827-1829. He was born about 1778-1780, he was a widower who came from the Ulverston area in Lancashire England. He apparently had a grown up family in Ulverston. His profession was that of a hooper, a person involved in the construction of barrel or cask making, his job was fashion and fix the metal or wooden hoops or bands that bring the barrel staves together to form the finished article.

Ambrose, like numerous English and Irish immigrants they descended upon Gatehouse in the early and mid-1800s, workers being required for the industries that were flourishing at the time, in Ambrose's case apparently there was a demand for barrels and casks for the breweries and the fishing industry, casks to pack the salted herring, and the wages were much higher than in England at the time in his line of work.

With his family grown up and having no ties as such, Ambrose bid farewell to Ulverston and set out for South-West Scotland to begin a new era in his life. It was not long afterwards that he met a young woman who in age was about 30 years or so his junior, her name was Margaret Galloway, she was 19 years of age, born in 1811. Margaret was living and working in Gatehouse. She was apparently a wayward young woman who did not see eye to eye with her parents, she eventually brought shame upon her family by having an illegitimate child at the age of 18. A child born out of wedlock was looked upon as a great sin, it was classed as unlawful. She had brought shame and disgrace upon her family, and was banished from the family home.

Margaret was the daughter of William Galloway, and Agnes Macnight of Airds, who lived at Loch Ken just a few miles from of Gatehouse. William Galloway was born in 1770. The Galloway's had four other children, a son Andrew, born 1806 who was drowned in Loch Ken in 1830, aged 24 years. Jane Hughan Galloway born 1815. Thomas Hughan Galloway, born in 1817, Agnes born in 1820, and Mary born in 1824, Margaret's illegitimate child was a baby girl who was named Elizabeth. The father was named as William Campbell, and it would seem that she had no desire to marry him.

Margaret Galloway married Ambrose Birkett on April 26th 1830, she was 19 years of age, Ambrose was about 52, she was 33 years his junior. Margaret had three children to him, all boys, James born 1831, Henry born in 1833, and Alexander born 1836.

Ambrose died in 1840 at Gatehouse, leaving her to bring up her their children. She was still only 29 years of age. They were living in the parish of Girthon, in Back Street as it was called in those days, today it is called Catherine Street. Margaret became destitute after her husbands death with no income as such, with five mouths to feed and their bodies to clothe. Her mother and father never forgave her for the shame she had brought upon the family and to herself, but they would not see the young ones suffer, her younger brother Thomas also took care of their wants until they became of the age when they could fend for themselves. They were all found positions of work when they became of age. Elizabeth Campbell, was now Elizabeth Birkett, Ambrose had agreed to accept her as one of his own, she was training as a seamstress, James the eldest boy was sent to Dumfries to the parish of Troqueer, now known as Maxwell Town which is a suburb of Dumfries, he went to be an iron founders apprentice, and acquired lodgings near to his place of work with a farmers widow by the name of Elizabeth Foulis. The second son Henry went into farm service with the Maxwells who were family relatives. Alexander the youngest son, was found a position in forestry work.

Henry Birkett

Whilst Henry Birkett was in farm service, he met and married a young lady by the name of Elizabeth Lansbury, she was from Dumfries, they had two children, both boys, James and Alexander. The family moved from Scotland to Whiston Cross, near St Helens in Lancashire England. Henry was very fond of horses, having working and being involved with them during his farm service. He set up and opened a teamster carrier service which ran between Liverpool and St Helens. He was also at the same time a publican, running the Whiston Cross Hotel. Henry's brother-in-law John Lansbury left Dumfries to move to Whiston Cross to help Henry run the carrier service. There were now three more additions to the Birkett family, three girls, Sarah the eldest, then Margaret, and Jane the youngest. Henry built up a thriving business and done well.

James Birkett

When James the eldest of the three brothers completed his apprenticeship as an iron founder, he was awarded a scroll and medallion as being an excellent apprentice. He stayed on with the firm for a period of time, and he then moved to Newcastle in North-East England. He began work in Newcastle with Mr. W. Shields. The owner of St. Peters Forge, the famous chain and anchor makers of Tyneside. He soon afterwards became a partner in the firm, on the death of Mr. Shields the firm became known as Birkett and Caisely. On the retirement of the latter James became sole proprietor, carrying on the business for some years employing 55 men plus apprentices. He eventually retired into an independent position after selling the business. He had become very fond of Newcastle and its people and made it his home, but never failing once a year to cross over the border into Scotland to visit his family, and place of birth, also making visits on occasion to see his two brothers.

James was elected a member of the Town Council in 1883, and represented the interests of the people of Heaton ever since. In 1892 he was raised to the magisterial bench of the City. He was a liberal and a home ruler.

James Birkett was held in high esteem by all, and particularly by the Heaton people who appreciated his efforts warmly, and always returned him to the council without opposition. He was presented with an illuminated address at the Heaton assembly rooms, the Mayor and most of the City council members being present.

James took ill returning from a council meeting on February 11th, 1889, he died the same day at his home number 37 Heaton Road, he was aged 67 years.

REFERENCE AT THE POLICE COURT

At the Police Court, yesterday, the Chairman (Mr. Cook) referred to the death of Mr. Birkett. He said the Bench and the City Council had sustained a heavy loss by Mr. Birkett's death. Mr. Birkett was an able and a painstaking magistrate, an excellent and indefatigable member of the City Council. The city had lost a valuable public servant, and it was with deepest regret that the Bench heard of Mr. Birkett's death.

On Saturday afternoon the remains of the late Councillor James Birkett were interred in Heaton Cemetery, Benton Road, in the presence of hundreds of people. A more numerously attended funeral has not been hitherto known in the east end burial ground, and the big concourse of personal friends to the deceased showed how close were the ties that bound the most popular personality in the east end of the city to his host of admirers and personal friends. The cortege left the residence of the deceased gentleman in Heaton Park Road at 3 o'clock the cemetery being reached about half an hour later, There were in the procession twenty carriages or more, while there was many people who followed on foot. At the cemetery the Mayor and a large number of members of the City Council and of Mr. Birkett's colleagues on the magisterial bench were also in waiting. The Liberal Association, the East End Liberal Club, the Irish National League, the bowling club with which Mr. Birkett had been so long associated, The Newcastle and Gateshead branch of the Ironfounders Society (of which Mr. Birkett had been a member for 43 years), and many other bodies were represented.

THE LATE COUNCILLER JAMES BIRKETT

James Birkett 1831-1896.
from a photograph.

Shortly after his death, a memorial clock was unveiled in Heaton Park to his memory, commemorating his services to the East End of the city. Mr. Birkett left a wife Mary Ann, who was from Gateshead, they had no children.

Alexander Birkett

Alexander the youngest of the three brothers started his working life at the age of fifteen, he took up forestry work in the dense and rich timber forests in and around New Galloway and Minnigaff, this was about 1850-1851. It was sometime after, whilst working in the Minnigaff area that he became acquainted with a specialist in the forestry field by the name of James Brown, James with his wife Elizabeth and their two children were Irish immigrants. They had arrived in Minnigaff in 1841, James was 25 years of age, Elizabeth likewise, Sarah was 2 years of age, James junior aged 6 months. James Brown was about 35 years of age when he and Alexander met and began working together, they became friends, and it would seem that it was partly due to the expertise guidance of James Brown, that Alexander became an expert in the timber trade, becoming a timber measurer, and eventually a sawyer.

Alexander Birkett 1836-1912.
From an engraving.

In 1857 Alexander Birkett aged 21, and Sarah Brown the daughter of James and Elizabeth Brown were married. Shortly after they were married they moved to the Dumfries area. It was there that their first child Alexander C. Birkett was born in 1860. Henry their second son was also born in Scotland, and first daughter Elizabeth in 1863.

It was about 1865-66 that the family left Scotland and moved to England, where they settled in Whitehaven, in the County of Cumberland, now known as Cumbria. Alexander taking up work in the local ship-yards where the work was plentiful, this being the reason for the leaving of Scotland. It was in Whitehaven that Ambrose their third son was born in 1868.

In was the same year 1868, of Ambrose's birth, that the family moved a few miles further down the coast to Maryport where industry was flourishing in and around the docks, the shipbuilding yards, and other industries. The family settled on the south side of the River Ellen at number 4 Glasson, as the area was known in those days.

Alexander's first job in the town was that of a general labourer on the docks, eventually he secured a position in the timber yards of the Ritson's, the well-known shipbuilding company as a sawyer, after a period of time he became foreman in the timber yard, and being responsible for the measuring, selecting, and the grading of the various types of timber required for the construction of the ships.

Martha their fifth child was born in 1870, and my grandfather John in April 1872, both being born at Glasson. The family moved from Glasson in about 1874 to St. Mary's Place in Kirby Street in the town, where James the 5th son was born in 1875, and Sarah the third daughter in 1879. The last of the family to be born was William in 1885, by this time the two eldest sons Alexander and Henry were both fully grown young men, and tradesman sawyers, both employed at the time in the shipyards. Ambrose the third son was now 17 years of age, after being employed for a time on the harbour and the docks, he became a carter, involved with the sale and delivery of fish, locally, and to surrounding areas.

By this time in 1885 my grandfather John was 13 years of age, and a scholar, as was James who was 11 years of age. Sarah was aged 6 years, and William having just been born.

Alexander Birkett who introduced this branch of the Birkett family to Maryport in 1868, died on the 30th of August 1912, aged 73 years. His wife Sarah died on the 24th of February 1922, aged 82 years.

John S. M. Birkett

My grandfather John, the fourth son of Alexander and Sarah, when not at home or school, could always be found on the docks or harbour side, as a young boy he

was infatuated by sailing ships and the sea, he would be found in conversation with seaman or with the local fishermen. His desire was to make seafaring his future career. In 1885 when not quite 15 years of age, himself and another young man of the town by the name of Messenger, stowed away on a sailing vessel out of the port. She was owned by the well-known local firm of Hine Brothers, The Company being called the Holme Line. Apparently the vessel of their choice was the sailing ship the *Castle Holme*. She was bound for almost a two year voyage, that would take them to Africa, Australia, China, and also to Canada, before returning to the home port.

The two stowaways were found hiding in a lifeboat when the vessel was well out into the Irish sea. They were brought before the captain, there was no turning back, they would have to work the duration of the voyage for their food, but without wages, and were informed by the captain if their desire was to become sailors they had the

John Birkett aged 17 yrs after his first voyage to sea of almost two years.

time and opportunity, as they would be away from home for a very long time.

There was one small comfort did eventually come their way, one member of the ships crew, an able seaman, jumped ship and went absent at one of the ports of call, so the captain being kind hearted, shared the missing sailors wages and tobacco ration between the two stowaways for the duration of the voyage.

When John Birkett returned home to Maryport he was not quite 17 years of age, but he was a fully qualified able seaman, and well complimented by his captain on his initiative and efficiency, and that if his desire was to make seafaring a career he had the capabilities to reach the top.

While on leave from his first voyage to sea it was then that he began courting his future wife. Her name was Ada Fletcher from the neighbouring village of Dearham, she was not quite sixteen and employed as a trainee seamstress.

John's future intention was one day to be the master of his own ship, he was a fine seaman, but he was to be greatly disappointed, for when he sat for his mates ticket, he could not pass the eye colour test, and found out to his dismay that he was colour blind on certain colours, and these were most important as to obtain a higher rank on board ship. But this did not deter him from carrying on in his profession as an able seaman, he was a young man who was proud of his profession as that of a sailor, and especially to be a crew member of a fully rigged sailing ship.

During his career as that of a sailor, he sailed mainly with the Holme Line of Maryport on ships such as the *Castle Holme*, the *Briar Holme*, the latter, which in his own words were "she was one of the finest and prettiest vessels afloat." he

The Callixene *built 1869, 1,344 tons.*

sailed also on the *Eden Holme*, and *Hazel Holme*, the other ships of the line on which he sailed were steamers, *The Forest Holme, Loughrigg Holme, Rydal Holme, The Derwent Holme*, and the *Ardmore*.

John also voyaged on vessels owned by Captain John Ross Suiter, of Camp Road, Maryport. The fleet was only a small one, consisting of four wooden sailing ships, the largest being the *Callixene*, full-rigged at 1,344 tons gross, built at St. Johns New Brunswick in 1869. The *Gladstone*, 1,057 tons, built 1860. The *Clyde*, 702 tons built 1860, Nova Scotia, and was owned by Mrs. J. Suiter. The other ship being the *Mersey*. These vessels traded mainly across the Atlantic in the 1880s and 1890s to Quebec in the season, and to the American timber ports. The firm unfortunately went into liquidation in 1896 after a series of misfortunes had presented themselves upon the small company.

John made his second voyage to sea after a short leave ashore, this was a voyage of nine months a short voyage in comparison to that of his first. His ship was the *Loch Eck*, a three masted iron barque trading out of Maryport at the time, she was owned by J. Wilson of Glasgow.

He was now 19 years of age, and aboard the *Callixene* out of Maryport. During the voyage and whilst in heavy seas, they came upon a vessel in deep distress. She was named the *J. C. Williams*, a small wooden barque of 860 tons net, built in Nova Scotia in 1874. At the time she was sailing out of Yarmouth Nova Scotia. She was manned by a crew of 17 hands, and there were two women on aboard. My grandfather recalled that her mainmast had gone straight through her, and that she was slowly sinking, the crew were in a state of complete exhaustion

Ada Fletcher aged 15.

and even the two women were taking turns at the pumps. They had to wait until the storm abated somewhat before they could put down the lifeboats, eventually the *Callixene* got down two lifeboats, and the stricken vessel one. The crew and the two women were safely taken aboard the *Callixene* and were put ashore three days later in Barbados. The *J. C. Williams* went down and was lost shortly after the rescue.

John Birkett's voyages of long duration were in his early years as a seaman, from 1886 until 1893. The long voyages were over when he and Ada Fletcher were married at Cockermouth register office on the 30th August 1893. John was aged 21 yrs and Ada was 19.

We now find Ada and John living at 77 Eaglesfield Street in Maryport with young daughter Martha, and newly born son Henry (Harry). Ada working from home as a dressmaker, and John sailing out of Maryport with the Holme Line. The year being 1897. In 1901 the family having moved from Eaglesfield Street were now living at number 1 Carey's Yard in John Street, having to find bigger and more suitable accommodation for their growing family. Martha was now 5 years of age, and Harry 3 years, with another child on the way, who was to be John junior, followed by Mary Ann.

John S. M. Birkett, photo 1907.

John finally gave up the sea in 1905, having spent twenty years continually sailing with only brief periods of leave spent ashore. He became a stevedore on the docks at Maryport and was made up to supervisor in charge of the loading of the Workington made steel rails, that were shipped out to Canada, Australia, and the Argentine, countries where over the last two decades he himself was a crew member on some of the ships that transported these heavy cargoes. The loading of steel rails into the ships holds was a very specialised job, great care had to be taken to be sure there was no movement of the cargo in heavy seas during a voyage.

It was now May 1910, the year my mother Sarah was born, the family were now living at number 4 Ellenborough Place, there had already been another addition to the family before her, that of Joseph the third son, another son was to follow which would complete the family, Alexander, the fourth son, who would always be known as Eric.

By this time, the eldest son Harry, was due to begin his apprenticeship at the Phoenix Foundry in Maryport, his ambition to become a marine engineer. Meanwhile his father John was now making regular trips from Maryport to Liverpool, being one chosen from West Cumberland to supervise the loading of steel rails being shipped out from the port, again for Canada, Australia, and the Argentine. These were busy times, but sadly they were not to last. The family moved house yet again, this time to Ironworks Cottage, which was situated in the proximity of its namesake, the Solway Ironworks.

The seed of the big depression that was to hit the country in the mid-1930s was

The Birkett family group.
Back Row. C. Zola, Flo Birkett, Harry Birkett, John Birkett Junior, Eric Birkett, Peggy and Joe Birkett.
Front Row. John Birkett, Sarah, Martha, Mary Ann and Ada Birkett.

sown in the early 1920s. It hit West Cumberland hard, and especially Maryport. The docks went into decline, and other major industries suffered heavily, some of

the smaller business's went into liquidation, with the result that employment suffered heavily, and even today in this year of 2004, the result of that great depression and its memory still abides with the people of what is now West Cumbria, and some of its traces are still visible to this day.

John Birkett finally gave up his position on the docks because of the decline in trade, men were being put on short time, others being paid off completely. He went into the retail fish and fruit business, and after a time he had built up quite a good delivery service, helped in the early stages by his elder brother Ambrose, who had also

John (Fabs) Birkett, son of William and Rose Ann Birkett. A well-known fisherman and local character. A powerful man in his youth who had a great knowledge of the Solway Firth. A rough diamond with a heart of gold, 1912-1986.

233

The Loch Eck.
Trading out of Maryport. John Birkett pictured extreme right, sitting on deck, his second voyage.

Ambrose Birkett (Ammy).
Maryport fish salesman. Photo at Gilcrux around 1908.

worked on the docks, but left to take up business in the retail sale of fish caught locally. In the early days the produce was transported by horse and carrier cart, until motorised transport came upon the scene. John's sons Joseph and Eric helped out with the business when available, also John junior when home on leave from sea. John served in both Royal and Mercantile Marine, he also became a member of the Royal Navel Reserve, after being invalided out of full time service through ill health.

Harry Birkett

It was during the First World War in 1917 that Harry Birkett took his first trip to sea, he was 20 years of age, he had completed his apprenticeship as an engineer at the Phoenix Foundry in Maryport and within a few weeks was aboard the SS Brodmead 5,646 tons (Blue Star Lines, London). Harry found adventure on this his first trip. The Brodmead was torpedoed on the 7th of Sept 1917 by the German submarine UB-49, west of Gibraltar. The steamer had been quite badly damaged, but was towed safely into Gibraltar harbour. His parents were informed that he was missing, and that the Captain and Wireless Operator were missing, one China-man had been killed, and 13 of the crew were wounded, and the only other information they could give at the time was that the only Euro-peans wounded were the 3rd Officer and the gunner.

Chief Engineer Harry Birkett.

Harry was not deterred by this incident on his first trip, and carried on deep sea voyaging after the war. He took his engineering certificates without difficulty, and finally he became extra Chief Engineer. At one period during his career he was con-sultant engineer for the installation of engines in new ships for the United Africa Company, and also served the Canadian Shell Transport Company in a similar capacity.

Harry by this time had married and was living at Walton Vale in Liverpool, which had become his home port during his long association with the sea. Peace

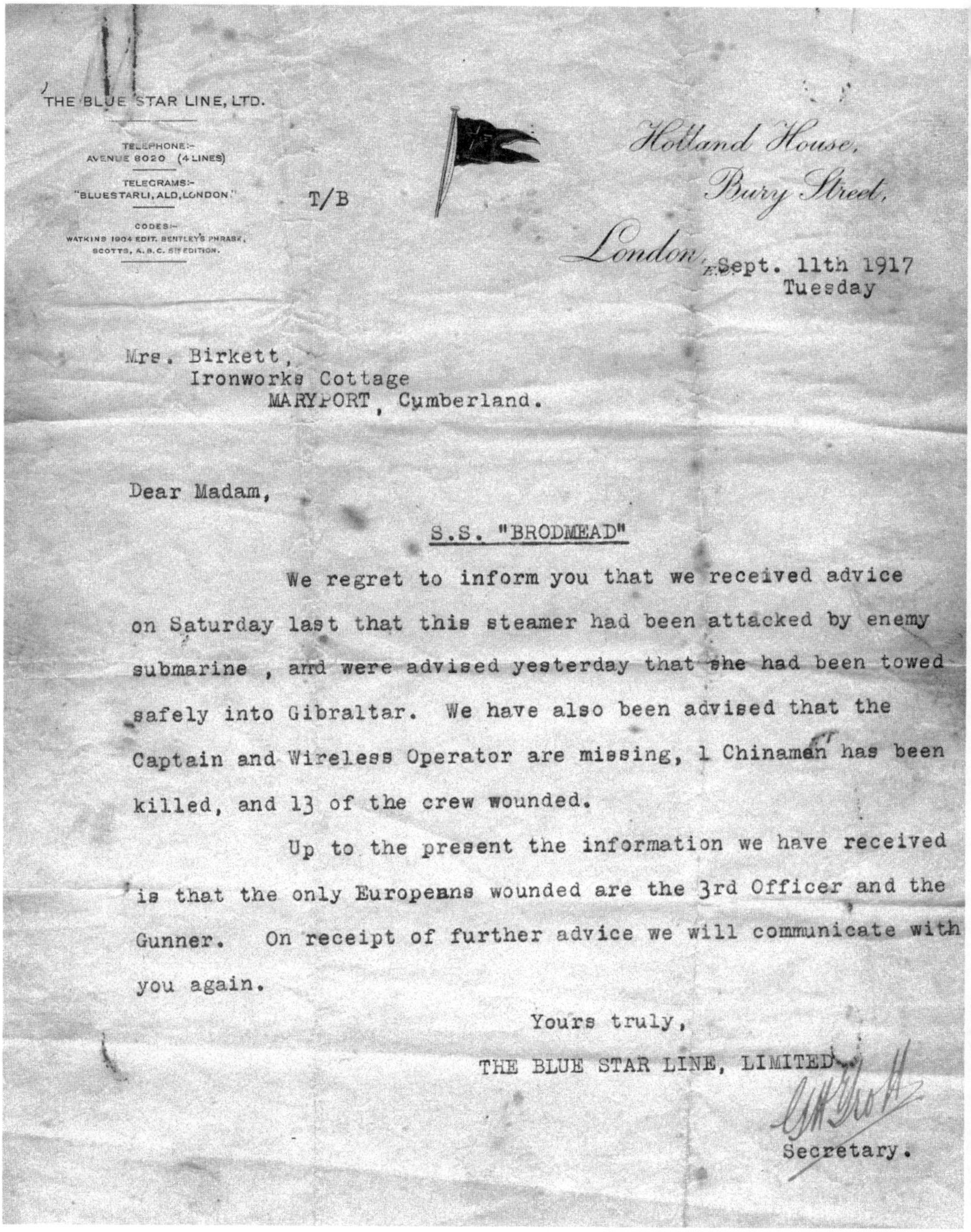

THE BLUE STAR LINE, LTD.

TELEPHONE:-
AVENUE 8020 (4 LINES)

TELEGRAMS:-
"BLUESTARLI, ALD, LONDON."

CODES:-
WATKINS 1904 EDIT. BENTLEY'S PHRASE,
SCOTTS, A.B.C. 5TH EDITION.

T/B

Holland House,
Bury Street,
London, Sept. 11th 1917
Tuesday

Mrs. Birkett,
Ironworks Cottage
MARYPORT, Cumberland.

Dear Madam,

S.S. "BRODMEAD"

We regret to inform you that we received advice
on Saturday last that this steamer had been attacked by enemy
submarine , and were advised yesterday that she had been towed
safely into Gibraltar. We have also been advised that the
Captain and Wireless Operator are missing, 1 Chinaman has been
killed, and 13 of the crew wounded.

Up to the present the information we have received
is that the only Europeans wounded are the 3rd Officer and the
Gunner. On receipt of further advice we will communicate with
you again.

Yours truly,
THE BLUE STAR LINE, LIMITED

Secretary.

Copy of letter.

236

was not long to reign for Harry, the Spanish Civil War found him again in the thick of the action, with ships running the blockade to take in vital foods and goods for the Government population, after a number of daring runs his ship the s.s. *Stanland,* was caught in an east coast Spanish Government Port by Italian and German bombers and blown apart, some members of the crew were killed, the others succeeded in getting another ship out of Spain, Harry being one of them. It was not long before he and some of the others were back on the same job on the on board the s.s. *Cimenco,* this carried on until the Government forces were reeling in defeat and the blockade closed the last available ports. Harry had a flair for adventure, he was an active man, a man who lived every day of his life to the full, seeking new horizons. Harry was by now a father with two young daughters, Patricia and Jean, but again this did not deter him from his love for the sea and ships, and like his father before him the call of the sea was too strong to ignore. He did try on two occasions to apply his profession ashore with the well known firm of shipbuilders, Cammel Lairds of Birkenhead Liverpool, but it turned out to be a dull proposition for a man of his type and character, so the return to the sea on both occasions was inevitable.

At the ending of the Spanish Civil War, Harry continued for sometime to sail with the Blue Star Line, meanwhile back at home in Maryport time was moving on, the family had moved from Ironworks Cottage to number one Mill Street, where they spent two to three years, before moving once more to 33 Curzon Street. The next move was 53 Curzon Street which was to be the last.

John and Ada's family were now all married and gone their separate ways. Sadly John junior had died through the decline of his health, he was only 37 years of age and was married with two children Allan and Eileen. Joseph after his Army service returned to the retail fish business, he married and had two sons, Norris and Joseph. Mary Ann had one child to her first husband Stanley Armstrong of Maryport she was named Iris, he was presumably killed in a bush fire after he emigrated to Australia, he was to have sent for her when a home was prepared for her and the child, but no more was heard from him. Mary Ann remarried and had a second daughter Alma. The eldest of the family Martha, had married and moved to London. Her husband was involved in show business, they had no children during their marrige.

Harry Birkett was now sailing in the South China Seas, for the China Navigation Company, the CNCo as it was referred to in those days, owned by the firm of Butterfield and Swire. The firm was founded by John Swire in 1872. Mr. Butterfield apparently disappeared not so long after the firm was founded, but the name remained unchanged for over a century until the 1960s when it became John Swire and Sons. Over the years the firm has developed into a large complex international trading group of which the China Navigation Company still plays an important part.

Harry sailed on two ships owned by the CNCo, the *Chinkiang,* and her sister ship the *Shansi,* the *Chinkiang* was built in 1898 by Scott & Co. of Greenock for the CNCo., Hong Kong, 2,004 tons gross.

These two ships were of six similar vessels built for the beancake bean oil trade from Newchwang and Antung in north China (close to Korea). The soya bean then as now an important feature of the Oriental diet. The ships soon acquired the nickname of "Bean-cakers". The ships were based in Hong Kong and crewed by British officers and Chinese ratings.

Harry spent quite some time in the South China Seas working for different companies, and became quite a popular figure among the local people of the coastal ports, becoming known as *Wenchow* Birkett. I have been informed that *Wenchow* (Wenzhou) is the name of a China coast port, but also the name of one of the CNCo's lower Yangtze River steamers built in Hong Kong in 1923 by Taikoo Dockyard and (owned by Swire). It is highly likely that Harry served on this vessel hence his nickname. *Wenchow* was eventually captured by the Japanese and sunk during World War II. Other ships Harry sailed on in his time spent in the China seas were the *s.s Taikoo*

The execution of Sheck Ah Yuen, Chief of the Canton River pirates.

Maru, the *s.s Yuan Ta,* the *s.s.Huichou,* the *s.s. Taitoma Maru.* He also witnessed the execution of (*Sheck Ah Yuen*) chief of the Canton river pirates, of which he was allowed to take photographs.

During the Second World War we again find Harry Birkett in the thick of the action. This time as chief engineer on board the *s.s. St Anselm* a British cargo ship of The Saint Line, 5,614 gross tons built in 1919. By the Northumberland Shipbuilding Co. Ltd The *St Anselm* was homeward bound from Calcutta for Hull, she was loaded with 2,150 tons of pig iron, 650 tons of linseed and 5,154 tons of groundnuts. She was torpedoed and sunk by U-66 (Commander Richard Zapp) in position 31.00N 26.00W. The ship evaded four torpedoes and was hit by two duds, the aft magazine was hit by gunfire which exploded and so doing blew off the stern, other parts of the ship also being under heavy gunfire. The ship sank in less than 15 minutes. Many Lascar seamen were lost when the magazine exploded. The Master, Captain. T. Ross and 17 survivors were rescued by AMC HMS *Moreton Bay* and landed at Freetown on the 13th July 1941. The

Pirates awaiting execution.

Chief Officer, Oswald McCurdy, and fifteen others which included Harry were adrift in an open lifeboat for 26 days, until they were eventually picked up by the Spanish steamer *Tom,* and landed at Buenos Aires. The men were totally exhausted when rescued, 34 men had been lost. Chief Officer, Oswald McCurdy, received the MBE (Civ) for services when the ship was torpedoed and for his conduct during a 26 day open lifeboat voyage.

Meanwhile a number of years had passed, during that time my father had come to Maryport with the Harbour And General Works from the South of England, who were to build the sea wall defences, he met Sarah my mother and shortly afterwards they were married. I was born at the outbreak of the Second World War in 1939, at 53 Curzon Street, where my mother was living with her parents, my father having been called up for service at the outbreak of the war until it ended in 1945. My brother Harry was born in 1947 at the Cottage Hospital Maryport.

My grandfather was retired by this time and taking a well earned rest, he had been a very active man since the day he first put his feet upon the deck of a ship, my grandmother had now only he and herself to take care of, some of the family had moved to the South of England, where there was more scope for work. Iris, Mary Ann's daughter had married a marine engineer from Fyfe in Scotland, who's parents were Scandinavian. Eventually most of the sons and daughters would emigrate to Australia, where I myself would make a short stay in the years ahead.

After suffering from exposure from the open boat voyage Harry Birkett's health broke down, which led to a rest period at Elk Ridge near Baltimore USA. After this period of rest and a visit to his family in Liverpool, plus a visit to

The St. Anselm.

Maryport to see his parents and friends, he was soon back at sea, when another ship went down under him by torpedo, this was just before the final defeat of Germany when sailing from London to Antwerp. When the war finally finished, Harry after home leave, made a trip to Baltimore to visit friends he had made whilst convalescing after his ordeal at sea. It was winter time, and the roads had a slight covering of snow and were rather icy, he was crossing the Boulevard when he seemed to slip, he fell into the path of an oncoming vehicle and was instantly killed, he was 47 years of age. Harry was buried in the British plot of the Lorraine Cemetery near Baltimore. Harry spent 32 years of his life at sea, and during those years wherever he may have been, he was involved in action and adventure. Going by the law of averages he should have been lost at least three times, nothing would be heard from him or of him for weeks or months at a time, then out of the blue he would show up or make contact, when all hope seemed lost. The family eventually gained the confidence that if he went missing whatever the odds Harry would come through, he was like the cat with nine lives. It seems a strange and unkind turn of fate, that after surviving every possible risk and hardship at sea in three wars, that he should be killed by a car in a small USA town where most of the people knew him and were his friends.

Footnote: Engineer Birkett had taken leave from a ship on which he had sailed on previous voyages, a ship of which he was very fond, while at home on leave on December 2nd 1939, he heard the news that his ship the Doric Star *of the Blue Star Line, had been captured and sunk by the German Pocket Battleship the* Admiral Graf Spee, *on that very same day in the South Atlantic.*

Harry and brother Joe.

John Birkett Junior.
while serving on HMS Resolution.

John
and Ada.

My grandfather John Birkett died in 1950, he was 78 years of age. Shortly after his death, his son Joseph and family emigrated to Australia, Joe sold his retail fish round to a gentleman named Bowman, who in turn gave up the business himself, and opened up a wool shop in the town for his wife. A year or so after Joe and family left they were soon followed by other members of the family, after a few years Eric and his family returned to live in England, and settled back in Buckinghamshire where they had lived previously before emigrating. My grand-

241

mother died in 1963, she was aged 90 years. The family had occupied 53 Curzon Street for almost forty years. My grandparents both lay at rest in the Maryport cemetery, to which I may add is a credit to the town and to the people who are responsible for its upkeep and appearance.

Maryport Cemetery.

A Message still at Sea

Whoever shall pick up this bottle, I pray
That they note they year, the month and the day,
So then at a glance 'twill be easily seen
How long in the water this message has been.
Now, why should all messages saved from the deep,
Be such as to make a man shudder and weep,
Why should they out of cruel disaster relate,
Of all hope abandoned and terrible fate?
Then let me for once from this custom depart,
And launch a few words which may gladden the heart.

So, if the wild ocean this bottle should send,
To some troubled skipper, Who's at his wits end,
To escape from his danger, or see his way through,
Let him from the bottle his spirits renew.
Or should some good comrade pick up these few lines,
Whose voyage it is peaceful, on whom the sun shines,
With whom all is well on the ship he commands,
'Twill do him no harm if with us he shakes hands.
Or perhaps the poor bottle on some sandy beach,
Of some honest landsman may come within reach,
Let him think as he reads this poor jingle at home
Of the sailor whose lot is the ocean to roam.
Be thankful when handling the bairn on his knee,
He is safe from the perils attending the sea:
The sun's shining and free is the wind,
We've long left our port of departure behind.
Fine weather we've passed through, no dangers have met;
We've rounded Cape Horn with the royals all set;
No sickness aboard us, no death do we mourn,
We're thankful "all's well" on the ship Golden Horn,
And, though not forgetting that trouble may come,
Rejoice that we're sailing for England and home.
We trust no disaster by us unforseen,
May now betwixt us and our hopes intervene,
That pleasant our future may be as the past,
And our voyage may have a bright ending at last.
So may we all sail on this voyage of life,
O'ercoming all perils, and dangers and strife,
In cloud or in sunshine, in calm or in gale,
Secure from disaster as homeward we sail.
Then, when the last harbour bar, death, shall draw near,
"All's well," may we meet it devoid of all fear;
The heavenly Pilot aboard us to guide
Our vessel, as into smooth waters we glide.
Naught carried away, upstanding each mast,
Forgetting with joy all the ills that are passed;
May we, through His mercy, as Peter expressed,
Abundantly enter the Haven of Rest.

Fletcher Christian and the *Bounty*

OST readers will be familiar with the story of the mutiny on **HMS Bounty.** It was in the year **1787,** that the British Government despatched the said vessel from Tahiti to Jamaica for the purpose of the conveyance of a fruit bread type plant. This plant was being transported to feed the slaves who laboured on the plantations, unfortunately the *Bounty* never reached her destination. Eventually when the breadfruit plant was successfully delivered the slaves refused to eat the food, but today it is still the staple diet among many of the Caribbean Islands. On the voyage 25 members of the crew mutinied, and set Captain Bligh and 18 members of the crew adrift in an open boat, the mutineers were led by Fletcher Christian, who was first mate on the *Bounty*. The mutineers then returned to Tahiti, where after a while nine of the mutineers led by Christian fled to the then uncharted Pitcairn Island. It was in 1808 that John Adams, and the descendants of the other mutineers were discovered by an American ship. Of the 16 that remained at Tahiti, 10 were captured and brought back to England to face justice. They were tried and three were executed. The voyage in the open boat by Captain and the other members of his crew is legendary, an epic feat of

Moorland Close Farm, Eaglesfield near Cockermouth. Birthplace of Fletcher Christian. Photo 1972.

A scale size replica of HMS Bounty.

seamanship, all were saved. There are varied accounts on the fate of Mr Christian, some say he returned to England. The most probable one being that he was murdered by a jealous islander while tending his small plot of garden on Pitcairn Island, He would most likely be a man who carried a guilty and a heavy heart, longing for the beautiful mountains and fells of his Lakeland home, his thoughts would carry him across a seemingly endless ocean, an ocean that the gallant little ship had crossed and carried him and herself to their final destination.

There have been many books written on the *Bounty* Mutiny, the two books which spring to my mind in order of detail and authenticity are as follows – **The Mutiny and Piratical Seizure of H.M.S. Bounty, by Sir John Barrow of Ulverston.** Sir John Barrow (1764-1848), who was permanent Secretary to the Admiralty. Sir John had access to unpublished documents official and unofficial, and to the papers of Captain Peter Heywood, R.N., a midshipman in the *Bounty*. This classic of maritime history was first published in 1831, it has been published many times since and is a remarkable account of the mutiny.

The other fine and detailed account on the incident is by **Mr. Glyn Christian,** who's family are directly descended from that of **Fletcher Christian,** his book being titled **Fragile Paradise,** first published in 1982. A well researched book on the trail of his famous ancestor, which took him across the seas to the Island of **Pitcairn.**

J.D.W.

Alexander (Eric) Birkett.

Father with cousin Iris. The Battery.
(Photo 1932-1933)

The Sisters – Mother Sarah (left) Martha (Centre) Mary Ann (Right).

Grandfather John Birkett with nephew and niece Norris & Iris helping themselves to fruit, Back Lane, Curzon Street, 1927-1928.

Brother Harry and Sultan, 1970.
Amersham, Buckinghamshire.

Myself with Mother, Tintern Abbey, Wales 1969.

Army Service, West Africa, 1959-1960.

Myself and Sheila (wife) Kendal, 1982.

We never made Las Vegas but we were happy.
Left to Right. Joe Fitzsimons, Mike Bell, Gordan Wignall, Myself, Les (fingers) McGlone,
David Hardy. Railway Hotel, Workington, 1956.

Left to Right. George, Joe & Maurice. Happy days 1959-1960.

Netherhall Maryport

Netherhall as it should be remembered in its heyday.

The decaying ruin and vandalised property, photograph 1972.
The building was eventually demolished and removed in the 1970s.

*Netherhall. The Peel Tower.
All that remains as a memorial to the
Lords of the Manor.*

*The vandalised interior of the once
Stately Home, 1972.*

*The Senhouse Roman Museum Maryport. Once the Headquarters for the Royal Naval Reserve, the building
was built by the Admiralty in 1885. It is now a permanent Museum which houses the Netherhall collection
of Roman alters and other artifacts for display to the public.*

Captain William Andrew Nelson of Maryport. 1839-1929. One of the finest Captains who ever graced the deck of a Sailing Ship. He spent 47 years in square-rigged sailing vessels, thirty-six of them in command. He never lost a ship. Photographed in Maryport by Samuel Bettoney, 1875.

The Auchencairn *in full sail four masted steel barque. Commanded by Capt. William Andrew Nelson.*

Cumbrian Dialect & Humour

Short funny stories and sayings

FUNNY stories and sayings usually stick in ones mind, quite a number of these are produced and directed by the speaker in a somewhat serious manner of which they do not realise at the particular time, they are as they think, being involved in serious conversation, and do not realise that they have created the birth of a saying or a story that will become well known and handed down through time. This also depends on the person to whom the story or conversion is being directed, the sharpness of the person on picking up the funny side, he or she's sense of humour, and being able to relate the story to others.

I myself have always had a good sense of humour, I was brought up in a home that possessed a serious side, but which always had to play second fiddle as you might say to the humorous side of life, so any conversation that was born of a serious nature would oft times end up with the family in fits of laughter.

For instance, going back many years ago in Maryport, I had arranged to call on a friend at his home one Saturday morning, on the way to his home I chanced to meet his mother in Crosby Street, we exchanged greetings, I then said to her "is he in?, to which she replied "If hee's nut in hee'l be oot, an if hee's oot it wont be lang til hee's back in agyan, hee est dooer vaneer hangan of it hinges, hee's in an oot like a spuggy feed'n its young." This answer was directed to me in a quite serious manner, and it was all I could do to keep a straight face.

A number of the following stories in this last chapter of the book are true, this I can vouch for as I was involved in some of them. I have travelled quite since leaving Maryport, but I can say in all honesty that I have never heard stories and sayings of the like that I recall from my own old home town. Naturally I have come across good humour elsewhere. In Kendal for instance, where I have resided for a good many years, I can find serious faces that in no time will be creased in laughter when a funny story is told or an unusual expression is used.

Humour can even be born from sorrow, we can shed tears at a bereavement, but even in sorrow someone is sure to pass a comment or remark that will raise a smile to tearful eyes, which will lighten the burden of sorrow carried by those who mourn their loss.

Today's Cumbria was formed by the amalgamation of Cumberland and Westmorland and also part of Lancashire to make it one of the largest Counties in England, this taking place in the early 1970s.

Returning to the subject of dialect, I have not gone into the explanation of this in the greatest of detail, its history etc. There are numerous books that can be purchased or obtained from local libraries on the subject of local dialect and origins, Cumbria has its own dialect society of which I am a member myself, Basically for readers information, our dialect is a mixture of Scandinavian (Old Norse), Danish, and Viking ancestry, the Manx connection, we have Celtic and Anglo Saxon, Icelandic, Welsh, Irish, Scotch, and not forgetting English thrown in, and again not to forget the Germanic sound in our dialect which is more pronounced in West Cumbria, which like the German language has a gutteral note to its spoken words, many of the local words are similar to German words, such as (watter for water, which in German is vassa.) The word kloset in German is for toilet, when as a young lad in Maryport, I heard on many occasions over the years as the toilet or lavatory being referred to as the kloset, and I can honestly say I have never heard it used anywhere else in this country on my travels, and I do recall as long as my memory takes me back, that it has been said by numerous people on occasion that the towns of West Cumbria, such as Workington, Whitehaven, Millom, and Ravenglass and especially Maryport that there is a most definite hint of Germanic flavour in our dialect. Maryport has always been known for its own brand of dialect sayings and expressions, to a visitor to Cumbria who is not familiar with the accent or dialect, it most probably sounds all the same from one end to the other, but to local people there is a great variation, and one can usually detect the difference in the dialect within a few miles. A good number of years ago I spent a bit of time in Australia, and while I was there I was asked on occasion what my nationality was, on a couple of occasions I was asked if I was a German or Russian speaking with a broken English accent. Being involved with the conservation of wildlife, mainly the European Wolf and Brown bear, I have over the past five years or so made frequent trips to Croatia, to stay with a friend who is involved in releasing these animals into the wild, animals which have been brought up in captivity as cubs, young animals found without a parent mother who has most probably been shot by a poacher for her pelt etc. These trips were spent in the Velebit Mountain range that runs along the Adriatic Coast. When a rest was required from the endless walking and climbing, tracking animals which had been released previously a year or so before, we would make for the coast to relax enjoy the local cuisine and enjoy a drink, and make conversation with the locals, which was not so easy for me not being able to speak Croatian, my friend who speaks fluent English, on more than one occasion when we were being introduced to local people he was asked if I was German or Norwegian. I do endeavour to speak in good understandable English when out of my own locality, but I find I am much more at ease and feel a great burden has been lifted from my back, when I am involved tucking into a local stew, that when served up contains so many interesting ingredients, such as a mixture of Marra's Gadgie's, Yowe's and Coo's, a great menu for the visitor to our beautiful County. We must endeavour to keep this dialect alive as it is slowly on the decline.

For the reader the words in dialect from the following stories and sayings, can with time and patience be translated from the glossary at the end of the book, naturally I have only written the words and meanings that relate to this manuscript, maybe at a later date I may indulge in another manuscript that will give a deeper insight into dialect history and origin, what follows is only intended to raise a smile from the face of the reader, so please read on and enjoy. Hopefully you will have been blessed with a good sense of humour.

Words phrases and meanings

The following selection of Cumbrian words phrases and meanings relate mainly to West Cumbria, as I remember them from my youth, the 1950s onwards, naturally a majority of these words and meanings etc. will be recognised in many other parts of the county. In this instance I am focusing mainly in and around the Maryport area, for it is a well known fact that Maryport has its own brand of dialect, there are certain words and sayings I remember being used by my grandmother who came from Dearham, a small village on the outskirts of town, she had a strong local accent, my grandfather also who was Maryport born, but who's parents were from Scotland, he too spoke with a definite local accent, but there were certain words he oft times used that's origin was Scots, which no doubt he had picked up from his parents and elder brothers. For instance, if he was referring to a vest or shirt he would call it his sark' which in Scotland means vest or shirt, a pullover was a gansey, and gallouses were a pair of braces. These words are very rarely used these days, unfortunatly local dialects are on the decline, this is mainly due to an influx of outsiders moving in and settling, bringing with them their own brand of sayings and words which the local youth pick up and add to their vocabulary, also television is another source which over the years has introduced words and sayings which are now used by the young ones of today, so sadly as I have mentioned previously our dialect is on the decline.

Introduction

Nivver is never
Nowt is nothing
Dooan't is do not
Clout is smacking
Weshin is washing
Marrer is mate
Lowpin is jumping
And a gyat is a gate
Cabbish is cabbage
Poddish is oats
Ah' cud gaa on fer ivver, but ah'd git a sore throoa't.
I will start by using a words of greeting, followed by a reply.

The greeting

Hoost'a gaan on marrer? Wat feetle?. Hoo yah deuh'n?. Hoost'a fizz'n? Hoo yah gittn on?.
Wat cheer marrer?. Wat sek fettle?. Wat fettle tin kettle?.

The reply may be as follows

"Chitter like owt marrer, Ah's better than great, Fit as a banty cock, Ahs as reet as rain, Topo marrer, Champion, Ah's as weel as can be expected, Nut si bad marrer, Ah's hoota fettle, Ah's nut si good, or a person might be – Ah's fair t' middlin, meaning – not good and not bad – (holding his own healthwise, or with the world).

I can recall two gentlemen in particular in Maryport who always replied to a greeting with the same reply, one would say "Ah's up an doon like a cork thats lost its bottle, apart fray that mi'lad, ah's o reet."

The other was in a poetic reply, "Ah's eether up er doon, an if ah's neether, ah'll be fair t'middlin, noo will that please tha?, and to finish the reply if he was ok, he would say –"ah's awreet John mi lad, hoos thisel?

If a person was a bit simple or an idiot, they would be regarded as one of the following –
Nut aw theer, Nut a full shillin, Wrang a't heed, Gitten a slyat lowse, Nut plum, Off his rocker,
Nut wise, A pilgarlic, Poddish brain, A reet gowk, Neah gumption, A numskull, Neah marbles,
My grandfather would refer to the above as – He es nowt int crows nest, or – He es neah oil in his lamp.
He's as dim as a clapped oot mantle,

A person who was worse the wear for drink he would be regarded as one of the following.
Tanked up, Full te't gunnles, Weel kettled or weel scuttled, Kalied, Full as a clog, Pie-eyed,
Weel oiled, Palatic, Three sheets te't wind, P ——— as a parrot, Weel plastered, Full as a kite,
 Stinkin drunk, Legless, He'd hed is share n'some bugger else's. Blinned drunk. Brimmin ower.

If something was tough or hard to chew, or to break up, it would be – As Tough as bulls lugs, Tough as teak, Tough as a hard shelled crab, Like chowin granite. The following one was also used by my grandfather, to which I have never found its origin, maybe a reader could enlighten me, I would be most obliged. – As hard as Nockmurton.

If a person was having a hard time, under pressure or harassment, they would be – Pusht fray pillar't post, Backset an foorset, Nock't aboot like a willywam, Swimm'n agynst tide an gitt'n neah spot, Being stuck up a gum tree wid neah way ah gitt'n doon. I remember my grandmother once using the following expression regarding a young lady in the neighbourhood who's husband had been giving her a hard time. – Yon poor lass, that fella's put her where a pund a cannels wadn't finn'er.

Another saying she used to use was, if the day or week had seemed to pass rather quickly, – Ah dooant know where this weeks gone, Its gone like snow off a dyke. Or –"Its cum'ta wi wadda thowt it."

If a person had been beaten up, or a football team, or rugger had been well beaten, they had been –
Weel snottered, Pulverised, Weel clobbered, They ed't stuffin nockt oota them, A good tannin, Brayed up, Weel hammered, A good rib ticklin, an a fyace lift t'gaa wid it, He'd gitten his cob battered.

If a drinking man was short of a copper er two (short of money), and needed a drink, he would approach a friend or acquaintance, or for that matter someone he only recognised by sight by the following –
("Noo then mi lad, ah bet thy pockets is weel stitched), (Esta gitten a sneck lifter), (Ah bet thoo's a lad wid neah wols in his pocket), (are yer sayin owt?) (any chance of a gargle marra), (Esta iveer seen a dry camel?, if nut thoos look'n at yan noo). (Yah wannt nowt suppen on thi own, thoo needs a marra, hoos aboot it?) ("Noo thou looks like'a lad that wad'nt see a fella suffer, Lets away doon't pub, its thy turran next). (Thy shoes is weel heeled, – or – thy clogs is weel caukered).

The following sayings or expressions I recall from the late 1950s and early 1960s. Git thi pipe (hang on a bit, or give me time). Dy'a waant jam on it (never satisfied) cackle n grunt (eggs and bacon). Mizzled (disappeard). Likerish o maks (Liquorice allsorts). Deed as a dockin (no life or movement). Flooted (flown the nest). Gis a gander (give me a look). Tissawivver (a matter of fact). Thi breeds buttered (you are doing alright). Being bubbled (a person being reported for theft, or something of that nature). A bobby dazzler (a real beauty). Jamfull (packed house, no room). Moonlight flit (gone without a word, no farewell, done a moonlighter). Slape fingered (a light handed thief, a one to watch). Being nobbled (doped or drugged). Its a doddle (very easy). Done a bunk (disappeard). Tekken french leave (doing as you please, and without authority). Wizzn'd as a walnut (weatherbeaten). When Xmas faws in June (probably never, no chance of a happening). Being diddled (cheated). Mair fyaces than't toon hall clock (a person who was not just two faced, but one of many). Weel jiggered (very tired). A jigger n chanter (a dancer and singer). Slowken n coddln (kissing and cuddling). Titivated up (looking smart). Gitten smittled (caught an infection). The great I am (self opinionated). Bannock feace (a flat faced and flat nosed person). Poddish kyte (person with a large stomach or midriff). Gittn't buckle in (being angry or upset at someone, not on good terms). Brass feaced, or granite chops (hard faced). Slobber chollars (fat faced, fleshy). As giddy as a gander wid yah leg (a chirpy, giggly all movement type person).

Shipping Brow Maryport leading to Harbour and Docks.
Photo April 2002.

Cumbrian Humour

with some short true stories

Hills and Mountains (*true*)

AN American tourist on holiday in the Lake District for the first time, he was staying in a well known Lakeland hotel, having made his introduction, he was now involved in conversation with some of the locals in the hotel bar, he was commenting on the mountains. I'm a little disappointed in your mountains fella's he said, I'm not saying for one moment that they are not beautiful, they are every bit of that. But they are just hills compared with the one's back home, I guess it would be a mite difficult to get lost in them. "Noo then mi lad, answered one of the locals, Foaks div git lost in them hills as thou coes them, an noo an agyan t'rescue lads esta gaa look'n fer them, and tha mun believe it er nut, t'lads bring yan er two doon deed on occasion." But in say'n that, ahv'e nivver heere'd on any Yanks gitten lost up theer, garn be wat ah's telt, thy lot can clim owert't lot in a mornin afoor brekast, an than swim't length'a Winnermere lyak afoor tea. "Tell me yah thing," wat dis yoor lot think aboot God putt'n Everest int wrang country? By this time the American tourist was beginning to look a little confused, and was being viewed by most of the people in the bar, some looking serious, and others wearing a slight, but expectant smile awaiting his reply. "I'm afraid I do not understand much of what you are saying sir, he replied. Well noo replied the local, mebbe thats just as weel, ah wadn't like ter git't blame on start'n t'third wurrald warr, cos oor islands es alus been mates. Noo ahv'e spokken mi bite, an ah'll bid tha good day, but just yan mair thing afoor ah gaa's, tek thi time on thi walks, er thoul end up wid nowt tah deuh hafe way throo thi hollida, cum on Bess lass he said, and off he went followed by his faithful border collie.

(Cockermouth 1973)

If in doubt ask

Excuse me Sir, am I on the right road to the market?
"Noo then ah's nut si seur on that, ah's a bit ona stranger messel, t'ony thing ah tell thou is, if thou's ont reet rooad thou waint be on wrang'n.

Storks and babies

Young boy asks his father – Fathar where dis aw them greet big stork birds gaa till ter bring't babbies back yam? Thou'd better gaa'n ask thi muthar aboot that son, he replied with a grin, she ken's mair aboot wildlife than ah deuh.

On oath

A man answering questions in court, – Oh aye, yis yer honner, ah saw it wid byath mee awn two eyes, an ah saw it wid Willie Dixons anaw, cos he wuz stannen reet next till'es.

Enjoy your flight *(true)*

A man who was a little slow on the uptake and a bit of a character was presented with his first opportunity to travel abroad on holiday. He had acquired all the necessary travel brochures and information from the local travel agency in Kendal, and had finally chosen to take a holiday in Spain.

He was due to take quite a ribbing from the lads in his local pub, as he had hardly ever set foot out of town, let alone travel to Spain. "I heer yer away t'Spain fe't holidays Kenny lad said one of the locals, aye' replied Kenny, ah cant wait, ah's look'n forard tll it," are yah fleean er sail'n? asked another, no replied Kenny, ah's away be air, oh aye, replied the local, amid the joviality which was now starting up in the bar, well mek sure yah dont git on a plane that es an ootside toilet, amid a roar of laughter. In great seriousness Kenny replied 'ahv'e gitten aw that sorted oot, ah's goin fust class, this reply was amid another roar of laughter, with some of the locals trying to keep straight faces. Another local then butted in and said to Kenny, who was by that time enjoying celebrity status, Well if yer goin ter Spain yer gonna miss yer favourite TV programme Coronation Street fer a couple a weeks, ya'h cant speak Spanish, an if its on oot theer itll be int local lingo "dooant worry aboot that eether replied Kenny, ahv'e gitt'n that aw sorted anaw, ahv'e bowt m'isel a laal telivision set that ah's tekken wid me, ah's nut as daft es you lot think, when ah do summat ah do it reet ah dooant need advice from you idiots". This reply followed again by roars of laughter.

(Kendal 1975)

The garden gnomes

Two women chatting in the corner shop while waiting to be served, after talking on numerous subjects, they had now arrived on the subject of gardening. Oh aye one was saying, my Sammy likes a tidy garden, "does thoo knaw, hee waint let't dog neer't lawn ataw, an he waint see a deed leaf liggin on it neether, hee's varra prood ont garden, twa's ony last week end gone, that he browta hafe dozen er them garden nomey's yam, er wativver the caw them, some er them es shovels, an some wid picks, tha's yan even es a weelbarra, yah know watt ah's on aboot". Her friend with a very serious and concerned look replied, "Divent think ah's rushn'ya, but when t' nomeys git finished at thy hoose, send them roond till oor spot t'gi that lazy bugger a'mine a hand, wid ooer garden its like a tip, hee es neah gaa in im ataw, tha's mair life in a cabbish".

The gannett *(true)*

Two men standing in conversation at the bar of a local pub, had their eyes fixed upon a male customer who had ordered a counter meal, he was quite a rotund person who evidently very fond of his grub and his beer, while awaiting his meal he had consumed three pints of bitter beer and a packet of pork scratchings, all within half an hour, when his meal arrived it was served with a large extra portion of potatoes and a plate of garlic bread. He then asked the waitress to fetch him another pint of beer, which she presented to him with a slight smile upon her face, picking up his utensils he forthwith attacked his plate, but not before he had consumed a full half pint of the beer without putting down the glass. The two men watching seemed spellbound, which I myself was being a witness to the beanfeast. Needless to say there was no etiquette involved in the spectacle. The consumer was oblivious to the watching eyes, he was more concerned with his plate, making sure there was no potato making a plan of escape from the awaiting jaws. Suddenly one of the two men watching from the bar made a comment, "Ev'ya ivver seen owt like that in yer life marra?, hee's like a bloody gannett, even a gannett wadn't mek a feul an a pig on itsel like that, lookster't way hee's knockin them taties back, hee es yan in his mooth, yan ont fork, an his eye on another, Aye' replied his mate, just afoor he dropped a tatie on flooer an it went under't chabble, it es neah chance gitt'n away, hee knaws its theer, its ganna git re-cycled like't other hafe styan, efter hee licks't gravy off his plate, (before the gannett left the premises he consumed two more pints of beer in rapid succsession, he then asked the waitress what time in the evening last meals

Maryport Crystal ale advert.

were served, "today Sir she asked?, yes he replied, the waitress with a large grin then said 8 30 Sir if we hev any taties left.

(*Maryport 2002*)

Do you want jam on it *(true)*

A local man was sitting in a cafe in Keswick, while outside the rain was coming down in sheets, and it was also very windy at the time, suddenly a family of four burst through the door, apparently tourists, mother and father, and teenage girl and boy. They commenced to take off their very wet outer garments etc., and whilst doing so, the young girl who was aged about fifteen was complaining bitterly about the weather, she was very close to tears "Why, she said in a raised voice, does it always rain when we come to this place", I'm absolutely fed up to the teeth with it, taking out a tissue and drying her eyes and face, she then started complaining that you could never see the mountains or the lakes properly because of the mist etc., and always having to carry or wear anoraks or waterproofs, the young lad who apparently was her brother but slightly older than she, said in a quiet voice "calm down and keep quiet, there are other people in here who have to put up with it," to which she answered "get lost". With that her mother and father intervened and told her to sit down and be quiet, which she then did muttering under her breath while doing so. It was at this time that the local man sitting by the cafe window decided to speak. Looking at the young girl he said "excuse me mi lass, ah's nut bein cheeky er pokin mi nose in, but when thou cus on thi holidays, dust'a cum ere ter see't Lyakes fells an awt greenery roond an aboot?, the girl stared at the man, just and so about being able to understand a few of the words directed to her spoken in the local dialect. Answering him she said "of course we come to see the scenery, why else should we come? an dust'a allus cum this time a'eer, int middle'a September?, with that the young girl answered rather sharply "its the only time of year we can come, when my parents here have their holidays, while this rather heated conservation was in progress, the girls parents were at the cafe counter ordering food.

The girl was by now getting rather flustered and beginning to raise her voice again, It doesn't matter when you come here she yelled, its always dammed windy and raining. The local man interrupted her and said, "where dust'a think young woman where awt lyak's cus fray, an awt greenery aroond these parts, if it wasn't fot watter fray up above, ther wad'nt be any lyaks, what dust'a waan't jam on it? With that the young girl jumped out of her seat yelling at the man "why cant you speak proper English you silly fool, what has jam and dusters got to do with the dammed weather, with that she stormed out of the cafe in tears. The girls parents were now back at the table, and wanting to know what had upset the daughter, this was relayed back to them by the son and the local man, The mother then saying I do apologise for her behaviour Sir, but she doe's have a point about it raining a lot, and I myself do not understand what you mean about the weather and jam and dusters, "can you explain? Aw 'reet I'll tell tha, replied the man, If a man wus starvin an somebody offered that man a slice'a breead, that man wad be varra humble an thankful, but if he complained till hee's angel ev murcy, that ther wus neah butter ont slice a breead, he wud git telt he shud be varra thankfull fer laal murcies, That's wat ah mean aboot ev'n jam on it, Be happy wid wat God gives, Tha's a lotta fowk in this wurald that wadn't mind a lokka lakeland watter droppen on ther fyaces reet this second an on ther crops anaw. Noo afoor ah bid yer good day ah'll just say this, if yon lass'a thine wus mine, ah'd give her backside a good dustin, an cut oot hur jam ration fer a few days, then with a grin he left the cafe. (A true story, being in the cafe at the time.)

(Keswick 1974)

An air line

A tourist driving through a small village in the County needed his car tyres checked, feeling they needed a little more pressure. Pulling into the small forecourt of the village garage he was at once attended to by the proprietor, to whom he asked, "have you got an air line please? to which the proprietor grinned and replied, "an airline marra, yer must be joke'n, we event even gitt'n a bus station.

Vehicle problem

Driver to the mechanic; tha's summat wrang wid mi vehicle, "oh yes what's the problem?"
Reply, – its nut rattlen enuf.

Farewell Rock-n-Roll *(true)*

An old friend and I were making our way up Shipping Brow in Maryport, when he casually asked, "dy'a recognise this fella commin doon't broo John? Coming down the Brow was a man nearly bent double, walking with the aid of a stick, I answered who, the chap with the walking stick?, as there were other people making their way up and down the Brow, Aye, he answered, I replied "no, I'm afraid I cant seem to be able to place him at all, who is he,? you should be able to place him John lad he replied, you being a rock-n-roll man in yer younger days, He was a rock-n-roll champion, he won cups an trophy's an aw sorts fer shekk'n his legs aboot. Then without the flicker of a smile he said, "It cant'a done him a lotta good garn be't looks on him, he looks like he's shook an rocked hisel t'deeth.

Dy'a ken John Peel

Compare asking for volunteers in the audience at a local garden fête to give a song, Does anybody know John Peel he asks? a man staggering out of the beer tent quite intoxicated and a little worse for wear shouts out, "Any bugger waw ses the div is tellen'a load'a lee's, Peel's been deed fer weel ower a hundred eer.

Fray Bentos *(true)*

Two men who were co-operators on a machine at a one time thriving shoe factory in Maryport on the Solway Trading Estate, had just closed down their machine to have their lunch break, which is known in West Cumbria as – bate, or scran time. The lads sat down and poured out a drink from their flasks, and opened up their lunch boxes and commenced to tuck in. Bill one of the two, casually remarked, wattst'a gitten int butties t'day Tommy lad? Tommy opening up one of his sandwiches, and at the same time trying to talk with a mouthful of one of Maryport's well known Haig's pie's, replied with crumbs flying in all directions," It looks varra like its corned beef agyan marra, Is it Fray Bentos, said Bill with a smile on his face, again through a hail of crumbs Tommy replied, ah evn't a clue where it's fray marra, but it looks like'a bit'a good tackle.
(Fray Bentos is a well known brand of corned beef. The word fray in West Cumbria dialect means from).

The Apache Restaurant (true)

Going back into the late 1950s, It would be about 10.30 p.m. one Friday evening, when a car pulled up on Curzon Street, outside what was then the Cooperative butchers shop. Two local lads, one of them middle aged, were making there way over to Grasslot which is the Southern end of the town after a nights drinking session, and were in as we shall say, good fettle. The car was travelling in a northerly direction more than likely towards Carlisle. The occupants of the vehicle were seemingly southerners, heading for the motorway. One of them called out to the two local lads, he enquired politely where the local Indian restaurant was situated in the town, Geordie, the elder of the two Maryport lads answered "didt'a say Indian restaurant marra,? with a look of disbelief on his face, thou's look'n fer an indian restaurant?, is ah drunk' er in'a dream, realising the situation was fact, and not fiction, Geordie being rather intoxicated, but at the same time trying to converse with the strangers in a teetotal manner, and as polite as was possible said, "Noo then son, ah's varra sorry ter dissapoint yer, but ah raretha think thou's ont wrong track marra, thou's pass'n through civilisation just noo, we in this laal toon hev neah Apache's er them Cherokees, thou's nut just int wrang toon mi lad, thou's in wrang country aw'tergither. Noo if thou's hungry, we hev't best fish n chip shop in this laal toon fer miles aboot, fowk cus fray aw hearts and parts ter ere, ter sample Ma Cueto's fish n chips an pattie's, thou wont git nowt better mi lad. With that the southern chap answered, "I can understand a little of what you are saying, but we are into Indian food, and that's what we are looking for." Geordie commenced to speak again, "well es ahv'e said thou's int wrang country if thou's look'n fer Geronimo, thou lett'a look

elsewhere. With that, the driver with a shake of the head closed the vehicle window, then with the other occupants all wearing bemused looks the vehicle pulled away. Geordie's mate, who had never spoke a word through the whole of this complete fiasco was doubled up with laughter, "What's thou chittering at, said Geordie with a serious look upon his face, these fowk shud be telt that this is a civilised toon, It waint be lang till some bugger's look'n fer General Custer. Geordie's mate through fits of laughter was trying to explain to him that the strangers were looking for a Tandoori type restaurant, Indian eating houses that were run or owned by Hindu's or Sikhs, and were not American Indians, but Geordie was adamant, "Ah divent care watt tribe he wus on aboot, we hev nin ere, noo ahv'e spok mi bite, this is Maryport an nut 't middle er Dakota.
(A true story, relayed to me by Geordie's mate. Sadly both have passed away, two real characters).

Out of work

A woman saw her next door neighbour out in the backyard beating the dust out of her carpets which were hanging on the clothes line. The electric hoover was in fashion at the time, but apparently this lady was partial to the old fashioned method, and to use a local expression, "was giving them a good clobbering". using a large fan shaped cane beater, and to use another expression of the time, "going at it hammer and tongs." Every time she brought the beater into contact with the surface of the carpet, she would say out loud, "That's fer bein oot'a wark in 1935, then another whack, that's fer bein oot'a wark in 1936, and another whack for 1937 and so on, until she was still whacking in 1945. The neighbour who was watching and listening to this then went indoors shaking her head, she said to her husband who was sitting by the fire reading the newspaper, "didn't Jack fray next dooer dee in 1940? aye, replied her husband, watt for? nay it doesn't matter she replied, but he still must be oota wark where ivver he went till."

Half way house

A shepherd coming down the mountain side with his dog, meets a rambler who is resting at the cabin which is well signed "half way house". The rambler asks the shepherd, "how far is it to the summit?.
The reply was, "ah dooan't think this cabins been shifted sen ah last past it, which is nobut two hoors sen, so it'll be as far as thou's cum awriddy, and with a smile carried on down the mountain".

No room *(true)*

My wife and I on a day out, stopped at a well known village not far from Maryport, we were rather peckish and fancied a bite to eat. The village on that particular day being rather quiet. We called at a cafe which was seemingly empty of the human form, but which had no sign or notice to inform that it was open for business or closed. The door being open we entered, and decided to sit down, the tables all clean and neatly laid out with an interesting menu to welcome the hungry traveller. We must have waited a full fifteen minutes or so without sign of staff or customer. We were just about to leave and try elsewhere, when suddenly a door at the rear of the cafe opened, a woman came walking towards us carrying what appeared to be a bundle of tablecloths, she walked right past the table where we were sitting without uttering one word, she went behind the cafe counter despatched her bundle, making the return trip past our table again without a look nor a word. My wife and I exchanged glances together a smile and no word spoken, just the hope that we had been seen, another ten minutes elapsed, again, on the verge of saying goodbye to the forlorn cafe, the same door opened once more, and this time a middle aged man presented himself, he was wearing a pinafore that practically came down to his ankles, he was covered from head to foot in flour, he looked like an apparition. Like the woman before him, he past by without a word, went behind the counter, carried out whatever his business may have been, and then set out on his return trip past our table to the door of mystery, again without word or recognition. By this time it was becoming a joke, the pair of us were having difficulty keeping straight faces. It was then we decided it was time to leave, we began to move, when suddenly the mysterious door again opened for the third time in a full half hour, towards us again came the woman who this time I challenged with the words, "Are you open today? "aye, she replied carrying on past our table, we are oppen if yah can find a seat", so down we sat again in the deserted cafe, the woman passing again on her way to the door of mystery, as she went through it out he came, again I made a challenge, "Nice day I commented, Is it he replied? ah wadn't know" and carried on to the counter. By now it was no joke, time to go, Then appearing out of the blue was a young lady, who with a smile of welcome asked, "can I take your order? to which when ordered and served was prompt, and well worth the wait. We often look back upon this story which always raises a smile, maybe it was their way of keeping us entertained, rather than having loud music blowing one's brains out. There is something to be said for the sound of silence, when a little silent entertainment is added.

Rommell (true)

In this following short, but true story, the reader must try to imagine that he or she was present at the time, It will allow their imagination to understand how funny the situation was, and accept that without the vocabulary of very strong language that was used by the leading person in this story, who also possessed a voice like a regimental sergeant major, even during the course of a peaceful conservation, that the story would seem rather dull. To add to the above ingredients, the man possessed one of the broadest of West Cumberland accents I have ever heard, he was also a man who could fly off the handle for the slightest thing and make one shiver, even though he was only of average height and build. The same man was a very kind man, who would lend a hand to anyone. The bark was much worse than the bite.

It was in the 1960s, that a very good friend of mine was about to go on holiday with his parents to London, my friend was about 19 years of age at the time. His father was a driver for a local haulage firm in the town, he was also a very keen motor cycle man, who had been involved with them all his life, so naturally this hobby rubbed off on his son. My own parents knew the family very well, and had done for many years. They had been to London on previous occasions, but had always travelled by either train or by coach. This time they had planned to travel by motorbike and sidecar, father at the controls, mother in the sidecar, and my friend riding pillion. They were booked into a Hotel in the Charing Cross area of the City. The following is what happened after quite a pleasant journey down South to their destination.

On their arrival to the outskirts of the City, they found that there were quite a number of road works in operation which were creating diversions, and very heavy traffic which was giving problems to the City drivers, never mind a motorbike and sidecar from up in God's country. They found themselves beginning to go round in circles, the noise and fumes from the traffic being tremendous, Fathers goggles which were like the type worn by a German Tank Commander began to steam up, which incidentally purchased from an army and navy store, they were attached to a leather cap which represented that of a German storm trooper, a pair of leather gauntlets were worn that came up to the elbow, he was also wearing a large leather overcoat that practically came down to his ankles, they could not hear each other speak, neither could they stop. Father was now beginning to come to the boil and blow his top, mother was in tears, she had been told off for trying to shout and tell him directions, she had been informed that it was he that was driving the —— motor bike, and to the son, if he didn't keep quiet he could jump off and —— walk. They had apparently gone around one particular system about six times, he was now really ranting and raving to himself. They again presented themselves to the same set of lights for the seventh time, while waiting for the sequence to change, alongside the motor cycle and side car came a large chauffeur driven Rolls Royce, the back window of the Rolls coming down, a gentleman leant out of the window and seemingly was about to ask directions, he got as far as "Excuse me my man, and was answered like a barrage of shot from a machine gun, "Fust of aw Ah's neabody's —— man, an If yer —— lost ask a —— copper if yer can —— well fin yan in this —— loony bin. My friend the son, said that at the time, he wished the ground would have opened up and swallowed them, as he heard all that was said, and felt very embarrassed for his mother, who was pretending to be asleep in the sidecar. But he said that there was one consolation, while his father was shouting and gesticulating, a lady next to the gentleman in the Rolls leaned forward, who was apparently his wife, my friend heard her say just before the traffic lights changed,

"It's no good asking this man directions darling, he's a German, and a wild one at that' and he look's like Rommel. As the lights turned to green, Rommel was heard to yell above the roar of the traffic here we —— well gaa agyan. That did not bring the story to its final conclusion, when they finally arrived at their accommodation which apparently was sometime after, there had been an error in the hotel booking, and they had to move to another hotel of the same company, needless to say the General would have not been amused. From then on he was always known with affection to some as Rommel, even to his son. A good man who expressed himself in his own way.

Piper and Paper (*true*)

It was in about 1959-1960, a local pub was running its annual trip to London for a long week-end. One of the trippers was quite a well known character, who was known locally as Piper. This apparently was his first outing to London, as the coach approached the City centre it was early evening, about 5.00 p.m., the local newspaper boys were now out on the street corners selling the evening newspapers, the coach was now moving quite slowly because of the heavy volume of traffic, the newspaper boys were as normal calling out in their very distinctive London accents – Paper- Paper, which in their accent sounded like Piper, Piper. The above named tourist, jumped out of his coach seat and said in an exited voice, "Ahv'e nivver been ter Lund'n afoor, t'bus esn't stopp't yit, an the knaw ah's ere. Ah can see this is ganna be yan hell' of a week-end"

Life after death

Two men chatting, "doe's thou believe in life efter deeth Willie, asks Geordie?, Ah bloody weel hope se'a replied Willie, co's tha's nut varra much afoor it."

Tom Pepper, – Kilroy – Jack Robinson (true)

Two lads at the bar of a pub in Maryport (**Top Tap**) about 1963. One say's to the other "See yon -felle'r ower theer waw's just cum in, aye' replied his mate, waw is he? "Ah's nut sure wat hee's nyam is, was the reply, But he disn't hafe fancy his'sel, an a bigger liar than Tom Pepper ivver saw't day t'be An be't way he gaa's on, hee's been till mair spots than Kilroy ivver went till." After short period of silence the other lad said "Ah wonder waw it is?, "Nay replied the other seriously, Ah wadn't be suprised if it wasn't Jack Robisson hisel". Come on, supp up lett's away.

Allonby return

Tourist, "excuse me Sir, will this road take me to Allonby,? Ay'e mi lass it will, an if thou asks it nicely it'll fetch thou back when thou's finish't thi business."

As the crow flies

A woman pulls up in her and asks a roadside council worker, "Excuse me please which is the quickest way to get to Bullgill from here?, taking off his cap and giving his hair a ruffle, he answered making a motion with his thumb towards the hedge that he was trimming and at the same time yawning, he then decided to speak, which was in a very slow and calculating manner. "If thou clims ower yon stile theer int dyke, an turrans left, an gaa est crow flee's its nobut a coupl'a mile, but thou'll need sum gum byuts, cos the's a gay clatter'a coo claps ower theer in yon field. Cum ter think on it, thou'd mebb'e be better gaan in thi car, Charlie es a bull lowse oweer theer, an its nut varra friendly like, while scratching his head and giving another large yawn the woman was climbing back into her vehicle, the council worker heard her muttering as she did so "Why can't you find a local person when you need one?, he must be one of them Polish refugee's.

Mr. Jim Thorburn, well-known Maryport cyclist pictured here with his Sparkbrook Trike. Which he acquired in 1968, the trike was built in 1897, and was in very bad condition. He fully restored it, and it has since travelled around the Country, and also abroad to rally's. It has been in Maryport since 1925. Jim has owned it for the last 36 years, and she is still going strong.

Words in Cumbrian Dialect
In alphabetical order

THE majority of words relating to Maryport and District is a verbal dialect and not a written one, although some do appear in the following glossary, which is not a complete one of the dialect, but should suffice the reader to translate the dialect into English.

Aboot – about
Afooer – before
Afoorhand – beforehand
Agyans't – against
Ah'd – I had
Ah'll – I will
Ah've – I have
Aheed – ahead
Akin – related
Alang – along
Alean – alone
Amang – among
Anaw – as well
Aneugh – enough
Angert – angered or angry
Anser't – answered
Argy – argue
Ash cart – refuse vehicle
Auld – old
Awivver – however
Awn – own
Awreet – all right
Awriddy – already
Awtagither – all together

Back end – autumn
Backad's – backwards
Badly – Ill
Bare pelt – stripped off, naked
Bat – to hit or strike
Bawk – wretching being sick
Beck watcher – water bailiff
Beck – stream or river
Behint – behind

Belang – belong
Beyke – bicycle
Bidivlled – Be-devil, to plague-torment
Biskey – teacake
Bletherin – crying
Bleud – blood
Bloffin – (blackjack) – small fish
Blustery – windy
Bo – ball
Boggle – ghost or apparition
Bonkers – off his or her heads
Bonnie – pretty
Brant – steep
Brass fyced – hard faced
Brassed off – fed up, unhappy
Brat – apron or pinny
Bray – to give a hiding
Breead – bread
Brek – to break
Brok – broken
Broo – brow-hill
Broon – brown
Brossen – full up, after a meal
Browt – brought
Bubbled – informed or reported
Buckie – whelk (shellfish)
Buckshee – free or spare
Byan – bone
Byuts – boots

Cackle or cackling – talking a lot
Canny – cautious
Cant'a – can you
Cap't – surprised

Cat lowp – short distance away
Catch'd – caught
Caw'd – called
Ceake – cake
Champion – very well
Chanc't – chanced
Chanter – singer
Chitlins – young birds
Chittering – talking a lot (noisy)
Chitter – very well
Chortlin – laughing
Chow – chew
Chowin – chewing
Chuck – throw
Chuft – pleased
Chunk – piece of
Churries – cherries
Clag – to stick, sticky
Clarty – sticky
Clatter – can mean noisy, or a lot
Clobber – clothes, or possessions
Clobbered – to get hit, or beaten
Clod – lump of earth. or clay
Clog or clogs – footwear
Clout – punch, or to strike
Clutter – a mess
Cockloft – attic
Cod bangin – cod fishing
Coddin – kidding (joking)
Coe'd – called
Cooch or Couch – setee
Coo – cow
Cop or Cop't – in trouble (thou's cop't it)
Coppled – fallen over
Covin – perrywinkle-small shellfish
Cowped – tilted over
Croaked – died, or past on.
Crood – crowd
Croon – crown
Cropper – to come a cropper (to fall)
Cuddy – donkey, or small pony
Cwol – coal

Dadderin – shaking
Daft – silly
Dander – temper
Darsen't – dare not
Daub – to mark, or cover over

Dayleet – daylight
Deau – do
Deead – dead
Deeaf – deaf
Deeath – death
Deek – look
Detarmint – determined
Devarted – devoted
Di's – does
Diddled – conned, cheated
Dissn't – does not
Dist'a – do you
Divil – devil
Divn't – dont
Doddering – unsteady
Doddle – easy
Doff't – to undress
Dollop or jollop – a good helping
Dook – swim
Dowter – daughter
Dub – small pool of water
Dueh'n – doing
Dueh – do
Dump't – thrown out, give away
Dyke – hedge, or hedgerow

E'ya – have you
Ee'a – here
Eead – head
Eether – either
Eft'a – after
Efterneun – afternoon
Egg on – urge someone to act
Eneaf – enough
Es – has
Est'a – have you
Etwixt – between
Evy'a – have you

Faddy – particular
Famished – hungry
Fath'a – father
Feace – face
Fergit – forget
Fettled – fixed
Feul – fool
Feyt – fight
Fidget or fidgety – restless

Fin – find
Flaysome – frightening
Flay – to frighten
Flewted – flown the nest
Fluke – or an unusual happening (one off)
Fluke – small flatfish
Flummox – fluster
Fo'en – fallen
Fo – fall
For'ad – forward
Fowt – fought
Fratch – argue, to fall out
Fund – found
Fust – first

Gaa – go
Gabby – Mouthy, – very talkative
Gadgie – a person (male)
Gaffer – the boss
Gammy – injury (gammy leg
Ganna – going to
Garn or Gaan – going
Gaumless – no sense (thick)
Gawkin – staring
Gezzlin – gosling
Ginnel – narrow passage
Git – get
Gitt'n – getting
Giveower – enough (stop it)
Glabbies – marbles
Gob – mouth
Gowk – a fool (foolish)
Gowld – gold
Gurn – to pull a fuuny face (gurning)
Guzzle – drink or eat quickly
Gyat – gate
Hagger – miner (hagging or cutting)
Heead – head
Heed – notice (take heed)
Hev – have
Hissel – himself
Hod'on – hold back, (wait)
Hoddin – holding
Hoo's – how is (hoo ist'a)
Hoor – hour
Hoose – house
Hoss – horse
Howk – to dig (howkin digging)

In't – in the
Intil or inti – into
Isn't – is not
Ist'a – are you
It'll – It will
Ivver – ever

Ivverything – everything
Jigger – dancer
Jiggered – tired, or worn out
Jinny spinner – sycamore seed (or a daddy longlegs)
Jip – a part of the body giving discomfort
Jonah – a moaner (bringer of bad luck)
Judder'n – shaking – shuddering
Kalied – drunk, under the weather

Kali – sugary powder
Keck up – to tilt
Kecks – trousers
Ken – to know
Kep – to catch
Kettled – drunk (weel kettled)
Kilt – killed (or as in the wearing of)
Kinns – cracked hands (chapped)
Kittled – tickled
Kizzn'd – burnt, dried up
Kloset – toilet
Knacky – handy
Knapp hand – very efficient
Knaw – know
Knaws – knows
Knock't – knocked
Knocking on – getting older
Knockin – knocking
Kyte – large stomach
Kytle – form of jacket

Laal – small
Laff'n – laughing
Laik – to play
Laiting – searching
lambaste – to hand out a thrashing
Lamped – -to be hit, or struck
Lang – sen – long since
Lang – long
Lanky – tall and lean

Lap – to cover or wrap
Larn't – learned
Larned – learned
Leater – later
Leeave – leave
Leet – light
Leetnin – lightning
Leets – lights
Lend – loan
Let on – to admit
Leukoot – lookout
Leuksta – look you
Leyfelang – lifelong
Leyk't – liked
Liggin – lying down
Lip – to give cheek (being cheeky)
Lish – nimble, fit, active
Lobbed – thrown
Lobby – hallway
Lok – a drop (an amount of liquid)
Lonnin – a lane or pathway
Lookst'a – look here
Lossin – loseing
Lowped – jumped
Lowse – loose
Lug's – ears

Maggie ann – margarine
Mair'n – more than
Maistly – mostly
Maist – most
Marra – mate – one of a pair
Masher – a gentleman, smart
Mea'd – made
Mebbe – maybe
Med as weel – might as well
Mekkin – making
Mek – to make
Midden – refuse heap, or compost heap
Middlin – half and half (average)
Min – oot – mind out
Mits – hands or fists
Mizzled – disappeared
Mizzle – foggy with fine rain
Moidered – harassed, or pestered
Mollycoddle – to spoil
Mooth – mouth
Moudy – a mole

Muck – dirt
Muffler – scarf
Muggy – close (warm damp weather)
Mun – must

Nabbed – stolen
Narra – narrow
Narve or Narves – Nerve or Nerves
Neah – no
Neahwhere – nowhere
Neame'd – named
Neb – nose (or peak of a cap)
Neet – night
Nifty – quick fast moving
Nigh on – nearly
Nip – pinch
Nobbled – fixed (drugged)
Nobbut – only just
Nocked off – finished work (or item or items stolen)
Noggin – measure of liquid (small measure)
Noppy – small and neat
Nowther – neither
Nowt – nothing
Numnut – idiot
Nut – head

O'maks – all kinds
Od'on – hang on for a while
Od – hold
Okard – awkward
Olas – always
Ont – on the
Oors – ours
Oot'a – out of
Ootasorts – not so good
Oppen – open
Ower fyced – too much to face
Owereered – overhead
Owerneet – overnight
Owt like – decent, reasonable outlook
Owt – anything
Owther – either

Pack't – packed
Parky – cold, chilly
Pas't – passed

Pelt or pelting – barrage (heavy rain, pelting down)
Pezzled – well beaten
Pickle – as in a pickle (in trouble)
Picky – hard to satisfy, choosy
Pict'r – picture
Pilgarlic – a simpleton, idiot
Pissibed – dandelion
Pluke – pimple or spot
Pobs – milky pudding
Poddish – porridge
Powk – poke
Prod – poke
Pudd'n – pudding
Puddled – not with it
Pull't – pulled
Pulverised – badly beaten
Punt – small row boat

Quack – doctor
Quandry – dilemma, uncertain
Queer do – strange
Quit – to finish

Raa – raw
Rag – n – byans – rag and bones collector
Raggy – frosty
Rag – lose your rag (temper)
Rake – a lot of
Ranty – to rant and rave (bad tempered)
Ratchin – searching, (looking for)
Razzle – rave up (drinking, on the razzle)
Read'n – reading
Reck'n – reckon
Reclec't – recollect
Reet – right
Riddy – ready
Rist – rest
Rive – to tear
Rum do – queer goings on
Ruttlin – wheezy (from the throat)
Sark – vest or shirt
Sarra – served
Scar – foreshore, or stony area
Scheulmaister – schoolmaster
Sconse – stone type table or seat
Scrat – scratch, scratching
Scrunt – apple core

Seelang – solong, or farewell
Seest'a or sist'a – look, or look here
Segs – hard skin, hands and feet
Sen – since
Set to – a fight
Seyam – same
Seyyap – soap
Shadda – shadow
Shampt – ashamed
Sharpish – quickly
Sheck – shake
Shive – slice of
Shud – should
Skelp – smack
Skiddadled – run away, ran off
Slape or Slyap – slippery
Slattery – wet
Slavvery duck – mixture of savoury meats
Slovenly – untidy, dirty
Slowkin – kissing and cuddling
Slowter – slaughter
Slumgullion – a thick meat and vegetable stew
Sluther gut's – eats and drinks to excess
Smatch – a smattering
Smiddy – blacksmith (or person – Smith)
Smittled – infected (infection)
Smo – small
Snagger – a turnip
Sneck – door catch (can also mean nose)
Snitch – nose
Snoot – nose
Soond – sound
Speel or spelk – fine splinter of wood
Spen – spend
Spitt'n – spitting (light rain)
Spokken – spoken
Spok – speak
Stannin – standing
Stoup – bent over
Strang – strong
Summat – something
Supping – drinking
Syam – same
Syun – soon

T'eal – tale
T'ean – taken

T'wad – it would
T'was – it was
T'winter – the winter
Tantrum – fit of temper
Ta – thank you
Taties – potatoes
Teable – table
Tean – took
Teem or tyum – to pour out
Tek – take
Telt – told
Telt – told
Ter – to
That'n – that one
The'll – they will
Thee or thou – you
Thersels – themselves
Thissen – yourself
Throstle – song thrush
Thunner – thunder
Till – until
Toak't – talked
Toakin – talking
Toffed up – dressed up (smart)
Toon – town
Top cwot – top coat
Towped – tipped, or leaning over
Trollop – woman of disrepute
Tummled – fallen down
Turran – turn
Twang – accent

Ud – would
Unna theer – under there
Unna't – under the
Upseyde – upside
Ur – her.
Urly – early
Vaneer – very nearly
Varra – very
Vext – upset
Wack – share

Wad – would
Waint – wont
Walk'n – walking
Wamp – wasp
Want'ta – want to

Want'ta – want to
Wark or wuk, – work
Warlic – mischief
Wasn't – was not
Wat'll – what will
Wativver – what ever
Watter – water
Waw – wall
We'r – we are
Weel – well
Weshin – washing
Wesh – wash
Wether – weather
Wev'e – we have
Whang – to throw
Wid – with
Willt'a – will you
Wind'a – window
Wisht – be quiet
Wrang – wrong
Wukkit'n – Workington
Wurald – world
Wuth – worth
Wuzzle – weasel

Yakker – an acre
Yakker – farm worker (farm labourer)
Yan or Yah – one
Yance – once
Yat or Gyat – gate
Yatterin – constant chatter
Yer – your
Yiss – yes
Yit – yet
Yon – an object, over there
Yonder – over there
Yowe – female sheep
Yowl – cry or howl
Yuk – throw

The White Star Liner Majestic.

Aerial view of Maryport.

Contractors at work on Maryport's New Pier in 1939. Debris from the Old Pier can be seen in the picture.

Ewanrigg Hall, Maryport – the mainland home of the Christian family. The building was partly destroyed by fire in 1904. Part of this fine building still remains today. The Christian family were originally from Milntown in the Isle of Man.

View from Mote Hill, Maryport, looking down to the River Ellen. The rounded railed area is from where the Broadside launches took place. The Ritson Shipyard was situated directly behind.
Photo: 2003